Staying on Course

A Biography of Robert H. Reardon

BARRY L. CALLEN

ISBN 0-9646682-4-6
Printed in the United States of America

ANDERSON
UNIVERSITY
PRESS

Acknowledgments

Gratitude is expressed for the editorial assistance of Jan R. Callen, the archival assistance of Douglas Welch, and the encouragement and helpfulness of the members of the Editorial Committee of Anderson University Press, Tom Bruce, Trish Janutolo, and James Morehead. Layout and cover design are by David Liverett who provided insight as well as artistic skill. Technical assistance also came from Tammy Burrell. President James L. Edwards and Dean Carl H. Caldwell reviewed this project at an early stage and were most encouraging.

Special appreciation is extended to Robert H. Reardon himself who endured many hours of taped interviews and endless questions posed to him by Barry Callen. He also opened his private document and photo files and even many portions of his private journal. Without such materials, an adequate biography would have been impossible.

Robert H. Reardon

Table of Contents

....

Introduction

....

Life is essentially a journey. It is the essence of reality that it should be process, and it is of the essence of our life that we should walk. We have many dangers as we walk, for the bypaths are many and some of them lead to dead ends.

—D. Elton Trueblood, *The Life We Prize*, 213.

Robert H. Reardon, minister, educator, and master of metaphors, once opened a new school year at Anderson College in Indiana by explaining to the faculty and staff that the year's beginning was like launching a ship. The voyage would be many months long, could be perilous at points, was eminently worthwhile, and had waiting for the travelers at journey's end a gracious port of rest and real fulfillment. He bid the campus leaders the joys of a wonderful trip through the turbulent sea of the coming school year. Avoid the ever-present dead ends, he warned; engage in the essence of education and life itself by sailing forward with vision and courage, traversing the many waves with persistent hope until the desired destination finally looms in sight at the end of second semester.

This nautical metaphor serves well as an appropriate image of Reardon's whole life, ministry, and campus presidency. He was a vigilant and courageous pilot who managed to keep the most important things in view and on course regardless of circumstances—and even to keep a sense of adventure and humor in the process of the voyage. He had an instinct for anticipating dangerous currents and steering the campus and sometimes even the larger church community away from bad choices.

The personal life journey of Robert Reardon has involved his family's immigration from the "old world" to the new, Ireland, France, and Germany to America, and pursuing new light and fresh spiritual life in concert with a body of serious Christians, vigorous church reformers known as the Church of God movement (Anderson). He has sailed some treacherous seas while guiding the Anderson College (University) campus for decades. This school has evolved from a tiny Bible training institution into a substantial church-related university, moving during Reardon's leadership from cultural outsiders to valued partners in the classic tension between "town and gown" in Anderson, Indiana, and far beyond. Reardon has paddled down the sometimes twisting river of reason and education in ways that made both of them serve rather than destroy true Christian spirituality. If, as Elton Trueblood says above, reality is a process and quality living involves a persistent walking that knows the eventual goal and carefully avoids the pitfalls along the way, then this very special man, Robert Reardon, has surely stayed on course and run a very good race.

Biblical Foundations

The real pioneer was Rev. Eugene A. Reardon, Robert's father, who visioned for the Church of God movement its best possible self-understanding as it wandered from its prophetic beginnings in the nineteenth century to a fresh search for its soul in the early decades of the twentieth century. Son soon followed father and carried on exceptionally well for additional decades that have reached the present day. Robert Reardon once wrote under the title "Off the Track" about this reform movement's unfortunate diversions into extremism, narcissism, dogmatism, and exclusivism (*The Early Morning Light*, 82-86; see chapter seven of this biography). He always has hoped to steady the ship, verify the course, and discipline the crew.

Dr. Walter Horton of Oberlin Graduate School of Theology, once a beloved seminary teacher of Robert Reardon, said at the death of Rev. Eugene Reardon in the 1940s that he saw father Eugene and son Bob in the biblical image of the prophet Elijah yielding his divine call and ministry to young Elisha. Much more recently, Rev. Ronald Fowler said that Robert Reardon has functioned as the prophet Samuel for the Church of God movement, bridging with informed awareness and deep sympathy the movement's pioneer period and its contemporary mission and challenges. He has stood between the times, helped past and present to dialogue constructively, and steadied the way of inevitable transition. Robert Reardon, as Elisha and Samuel, has maintained what he has understood to be vital, keeping many things on a steady course, even while he often was moving with courage into uncharted territory.

Advice and Testimonies

A personal word is in order. Robert Reardon has been crucial in my own professional journey. My writing of this biography is in part an exercise in personal memory and a gift of love and appreciation. President Reardon is the one who asked that I remain on the Anderson campus in 1966 after my first seminary degree to pursue teaching responsibilities at the collegiate level. When I was being recruited to the faculty of another campus two years later, he urged me to stay with Anderson. I accepted; he was right and I am grateful. A few years later he showed great confidence in me by asking that I assume the major responsibility of the deanship of Anderson School of Theology. When I accepted, nervously and appreciatively, he gave me crucial advice that I have never forgotten, advice so typical of him.

An experienced administrator himself, President Reardon said to me privately, "Barry, now that you are a dean you will always have critics. Get used to it. They can be tolerated. If they are the right ones, you will be able to sleep at night. Here is how you can be sure that you have the right critics. Fix your eyes on the star that is your own divine calling and then follow it no matter what. When critics emerge who are unhappy with your faithfulness to the course that is right for you, they will not prevail because you will know that you are on the right course!"

This advice to me exemplifies the whole life lived by Robert H. Reardon. The issue has been that of staying on the right course no matter what. Crucial to viewing properly Reardon's steady hand at the wheel is one key fact. Staying on course for him means both the conservatism of worthy tradition and the progressiveness of fresh frontiers that move yesterday forward into new tomorrows with courage and creativity. To the conservatives in the church, he often has appeared a dangerous radical. To the liberals he sometimes has been viewed as "holding the line" too tightly for their taste. Critics are always present when one is active on the public playing field. For Reardon himself, a very visible public figure, survival has been a matter of being rooted deeply in the treasure of biblical revelation that is both final and freeing, foundational and yet forever new.

During his retirement years beginning in 1983, Robert Reardon wrote about his early life in his book *The Way It Was* (1991). The back cover carries brief statements about him. They are admiring observations made by four of his dear friends. Noting the identity of these people reveals much about this most unusual man and serves well as a preface to his whole life story. Bill and Gloria Gaither, leaders in the world of gospel music, said: "Every movement needs a storyteller to record the way it happened, to recognize why it is needed, and to preserve the vision for those who may never otherwise know the reason for the heritage they've been given. No one tells the story better than Bob Reardon."

Two others, had much to add. Carl Erskine, legendary pitcher for the Brooklyn Dodgers baseball team, reported that Reardon "sees the church's spiritual and cultural influence on the Anderson, Indiana, community in a marvelous, highly personal light." Then there was Charles M. Schulz, the beloved cartoonist of Charlie Brown fame: "There is much to be learned from the struggles of Bob Reardon as we read how he moved through his younger years, immersed in the religious conservatism and isolation of another day, to eventually be the guiding force behind Anderson University. My admiration for what he accomplished knows no bounds."

Here, then, is a brief composite of Robert H. Reardon: storyteller; preserver of the vision; interpreter of the heritage; spiritual and cultural leader; force in Christian higher education; friend of the famous; simple Christian believer of humble origin. He has believed deeply, fostered change when progress was crucial, and resisted change when perversions of a valuable past pressed dangerously from all sides in the attempt to force a less-than-ideal future. As a sailor through many troubled times, Reardon has been a specialist in the art of staying on course.

The original pilot of the Anderson campus was the beloved Dr. John Arch Morrison, the first president. Anderson College Press was privileged to publish his autobiography in 1962, titled *As the River Flows*. Now, forty-two years later, Anderson University Press is pleased to publish the biography of the second president of Anderson University, Dr. Robert H. Reardon. The first man charted the way as a pioneer; the second man faithfully stayed the course as a determined pilot who had to travel through some very different and sometimes stormy seas. Remembering his journey is a good way to gather wisdom for facing the yet unknown future.

Sources of Material

A word about sources is in order. Where did all the information in this biography originate? In my role as Dean of Anderson School of Theology from 1973 to 1983, I (Barry L. Callen) was called to administrative service by Robert Reardon and functioned closely by his side, seeking to observe and learn from him. In the 1989 to 1992 period, I researched and wrote the history of Anderson University (*Guide of Soul and Mind*), including the making of a series of audio taped interviews with Robert Reardon and many others in his campus administration and in wide circles of the alumni and friends of the campus. I also gathered materials for my book *Faith, Learning & Life: Views from the President's Office of Anderson University* (1991), including a detailed review of the writings, speeches, Christmas cards, and charges to seniors by Robert Reardon over the years.

Then in 2002, when this present biography was conceived, Robert Reardon agreed to my request that he participate with me in a new series of taped interviews that were both personal and institutional. A dozen were done over a two-year period. The Anderson campus also conducted in 2002 several hours of videotaped interviews with Reardon as part of an historical archives project. This aging President-emeritus has been most generous in sharing his time and memories about many things of a personal, institutional, and church related nature. In 2003 he even opened to me large portions of his private journal, none of which had been seen previously by anyone. In these pages, then, it may be assumed that comments attributed directly to Robert Reardon and not documented otherwise are from these audio and video taped interviews or his private journal.

Several other persons were also gracious to share their memories about and evaluations of Robert Reardon. Included were members of his immediate family and former colleagues from various settings. Where direct quotations of these people appear with no specific source citation, they come from these recently taped interviews. In addition, three of Reardon's personal publications have been crucial sources. They are *The Early Morning Light* (1979), *Robert H. Reardon: Some Anderson College Reflections, 1947-1983* (1983), and *The Way It Was* (1991). Also of note is Reardon's 1943 masters thesis written at Oberlin Graduate School of Theology in Ohio (see Appendix E) and the 1984 volume

Educating for Service edited by James Earl Massey and published by Warner Press in honor of the then recently retired President Reardon.

What follows in these pages is a life story in words and photos, including several appendixes featuring key material of particular interest to graduates of the Anderson campus in the 1950s, 1960s, 1970s, and 1980s. This biography is about Robert H. Reardon, a deeply Christian man, a committed husband, father, and grandfather, a sensitive minister of the gospel of Jesus Christ, and a respected leader in the worlds of Christian higher education and the Church of God movement. It is about the crucial ministries of his father Eugene and wife Geraldine, the campus leadership of John A. Morrison, Robert A. Nicholson, James L. Edwards, and a host of others. It also is about the idealism, accomplishments, and struggles of the Church of God movement from the first involvement of a Reardon in the nineteenth century to Robert Reardon's continuing involvement in the twenty-first century.

May the telling of this dramatic story be informative and inspiring, recalling a remarkable past for the sake of pointing the way to what can be a remarkable future because of God's continuing intention and enabling grace.

Barry L. Callen
Anderson University
June 2004

CHAPTER One

Early Morning Light

···

Robert H. Reardon was born in April, 1919. When he was seventy-two years old, he recalled the old saying that a person who does not know or understand anything that happened before he or she was born is virtually an orphan. He mused in the opening lines of his 1991 book *The Way It Was*, "I have a thousand questions I wish I had asked my parents about the world in which they grew up. When I was young, only the present interested me. But I suppose most of us come to a time in our lives when we are reluctant to have the experiences of our past buried with us." Robert Reardon had come to that time himself by 1991 and chose to share some of the memories of his own growing up. He had many stories and he was a gifted, even a legendary storyteller. By the 1990s he was so well known and deeply loved that thousands would have judged themselves orphaned without some knowledge of this man's growing-up world.

What the Robert Reardon of 1991 knew much less about than his own growing up years were the years and stories that had shaped earlier generations of his personal family heritage. What he did know he treasured. This knowledge, even if only fragmentary, helped to keep him from feeling orphaned and now adds to the life stories of the rest of us. Fortunately, much now is known and can be told about important things prior to that day in April, 1919, when little Robert joined the world in Chicago, Illinois (see Appendix H for a brief family tree). Good remembering of key yesterdays can enrich the living of our todays and tomorrows.

Pain in the Old and New Worlds

Robert H. Reardon's father, Eugene Alanzo Reardon (b. 1874), was a key member of the earliest generations of the Church of God movement (Anderson), the story of which Robert Reardon would later review in his book *The Early Morning Light* (1979). Eugene was born in October, 1874, to

Timothy and Anna (Nash) Reardon, then living in West Liberty, Ohio. The family history of Anna, now known at least in part, had been battered with considerable pain.

Anna Nash was born in or near Limerick, Ireland. Her paternal grandparents immigrated from Limerick to the United States in 1845 with their son John. Their departure from Ireland was during and surely because of the worst years of the great Irish famine. Anna's parents stayed in Ireland, choosing to care for their children where they were and the best way they could (assuming that they had not already died). Circumstances grew ever more grave. The first Nash daughter, Lottie, was sent away to the new world to join her Uncle John, by then a successful Irish businessman living in a handsome farm home just east of West Liberty, Ohio. Then by ship in 1870 came Lottie's sister Anna, also fleeing to the home of Uncle John. She survived the voyage and joined her sister and the seventeen Nash children in this devout Roman Catholic family that was managing much better in the United States than were their desperate relatives back in Ireland. Three years after Anna's arrival in Ohio, on Thanksgiving day and at age sixteen, she was married to a local West Liberty man, Timothy Reardon (1851-1914), aged twenty-two.

Timothy and his brother Dan Reardon were construction masons. Their names are still visible on sidewalks in downtown West Liberty. Their father, Owen Reardon (b. 1819), and mother Mary (b. 1826) had immigrated from Cork, Ireland, also fleeing a terrible famine. Since the first child of Owen and Mary was born in Mississippi in 1847, apparently they had immigrated through Virginia on their way south. Then, sometime before the Civil War, they had migrated northward to Ohio where their other children were born. Timothy (b. 1851) was the first to be born in Ohio and Dan the last in 1863.

The Irish-American Reardons would now be new world people for the generations to follow. Eugene Alanzo Reardon (b. 1874) would be the first of the three children born to Timothy and Anna (Nash) Reardon, followed by Nellie (b. 1877) and Isabel (b. 1878). Being good Roman Catholics with a proud Irish heritage, the Reardons had all of their children baptized. The site was St. Patricks cathedral in Bellefontaine, Ohio. Eugene's baptism was on November 14, 1874, at the hands of Father N. R. Young, the local parish priest.

Timothy and Anna Reardon lived close to the river that ran by West Liberty. Their son Eugene became a good swimmer and had a set of clothes that could be shed entirely by opening only one button—instant and uninhibited entrance into the old swimming hole! But such informality was to have its limits. There was a dignity and formality about Timothy Reardon that he sought to convey to his son. For instance, one day they were on a main street in West Liberty as a prominent town personality passed by with his team of horses. Being familiar to everybody in town, young Eugene did not hesitate to call out to the man as he passed by, saying loudly, "Howdy, Joe!" Although the man responded pleasantly, Eugene's father did not. The boy was quickly chided. "Son, you never should address a man older than yourself by his first name—never!" Eugene would not forget this strict instruction and one day would pass along to his own son Robert a sensitivity to the proper formalities of public relationships.

When Robert Reardon (Eugene's son) was president of Anderson College in Indiana many years later (1958-1983), there was an occasional rebellious student who would call him "Uncle Bob" or even "Bobbie." While appreciated to the extent that these informalities usually were expressions of respect and even affection, Robert would be very cautious about them, even critical. Once in the 1970s, while Dr. Barry Callen was Dean of Anderson School of Theology serving under President Robert Reardon, a seminary student said casually in the President's hearing that he would go down the hall and "talk to Barry" about something. The President reprimanded the graduate student for referring to his Dean by his first name. He proceeded to make a point of reporting this inappropriate behavior in his seminary chapel address later that day. Older men and especially leaders were thought by Robert to deserve the routine formalities of public respect. This thought had come from Timothy to his son Eugene and then had been passed on to his son Robert.

Unfortunately for the nineteenth-century Reardons in West Liberty, Ohio, and despite their new-world location that was much more favorable than all the suffering back in Ireland, pain would continue to stalk the family. The Irish famine had been escaped, but not serious trouble of other kinds. Anna Reardon became homesick for Ireland. It is said that when she took to bed with illness, her husband Timothy would comfort her by singing, "I'll Take You Home Again, Kathleen." She must have found it wrenching indeed to have been sent away to America when only thirteen. Her life turned out to be all too short. Anna died at the home of her sister Lottie in 1885, probably in a flu epidemic. She was only twenty-eight and left behind her husband Timothy and the three children, all under the age of eleven.

Anna's premature death seems to have driven Timothy closer than ever to the crutch of alcohol, a longstanding problem of his. He would live another twenty-nine years, but mostly alone, unable or unwilling to keep his family together. The children did the best they could by living with relatives and in foster homes. Liquor was a scourge that visited numerous Irish families and it surely played a hurtful role in the case of Timothy Reardon, Robert Reardon's grandfather. There was a deep dysfunction that troubled the Ohio Reardons—most of it now undocumented. It is said of Timothy that he never refused a drink except once during the winter when he had his earmuffs on and did not hear the invitation! His daughter Nellie would come to suffer from paranoia and finally was committed to a state hospital in 1920. Daughter Isabel fared little better in the long run. Something eventually went wrong in her marriage and she died in the West Liberty County Home.

Life, while full of fresh promise, turned out to have its real downsides for these Reardons, even in the better setting of the new world. Despite this unfortunate fact, a wonderful story lay ahead that could not have been imagined in the years of the family's struggle in West Liberty, Ohio. The fuller and surprising Reardon story would flow through Timothy and Anna's son Eugene, to his son Robert, and then extend with Robert from his birth in 1919 far ahead into the twenty-first century.

Eugene Reardon Joins the "Saints"

Key to this larger Reardon story is the bridging person of Rev. Eugene A. Reardon. Only a boy barely eleven at the time of his mother's premature death, Eugene suffered from the harsh fact that his father proved an unreliable parent. Further, his Roman Catholic relatives showed little interest caring for him. Maybe this was because they had large families of their own and felt that it was Timothy's responsibility. Whatever the case, in future years Eugene would share very little about these difficult times of his youth. They must have been a heavy burden for a sensitive boy who seemed to have few advantages and limited options, all no fault of his own.

Eugene finally did manage to graduate from West Liberty High School in 1892, after which he taught school in the area for several years. While this sustained him for the time as a single young man, his unexpected future lay elsewhere. A high regard for education in the church's life would be vital for

Eugene's future. It also would be vital for the future of a man from Missouri named John A. Morrison whom Eugene later would learn to love, for Eugene's own son Robert, and for a little college campus in Anderson, Indiana, that would be launched two years before Robert's birth in 1919 and would become the central focus of it all.

The eventual destiny of Eugene was sparked by a dramatic personal event. It was through some Protestant friends who supported him that Eugene became a consciously dedicated Christian, giving his young life a whole new direction. Soon he became aware of meetings in his home area of West Liberty, Ohio, being convened by prominent leaders of a young Christian reform movement called the Church of God. Included were outstanding Christians like A. J. Kilpatrick, Barney Warren, and Sam Speck. Warren was a musician and associate of Daniel Warner, the primary pioneer of this reform movement that began in the late 1870s.

In 1891, Warren launched a new ministry in the Springfield, Ohio, area. Many persons were converted through his evangelistic labor, some later becoming influential ministers in the Church of God movement. To many promising young leaders, it was the courtesy, musical inspiration, and personal wisdom of Warren that made a significant difference. Young Eugene Reardon now came to be included in this privileged group. Warren's gentle disposition and rich spiritual life were compelling to him. They stood in stark contrast to much of the harsh and highly judgmental preaching common in the early days of the Church of God movement.

Eugene Reardon was converted to Christ near the end of a 21-day revival meeting in 1892 that met in a barn on the Simon Yoder farm at a place called Three Corners just outside West Liberty. He then made the dramatic decision to leave the Roman Catholic Church—quite a step in the context of his Irish Catholic family. Eugene was rebaptized as a born-again Christian and took a public stand with the Church of God reformation movement. This particular church association was chosen in large part because of his relationship with Barney Warren who shared the message of the new reform movement and planted a congregation of the "Saints" in West Liberty. The Yoders and the Mennonite family of Jonas Hoolie became like personal families for the needy and appreciative Eugene Reardon, now a young Christian with new Protestant identity and a big future ahead.

Reardon, now a very sensitive young Christian, was saddened by the

Faith Missionary Home, Chicago, Illinois

considerable brokenness he saw in the churches of the area and was energized by the vision of unity in Jesus Christ being proclaimed by this new movement. Soon Yoder and Warren became aware of Eugene's sense of ministerial calling. The reform movement had no Bible schools or seminary, so Warren encouraged him to leave teaching and Ohio and join the religious family of the Faith Missionary Home in Chicago that was associated with the Church of God movement. It was housed in an old church with a three-storey apartment house attached, a place where missionaries without personal homes could live temporarily and traveling evangelists and other ministers could spend time, rest, learn from each other, and serve human needs on the surrounding streets of the big city. There young Reardon could "wait before the Lord," travel with seasoned Church of God ministers, and have his ministerial skills honed and his call clarified.

This "home" was an example of the mentoring method of ministerial education, the "sink or swim" approach typical of the time in the young Church of God movement. Several such homes were located in large cities across the United States. Eugene Reardon determined to follow the reforming vision of the young movement and the advice of Brother Warren. He went to Chicago to learn and serve however he could, taking with him in his mind a model of ministry that had been shaped in part by the Roman priesthood he had known. It was a model featuring the virtues of poverty, obedience, and chastity, all of which he would practice for some years in the big and windy city. The future was wholly unknown, but, because it was God's future, it was open and hopeful.

The young Reardon moved to Chicago in 1897 as a single man aged twenty-four. Some of his Roman Catholic relatives suggested unfairly and very hurtfully that Eugene was being irresponsible because he was abandoning his two needy sisters. Of course, such relatives already were openly displeased about his departure from the traditional Catholic faith. The subtle accusation of sibling neglect was hard for Eugene to bear, but answering the call of God was chosen by him as the only path of personal integrity. Young Eugene, like his son Robert would do in the next generation, saw what appeared to be God's way and determined to follow it and stay on course whatever the cost.

Years of Bitter Herbs and Unleavened Bread

Beginning in 1895, Gorham Tufts had operated the Open Door Mission that housed, fed, and evangelized large numbers of poor men in Chicago. In 1898 Tufts was sent by the Church of God movement to India to distribute funds to the starving with money raised by the Church of God in the United States and Canada. George and Mary Cole then came to carry on the Chicago work. Arriving by train shortly after the Coles' work had begun was young Eugene Reardon. He joined the Coles at the Faith Missionary Home in his quest to pursue the humble paths of Christian ministry. This home and others soon located in Denver, Kansas City, New York, and Spokane were significant outposts for the young reform movement and played several very practical roles until they diminished in prominence in the 1920s. The one in Chicago became Eugene Reardon's home in 1897.

Enoch E. Byrum was a key early organizer of the Church of God movement, with the focal institution being the Gospel Trumpet Company based in Moundsville, West Virginia, from 1898 to 1906, and in Anderson, Indiana, from then on. This company published the movement's evangelistic and instructional materials and sent them to the missionary home outposts for distribution on the streets, in train stations, wherever people could be reached. Through the pages of the *Gospel Trumpet*, editor E. E. Byrum asked for and received considerable funding to assist this ministry of publication and its distribution outposts. The missionary homes provided hospitality centers for traveling evangelists of the movement when they were between meetings and functioned as training centers for young ministers who could interact with more seasoned leaders—exactly what Eugene Reardon had come to Chicago to do. These "homes" were Christian communities operated on a faith basis, places of refuge, ministry, instruction, and evangelism. They were experiments in Christian communal living that provided transitional vehicles from the early Church of God movement's strong aversion to virtually all organization in church life to the time in the 1920s when there were more settled congregations, a college, and national ministry agencies that would be supported cooperatively.

Young Eugene Reardon moved into the Faith Missionary Home, joined its "family," and became another recipient of its instruction and an enthusiastic new agent of its ministries. He would spend a total of twenty-two years at the Chicago home, never receiving a salary, even in the later years when he was the superintendent. Living quarters were cramped and clothes often were secondhand, but idealism ran high enough and faith was strong enough to overcome the harsh realities of the place. Here is the testimony of Rev. Reardon, published nationally in the *Gospel Trumpet* (January 17, 1901):

> I am glad to have this testimony, that I please God. Salvation is surely the sweetest thing I have ever found. Oh, how real God is, and how sure his word!... I am so thankful that God has a people who will be true to him.... How glad I am that the Lord has saved me from sectism and set me into the one body, the church of God, the bride of Christ.

The Chicago ministry was significant and grew over the years. Reardon was part of the big process of the home's building its own facility in 1903-1904 at 300 West Seventy-Fourth Street. However, he was unsure of his future at first, not being judged a particularly good ministerial prospect by some of the older ministers. After all, he had been a teacher and was thoughtful and soft-spoken, lacking the flamboyant personality that could gather and excite crowds. The reform movement was spreading mainly because of effective evangelism and prominent preachers like D. S. Warner and H. M. Riggle. At one point there actually was a move to send Eugene home to Ohio, but Mary Cole successfully resisted this idea. Time would prove her wise. The young Reardon persisted in his learning and serving and was formally ordained to Christian ministry early into the twentieth century at the hands of Rev. A. J. Kilpatrick.

By the time the Coles left the Chicago work in 1908, Reardon's organizational skills and quiet wisdom had become recognized and appreciated. He was appointed the superintendent of the missionary home and later the full-time pastor of the congregation that functioned in it. The church apparently could be served well by a man whose gifts did not include the flamboyance that excites large crowds. Although respect and increased responsibility eventually came Reardon's way, this is not to say that there were not great frustrations. At one point the problems had mounted, Reardon was really frustrated, and his friend Rev. Kilpatrick was visiting Chicago. The older man heard Reardon out and then knelt down with him, laid his hands on the struggling young minister, and prayed, "Lord, save this man from the sin of immediate results!" This was an important prayer. As it would turn out, Reardon was in the ministry for the long haul. To his substantial faith he managed to add patience over the years.

Beyond the roles of administration and pastoring, Reardon also became involved directly in the planting of congregations of the Church of God in the Chicago area. Of particular note is the one at Langley Avenue. There is an important story attached to this church planting. The Missionary Home in Chicago had attracted a group of African-American converts who were a few of the many migrants from the South to Chicago. These persons became part of the interracial congregation at the Home and were well accepted. However, there came a time in 1915 when they were not fully satisfied with aspects of Pastor Reardon's ministry style. He was hardly charismatic in his preaching and the music lacked qualities that they earlier had grown to appreciate. These brothers and sisters of color, with their somewhat different cultural preferences, approached their beloved pastor, whom they respected and trusted, sharing their concern and an idea. Could he help them establish their own congregation? They were committed to the Church of God movement, but were feeling the need for some independence from the restrictions of the Home itself.

While not an outwardly expressive man and being wise enough to realize that he was facing a cultural divide, Rev. Reardon managed to avoid the easy response of being defensive. Instead, he offered to assist them in fulfilling their dream. A key part of his help was his knowledge of Sethard P. Dunn, a Black native of Louisiana who had become committed to the Church of God movement. Reardon contacted Dunn and encouraged him to come north to shepherd this little flock in a new Langley Avenue location. Sunday may be the most segregated day of the week, but often there are reasons for this other than racial discrimination. In this case, Southern Blacks were attracted to the Church of God movement, appreciated the primarily White congregation and its leadership at the Home, but still felt the need to worship in their own way and handle their own life as they saw fit.

As Robert Reardon would proudly recall much later, his pastor father was blessed with social intelligence, seemed to understand the unusual circumstance being faced, and was prepared to help without discrimination or defensiveness. Later, son Robert would be the President of Anderson College in Indiana. On this campus one day there would stand Dunn Hall named in honor of Rev. Sethard P. Dunn. Behind the scenes, this men's residence hall also honors Rev. Eugene Reardon.

On Mission in Egypt

Eugene Reardon, still a single man, soon found his arena of service expanding well beyond the Chicago area. Enoch E. Byrum and a small company of others were on their way to India in 1904. They stopped for several days in Egypt, visiting Alexandria and Cairo and distributing literature of the Church of God movement. Results were slow in coming, but they were real nonetheless. Two years later, in response to the invitation of Hanna Arsanious, an Egyptian Christian who had read Church of God literature and written to the United States asking for someone to come and help, George P. Tasker and Hiram A. Brooks arrived in Egypt. They made an extended visit there even though their main goal was India. Their meetings were conducted particularly in Alexandria and Assiut in Upper Egypt. With need for a Church of God missionary to Egypt now obvious, they sent for E. A. Reardon who immediately left the Missionary Home in Chicago and arrived in Egypt even before Tasker and Brooks had gone on to India. This would be quite a challenge for a young man from rural Ohio who had been living communally in Chicago and had no previous international experience. Much later his son Robert wondered if he would have had the courage to launch out on faith in this dramatic way.

Coming in Egypt in 1907 with no knowledge of the Arabic language but with dedication to the major ministry need there, Reardon remained for seven months, living in Assiut, laboring patiently in the midst of considerable difficulty, and helping to build the foundation of the new work both in Assiut under the leadership of Mossad Armanious and in Alexandria under G. K. Ouzounian. The Alexandrian brother was a medical doctor and minister of the Seventh-day Adventist church. Reardon gave him three books published by the Gospel Trumpet Company on the subjects of sanctification and the Sabbath. The young missionary then was asked to preach. He did and made a deep and positive impression on several people. After returning to Upper Egypt and completing his work there, Eugene Reardon again was in Alexandria preparing to sail home. In his mail from the United States came a copy of the just-published book *The Revelation Explained* by F. G. Smith. While saying farewell to his new friend Brother Ouzounian and seeing his interest in this book, he gave it to him. Reading Smith helped this brother be "won to the truth" and established him in the Church of God movement that Reardon proudly represented.

Missionary vision and passion had now joined education and pastoral ministry as things deep in Rev. Reardon's heart. On his way home from Egypt to Chicago, he stopped in Essen, Germany, to counsel German church leaders on how to establish and operate a missionary home. He then visited Ireland, his ancestral homeland. F. G. Smith went to Alexandria, Egypt, in 1913, solidified the earlier contact of Reardon with Ouzounian, and later expressed genuine appreciation for Reardon's pioneering missionary work. When the Church of God in the United States began publication of the *Missionary Herald* in 1910, E. A. Reardon was a regular contributor of articles. Now a teacher-pastor with missionary experience, he wrote in the January 1910 issue of the "tremendous responsibility now resting upon the saints of God" to be "zealous for the salvation of the lost." He spoke in the September 1911 issue of a divine call to missions, but warned that those sensing a call should examine their motives for selfishness, ambition, and the mere glamour of travel. In the March 1910 issue of the *Missionary Herald*, Reardon wrote of the urgent need for missionaries in Egypt and spoke lovingly of a land

> . . .strewn throughout the length of the Nile valley with temples
> and monuments so hoary with age that to trace their origin would
> land one in the dim, forgotten past. They seem to arise out of the
> eternity behind us, shrouded with the mysteries of by-gone ages,
> and speak to us of the awful age of time.

There were Reardons who had fled the struggles of old Ireland; now a Reardon had a more widened view of time and geography and hoped to help enhance the global impact of the gospel of Jesus Christ. On his 1908 return from Egypt to the "family of the saints" in Chicago, Eugene Reardon spent time on a much more personal subject. He continued courting an unlikely young woman named Pearl Horman. The courting had to proceed under the watchful eye of the "saints," a restriction that was one reason he amusingly called these Chicago years ones of "bitter herbs and unleavened bread."

Transitions in Home and Church

Pearl Horman's grandfather Henry had immigrated in 1849 from a little village near Hanover, Germany, fleeing originally to New York City when he was being conscripted into the Prussian army and his family was opposing his romance with a Roman Catholic girl, Mary Rollings. Mary joined Henry in the new world a year later. They soon married, built a log cabin in Crawford County, Ohio, and six years later went into the shoe and boot business in Madison, Wisconsin. Later moving the business to Milwaukee Avenue in downtown Chicago, it flourished and the Hormans came to think of themselves as among the socially elite. They lived on the third floor of the home, made their shoes and boots on the second floor, and ran their business on the ground floor—a very European way of doing things. They were prominent in the Evangelical Lutheran Church in Chicago, where the Horman's son William met and soon married Lydia, a daughter of the Miller family that had immigrated from Alcase Lorraine in France. One of William and Lydia's children would be Pearl Horman (b. 1883). See Apendix H.

How would Pearl, coming from a successful merchant family prominent in the Evangelical Lutheran Church, become related to a group of Church of God "saints" in a communal missionary home located far away from Chicago's downtown "Loop"? It was because Pearl's father, William, had smoked since his boyhood days, would die of lung cancer in his forties, but before his death somehow heard of the healing ministry of the Church of God "saints" in the city and made a visit to the Missionary Home where Rev. Eugene A. Reardon was. While he did die of his cancer despite prayer to the contrary, William's final period of life drew spiritual strength from the ministries of the Home. His wife Lydia affiliated with the Church of God and brought her four girls with her. Also affiliating were Lydia's sisters, Sarah and Lizzie Miller. They all needed a new home now and the saints became their family. Sarah Miller soon became the matron of the Missionary Home while Lizzie Miller did the cooking.

Left to right: Cora, Edith, Marion, and Pearl (Reardon) Horman.

Key to the future was the fact that one of Lydia's daughters, Pearl, did secretarial work for the Home and soon was being courted by the superintendent of the Home, Eugene Reardon. She would become his wife in 1908 and later the mother of Willard and Robert Reardon. Pearl's best friend, when she heard that Pearl was intending to marry E. A. Reardon, a man who had no personal home and received no salary at the Missionary Home, said to her, "There are few people who can say, 'Blessed be nothing!'" Tough and austere as life at the Home was, it was hardly nothing. There was a fullness and richness about it because of the sense that God was in it and those who lived and ministered there were truly about God's business.

Pearl Horman had become a serious Christian woman. Her testimony of Christian faith was published in the *Gospel Trumpet* (April 18, 1907) and titled "Working For Jesus." It read in part:

> Am I doing all I can for the Lord and dear lost souls?... How interested and concerned we should be about the salvation of others!... We have this glorious truth and should do all in our power to spread it. There are numbers of sects who, with their

wrong doctrine, are working so diligently.... Very, very soon our time of service in the Master's harvest field will be ended.

Eugene and Pearl Horman married in 1908, with the officiating minister being Rev. Barney Warren from Ohio, the special friend so influential from Eugene's earliest contacts with the Church of God movement and in his decision to move to Chicago. The honeymoon was in the communal Missionary Home.

The first of the two sons born to Eugene and Pearl Reardon was Willard, who arrived in December, 1912, in the Missionary Home. It was a difficult delivery. There was a doctor present, even though doctors were not particularly popular among Church of God people at the time—faith healing often was preferred exclusively. Just before he was six years old, little Bill began kindergarten at Harvard School just two blocks away from the Missionary Home. He often played in the storeroom on the third floor of the Home, especially loving an old electric train he had access to. This was an early sign of his mechanical ability and future in the field of engineering. It was an adventure for him to go shopping with his Aunt Lizzie. There were numerous vegetable markets, bakeries, butcher shops, and fish markets in the immediate area. He especially disliked the fish markets with their sawdust floors and awful stench. What they bought at these places was often supplemented by foodstuffs of various kinds donated and brought to Chicago by truck from church people living on farms in the region. Times were hard, but God's people were good and they managed.

Willard's brother Robert was born on April 27, 1919, in the Missionary Home then located at 300 West 74th Street in Chicago. He received the middle name Horman as his mother's way of maintaining ties with her family. Thus, Robert was a combination of his German (Horman) and Irish (Reardon) heritages. Joseph T. Wilson, founding principal of Anderson Bible Training School in 1917, came to Chicago in 1920, held baby Robert in his arms, and offered a prayer of Christian dedication. Wilson had no idea about how significant this little boy one day would be to the little school he had just founded in Anderson, Indiana. It would be a long way for Robert to get from the humble streets of urban Chicago to the elite halls of American higher education. Long or not, in time Robert Reardon would make the journey successfully.

Pearl's pregnancy with Robert was difficult. She again had some medical assistance in the Home at the time of the birth. It was a woman, Dr.

Duncan, with an "M.D." of the day, but hardly a true medical professional by today's standards. Bob's birth resulted in a serious illness for Pearl. Later she testified to being healed by God from this "cancer." Robert himself would later observe with some amusement about the earliest boyhood years of himself and his brother Bill: "No neckties were to be worn by the saints, and no wedding rings by the women. So you can imagine the scene when father, with his clerical collar, vest, and black suit, looking every inch like a Roman priest, and my lovely young mother, two children in tow and without a wedding ring, would board the streetcar in the Polish-Catholic neighborhood!" (*The Early Morning Light* 9). These saints of the Church of God were sure about who they were even if others did not always understand.

A Reardon family joke is that, after Robert was born and his father

Reardon Family, 1920. Pearl and Eugene with their sons Willard (above) and Robert.

Eugene had taken one look at him, the father immediately left with F. G. Smith for a year-long missionary tour around the world! It is probable, of course, that the looking and the departing were not connected directly. The birth was in April, 1919, and the tour began in late June. The tour was a key and very visible event for the church generally. While an inevitable strain on the Reardon family, it was a burden gladly carried. Eugene being gone for an extended period of time certainly was a significant sacrifice for Pearl personally, but she carried on with grace, fortitude, and the help of her family of saints. She was dedicated unconditionally to her husband and the cause of Christ that he was serving. The 1919-1920 tour was well publicized in Church of God circles across North America and stimulated much new interest in the church's sharing of the gospel of Christ worldwide. It also stimulated a new concern in Brother Reardon that would flavor his future ministry.

Since 1916 F. G. Smith had been Editor of the Gospel Trumpet Company, by then located in Anderson, Indiana. His influential writings were coming to comprise much of what he and many others considered the "standard" literature of the movement. He appeared to be the self-appointed watchdog for any signs of creeping "man-rule" in the church and seemed to be presenting himself to Rev. Reardon and others during the world tour as the leader of the Church of God movement. F. G. and Eugene wrestled with this while on board ship, with Reardon making clear to him that Jesus is the head of the church. Smith, of course, did not disagree with this, but he nonetheless did appear to believe that he was intended by God to guide and protect the reformation movement from all dangerous perversions of its critical role in God's plan (meaning the role as he understood it, of course).

Although Reardon and Smith were good friends and trusted colleagues in ministry, and Smith sat under the preaching of Reardon Sunday after Sunday at Park Place Church in Anderson, they had come to have a somewhat different perspective on matters of church authority and leadership. Reardon worried about Smith's great influence in the movement and questioned the rightness of his view of the Book of Revelation that helped support that influence. There even was a failed attempt by Smith to block anything being published by the movement that disagreed with the movement's early "standard" literature—much of which he had written himself. Then in 1930 Smith was voted out of the Editorship of the Gospel Trumpet Company in an upsurge of more democratic tendencies in the church. Eugene Reardon played a key role throughout, resisting the inordinate dominance of Smith. The years immediately ahead would provide a context where this difference of perspective would have to be faced squarely, sometimes painfully and publicly. Such a confrontation with Smith's general position would extend on into the later and very prominent ministry of Rev. Reardon's son, Robert.

Respect grew for Rev. E. A. Reardon over the years and across the church. Historian Charles E. Brown describes him as "a man of dignified bearing, neat in person and appearance, orderly in mind, sound in judgment, pure in heart, [a man whose] judgment carried great weight with the brethren"

(*When the Trumpet Sounded* 202). Hardly a radical, he nonetheless was a creative and sometimes courageous innovator. For instance, Rev. Reardon decided that sporadic and secret giving to the local church by members putting money in a box by the door was a poor way to do the Lord's business. So he preached on tithing at Park Place Church in Anderson and then instituted an envelope giving system, the first in any Church of God congregation. Such steps brought him prominence locally. Respect for him nationally also evolved for a variety of reasons and led to a series of major responsibilities coming his way.

In 1907 the Gospel Trumpet Company in Anderson, Indiana, constructed an "Old Peoples' Home" for the care of many of the aging saints of the movement. Among the nine persons named as trustees of the association administering this Home was E. A. Reardon. Further, when the ministers assembled at Anderson Camp Meeting in 1909 and by common consent identified "certain brethren" who should be recognized as having responsibility for the movement's foreign missionary work, one of the seven men named was E. A. Reardon. Later, when the General Ministerial Assembly of the Church of God first organized in Anderson, Indiana, in 1917, Brother Reardon was elected as the Assembly's first Chair, a major vote of confidence indeed. Such prominence was in sharp contrast with the near decision some years earlier to send Eugene from the Chicago Missionary Home back to Ohio because it was not clear to some that he was good ministerial material!

The October 1915 issue of *Our Ministerial Letter* was sent to all ministers of the Church of God movement. It featured the major essay "A Message to Young Ministers" written by E. A. Reardon. This essay reflected the obvious wisdom of a mature Christian man addressing the next generation of church leaders. He urged "proper respect for our older brethren in the ministry" and expressed deep gratitude for "the kind advice and the faithful reproofs of older brethren that watched over my early ministry" (12). Reardon also offered the sincere hope that "the church of God will soon awake to her responsibility to give her sons and daughters more encouragement to enter the ministry and a better chance for preparation" (3). Note the small "c" on "church" (Reardon not wishing to think of the reform movement of the Church of God in a provincial and denominationalized way). Note also the inclusion of "daughters" in ministerial leadership and the dream of formal education for ministry coming soon to the movement. Such wishes, inclusions, and dreams were in the heart of Rev. Eugene Reardon. Soon they also would be very much in the heart of his son Robert.

After the Anderson Bible Training School was launched in 1917, Eugene Reardon was invited to be its first guest lecturer. The General Ministerial Assembly of the Church of God placed an immediate ban on the granting of any diplomas to students who completed programs at this little school. This was done to highlight the ministerial gifts of the Spirit and protect against human arrogance based on human "papers." E. A. Reardon was the minister who presented the 1923 resolution in the Assembly that successfully lifted this ban. He had been a teacher and felt that such a restriction was unfair to students. The little school's slogan, "where spirituality predominates," should not mean that the lives of the spirit and mind are inherently in conflict.

Reardon's relationship with the school soon broadened further. Beginning in 1920, he was the pastor of Park Place Church of God where most of the faculty and students attended. When the growing school was separated from its founding parent, the Gospel Trumpet Publishing Company, in 1925 and gained its own corporate life and board of trustees, the proposed articles of association to govern the independent school that were adopted by a resolution in the General Ministerial Assembly was moved by E. A. Reardon. The first executive committee of the school's trustees was composed of five key leaders, including E. A. Reardon. John Morrison, the school's first president, said later that Reardon "never feared the face of man.... I always thought he was just a little happier in the midst of a fight for a good cause than he was when all was peace and calm" (*As the River Flows* 149). Later there would be similar characterizations of his son Robert. Both father and son clearly thought that the school was "a good cause" indeed, one worth fighting for if necessary. At various times it indeed would be necessary.

Eugene Reardon exhibited leadership in more ways than occupying influential offices in the church's life in North America. He was a man of principle and courage who came to prominence in the 1910s and 1920s when the Church of God movement was experiencing significant change. Historian Merle Strege characterizes this change as a shift from decrying human organization in church life to the reform movement itself institutionalizing and thus risking the very danger it denounced (in Douglas Welch, *Ahead of His Times*, ii-iii). There was a struggle between movement exclusivism and inclusivism, a come-out sectarianism and a reach-out ecumenism. George Tasker, early Canadian missionary of the Church of God to India, was an inclusive voice, a man ahead of his times who paid the price when he was "fired" by the Missionary Board of the movement in 1925 for failing to hold to an inward-looking movement, an exclusivism that the Board insisted he should push in his teaching role with the Indian believers. Tasker had a different vision and refused.

One courageous voice that supported Tasker was E. A. Reardon, who reported boldly in *Our Ministerial Letter* in 1915: "Those who come out of Babylon under a harsh preacher are frequently born of a wrong spirit.... They will likely worship the reformation instead of the Lord, and with their sectarian spirit they will hold the reformation in exactly the same way that the sectarian holds his sect, and be more loyal to it than to God and his church" (8-9). These were sharp words from a prophetic man who, because of his view, was not appreciated by all, but was deeply loved by most.

Rev. Reardon became a point man for those who loved the reformation movement of the Church of God in a non-sectarian way. He intended to help steady the course of the movement and reset its sails in a time of significant change and occasional turmoil. While later pastoring in Denver, Colorado, for instance, he traveled back to Indiana to deliver the 1929 commencement address on the Anderson campus of the Church of God. He was awarded an honorary Doctor of Divinity degree by the appreciative school and was identified in the May, 1929, issue of the school's *Broadcaster* publication as "a devout and fearless preacher of righteousness" who also "is deeply in sympathy with youth and youth problems."

The school's president, John A. Morrison, was chair that year of the Camp Meeting Committee that set the program for the large annual gathering in Anderson, Indiana. National church tensions were nearing a boiling point among the ministers at the close of the 1920s, including the "trial" of professor Russell Byrum of the Anderson campus. He was being accused of using his own ideas to lead astray the college students (i.e., away from some of the ideas of F. G. Smith). President Morrison asked E. A. Reardon to address the annual Assembly of church leaders in a straightforward manner. Reardon did just that. Important issues deserved a fearless presentation and Reardon was the right man to do it. Reardon believed that the Church of God movement was in danger of straying into territory that would undermine its divine calling and seriously compromise the integrity of its reforming mission. A prophetic voice was needed to grasp the wheel and steady the course. Reardon was set forward as God's man for the hour. It would not be comfortable, but it seemed necessary.

In his opening address to the 1929 General Ministerial Assembly, Reardon said the following with deep conviction: "There is no one body of people on earth who can claim an exclusive right to Christ and to all his light and truth.... The expectation that all sheep of the Lord are eventually coming to us as a movement is not at all necessary to the success of God's plan." He spoke forthrightly of the "critical and narrow spirit in our own work" and announced the following to some approving and many skeptical ministers: "We are missing much because we have cut ourselves off from association and fellowship with other Christian people who in many respects could enrich us."

The man who was said to lack the flamboyant style so admired in the early Church of God movement nonetheless spoke clearly and was heard well by all. He dared to warn: "I can see a tendency to sectarianize the movement.... There is such a thing as stressing the reformation to such an extent as to cause our people to be reformation centered—reformation sectarians." Eugene Reardon had warned earlier in the October 1915 issue of *Our Ministerial Letter*: "Some seem never to be in their element unless they are threshing Babylon, exposing false teachers, or clubbing wolves. Such preachers rarely give the sheep a good meal" (9). Brother Reardon had spoken his mind plainly and there would be consequences—the risk a prophetic voice always faces.

Many leaders in the 1929 General Ministerial Assembly disagreed with these forthright comments and "open" attitudes of Reardon. Lines were drawn and an organized response followed. The Assembly proceeded to vote Reardon out of several offices, except for his continuing membership on the Missionary Board. Knowing the results of the voting, Reardon again addressed the Assembly. The air was electric. Would he be defensive, even vindictive? No. He said only this: "The brethren gave and the brethren have taken away. Blessed be the name of the brethren." There was the usual Reardon dignity. Loss was accepted with grace. Integrity remained unscathed. Respect and even reelection would return very soon.

Meanwhile, the "heresy trial" went on in the basement of Park Place Church. Russell Byrum was under attack for some attitudes and opinions he shared in the Anderson College classrooms that were similar to Reardon's comments to the Assembly. Reardon was one of several asked to speak on Byrum's behalf. He did and Byrum was exonerated. Even so, the results would be painful and stretch over many years to come. Byrum resigned his teaching position for what he saw as the good of the school. The outstanding theologian of the Church of God movement of that time went to building homes, never again to return to teaching or writing. This was a low point in the history of the movement.

While many ministers had not agreed with Reardon's 1929 Assembly statements, subsequent events made clear that he had been heard well by many of them. The very next year, in fact, with John Morrison and Eugene Reardon deeply involved, the Gospel Trumpet Company refused to elect F. G. Smith to a new term as its Editor, a shock to the conservative leaders in the church and a true watershed in the church's life. "Democratic" forces were gaining prominence in a movement dominated previously by several strong personalities—especially F. G. Smith.

E. A. Reardon was involved deeply in the pioneering and then institution building phases of the Church of God movement. Years later his son Robert would also play key stabilizing roles in the church's ongoing sense of calling and program direction. It was perceived by both father and son that the Church of God movement was a genuine movement of God. They both, in their differing times, circumstances, and ways, would find themselves seeking to steady the movement's course, keeping it both properly rooted and forward looking. Such an endeavor proceeded in relation to proclamations about "early morning light."

The Church of God movement believed deeply in the earliest generations of the Christian faith tradition and the work of the Holy Spirit among them. It was believed that, after centuries of church compromise and sin, God now was shining a fresh light on the church, the light of the church's early morning. Rev. E. A. Reardon was caught up in the exciting vision and life of this church reform movement from some of its earliest years in the states of Ohio (his original home), Illinois, and Indiana and in the country of Egypt.

The personal ministry and witness of E. A. Reardon became more light, welcome and clarifying light, that soon would illumine the life and ministry of his son Robert who, in 1979, would write a book titled *The Early Morning Light*. Robert Reardon called his book "a friendly reflection on some of the main events in the life of the Church of God reformation movement during the first fifty years." Robert's father was a key player in those early years, as Robert himself would be in the second half-century of the movement's life. The movement was one of dreamers who longed for the church to discover her essence, her Lord, her rightful mission and destiny. Both Eugene and later

Robert Reardon shared the dream and were determined to keep on a steady course the fresh effort to implement its fulfillment.

When Eugene Reardon returned in 1920 from his world tour with F. G. Smith, he learned that Rev. H. A. Sherwood had resigned the pastorate of the Park Place Church of God in Anderson, Indiana. Reardon soon was called to replace him. His answer was affirmative. Thus, Eugene and Pearl Reardon ended a ministry of two decades at the Faith Missionary Home and left the windy city on Lake Michigan for the much smaller industrial city of Anderson on the White River in central Indiana. It would be in Anderson that the boyhood of Robert Reardon began.

CHAPTER Two

A Hoosier at Heart

W hat is a "Hoosier"? It relates to citizens of Indiana, but nobody even in Indiana seems to be sure about an exact definition. One suggestion is that a Hoosier is a person born or living in Indiana who is industrious, hospitable, down-home, and enjoys popcorn, race cars, and basketball. Most of this definition certainly describes Robert H. Reardon rather well. He has always considered Anderson, Indiana, his home. In part, this is the result of certain events in the early twentieth century, more than a decade before his birth.

About one hundred and seventy newcomers arrived in Anderson, Indiana, in 1906. They represented the leadership of a Christian reform movement migrating from Moundsville, West Virginia, to benefit from promised economic advantages for the company. With them came the Gospel Trumpet Company, the publishing work and heart of the cooperative life of the young Church of God movement. On September 23 of that year these people gathered in the company's newly rented home at Ninth and Central in downtown Anderson for the first Church of God worship service in this city. A young congregation was born. In 1916 it resettled on a cabbage patch on the corner of Eighth Street and Union Avenue (College Drive) in a domed building that would seat about eight hundred people for worship. This was in a community called Park Place on Anderson's east side very near to where the publishing work by then had built its own permanent home and where the campus of Anderson University one day would be.

This new congregation, now called Park Place Church of God, soon arranged for a formal dedication of its impressive new structure in November, 1917. The speaker for this very special occasion was Rev. E. A. Reardon of Chicago. Following the two-year pastorate of Rev. H. A. Sherwood, in 1920 Reardon was called back to Anderson, this time to be the new Park Place pastor. He would serve there for a total of eighteen years, in two segments of time separated by his years of pastoring in Denver, Colorado. During those years when the Reardons were away from Anderson (1926-1933), Park Place was pastored by Albert F. Gray. Both before and again after Gray's pastorate, Anderson was the home of the Eugene and Pearl Reardon family.

Young Bob Reardon was one year old when the family's Indiana residence initially began. He later would identify himself as "a child of the church," with the Church of God movement especially in mind. One day he would be a teacher-minister and church leader who also had business and political skills that would interact with educators, governors, foundations, church leaders, and business corporations. But first came a Hoosier childhood in the midst of a strong and nurturing church community. Whatever the significant superstructure of his life would one day be, the church always would remain the underlying foundation, with Anderson, Indiana, the primary location.

Childhood Among "Our People"

Pastor Eugene and Pearl Reardon lived at 914 Walnut Street on the east side of Anderson, Indiana, a short walk from Park Place Church of God and the Gospel Trumpet Company. Comprising this household were the pastor and his wife, the two boys, Willard and Robert, along with Pearl's mother, Lydia Horman, and Lydia's sister, Sarah Miller. The Reardons first lived on Central Avenue when they arrived in town in 1920, but soon were able to purchase the house on Walnut Street just being built at the time. The purchase money was loaned to Eugene and Pearl by Lydia and Sarah who had gotten it as modest gifts from their brother John Miller who enjoyed monetary success as founder of the Chicago Tanning Company. What developed in Anderson might be thought of as a little "missionary home" on Walnut Street, reflecting in some ways the Faith Missionary Home in Chicago that the Reardons had been key members of for many years. Lydia, the mother of Pearl, was a wonderful cook and "Aunt Sarah" was the home "matron," while Eugene pastored the church and Pearl kept the home and assisted her husband by typing sermons and doing some home visitation with him.

Rev. Reardon was a very proper man and the "saints" of the church had very watchful eyes. Early Church of God people often were called "the saints," reflective of their strong "holiness" commitments and intentional separation from "the world." There was to be no appearance of evil, including how the pastor went about his work. This is why the couple often made the pastoral calls together. Robert describes his father as "a warm, outgoing person with considerable social intelligence." Pastor Reardon projected dignity and order into the worship life of Park Place Church of God, always dressing for morning services in a knee-length Prince Albert coat and gray striped trousers. He delivered God's Word with both authority and kindness, standing erect, with his Irish face aglow and blue eyes shining. The pastor's children were also supposed to maintain at least a semblance of dignity. That did not always come naturally for young Bob.

Women in this church fellowship rarely were employed outside the home in the early 1920s, laboring instead with numerous family tasks involved in rearing the children and overseeing the seasonal

Robert Reardon riding in a homemade car.

canning of garden food for the winter. Pearl Reardon, however, did decide one day that she wanted to learn to drive the family car. Eugene gave her lessons in the nearby Maplewood Cemetery where there was limited potential for a serious accident. Their son Bob recalls with considerable amusement one day when his mother decided to go to some meeting and insisted on driving herself there—unaccompanied. He watched anxiously as his father worried over her departure. In fact, Pastor Reardon actually hurried on foot as far as he could to see that she was successful in making the first turns on the route. God was merciful and she later returned safely. One place in the 1920s where women were really equal (at least in principle) was in the life of the Church of God movement itself. After all, in Christ many human classifications are supposed to lose their discriminatory meaning (Gal. 3:28).

The annual cycle of church life in Anderson organized itself around the great North American Camp Meeting that convened in June each summer. Bob and his friends were allowed to wander around the grounds that were close by the Reardon home. Eugene and Pearl considered it safe for their boys to move freely among the "saints." The boys especially liked the lunch stand. Six-year-old Bob managed on occasion to beg from his friend Steele Smith the needed nickel for an ice cream cone. Sometimes the boys would amuse themselves by looking at the license plates on the fascinating cars that had originated in many states and now sat quietly around the Anderson grounds.

Thousands of people gathered regularly in the big tabernacle where the singing was wonderful and the preaching powerful. Rachel Lord often sang and Sister Cotton, a saintly black believer, would run up and down the aisles waiving her handkerchief and shouting the glories of God. Rev. John Morrison, the first president of Anderson College beginning in 1925, was known to be cautious about some of this emotionalism, which he called "whooping it up." Even so, much of the emotion in the services was heartfelt, genuine, and centered in the amazing grace of God that is life changing. Thousands of stories could be told. One of special significance involves a young girl named Geraldine Hurst from Princeton, Indiana. She was saved as a ten-year-old in one such service and years later would become Bob Reardon's wife.

Bob sometimes was moved emotionally as a young boy by the sheer electricity of these camp meeting occasions and by the resounding songs sung with great passion, like the one by William J. Henry that occasionally poured forth from eight thousand voices while the boy sat understandably impressed:

> Let the fire fall on me, Let the fire fall on me,
> The fire of Pentecost, consuming sin and dross,
> Let the fire fall on me.

Although this singing could be heard blocks away at the Reardon home on Walnut Street, Bob usually sat in the large tabernacle on a wooden bench, sawdust on the floor, people packed to the doors, caught up in great waves of thrilling songs. His memory of it? "What an experience!" (*The Way It Was* 12). It soaked into the very fabric of his being. He would love church music all of his life, one day becoming a skilled organist.

Young Bob Reardon was not without some of his own "sin and dross" on which a little divine fire might have fallen helpfully. He would never forget a Sunday morning service at Park Place Church when he was sitting on his mother's lap quite disinterested in his father's sermon. He kept squirming and kicking the back of Sister Sherwood's seat. Pearl Reardon tried as a good mother to handle the situation, but with little success. The problem caught the minister's eye and the sermon was suddenly stopped. Things were now serious indeed.

As Bob recalls the small nightmare that soon followed, his dad "paused, closed his Bible, and, as about eight hundred people watched, he walked down off the platform, lifted me firmly from mother's arms and headed for the vestibule. It was in the sanctity of that south vestibule," Bob confessed much later, "that I got my first instruction on what kind of behavior was appropriate in church. It was punctuated with several whacks that resounded clearly in the awful silence of the assembled saints…. Father carried me back to mother's arms, restored and in my right mind, whereupon he walked sedately back to the pulpit and finished his sermon" (*The Way It Was* 3-4).

Another awkward incident featured Bob stealing some cherries from a tree next door to his home. His father somehow found out about it and Bob suddenly had more than a bellyache. He was made to apologize to the neighbor—"not one of the best days of my life." As he reported this to the Anderson College chapel audience on November 21, 1978, his father "was not a man to be moved to fits of anger and abuse his children," but, when the occasion called for it, he was a good man with a razor strap. "Everything I am today," reported the then President Reardon, "probably goes back to dad's use of the razor strap that used to hang on the back of the bathroom door."

Despite such definitive discipline, Bob did not know his father as a "stern, sober, unbending puritan." There was an abundance of love that allowed both of the Reardon boys "to think of God as our heavenly Father who loves and disciplines his children" (*The Way It Was* 4-5). Even so, sometimes Bob pushed his parents rather hard. Once he came home from Park Place Church and suddenly announced to his parents, "I am never going to Sunday school again!" His mother asked, "Well, Bobby, why don't you want to go to Sunday school?" His abrupt reply, full of faked fear, was, "Because there are bears in the basement!" What he failed to report was that the "bears" were Bessie Byrum, Eunice Morrison, and Birdie Smith—very strong church women with whom he no longer wished to deal.

Soon after the dramatic churchly correcting, Bob confesses coming into his home with his "pop gun" under his arm and announcing proudly that he had just shot off a piece of the Moon! Some of his friends later would hear this story and make the humorous observation that "this gift of exaggerated prevarication was the first shadowy indication of his future vocation as a college president!" (*The Way It Was* 4). It later would be observed of Bob that he worked creatively around the fine line between virtual prevarication and strategic maneuvering of the facts in the service of many good causes.

Early in life, Bob learned to dream, risk, use his imagination, and state his case impressively with a good story. He one day would become a very cultured and sophisticated man, but never would he forget or fail to appreciate the mundane realities of his early years. For instance, Noah Byrum lived where the stately Park Place Church of God building now stands. Byrum raised chickens and occasionally little Bob Reardon was sent there to reach into the pen and catch a chicken that was being given to the pastor's family.

The home of the Reardon family was a loving one, conveying to the two boys a sense of strength and safety. A lingering childhood memory of Bob involves his father's habit of walking regularly. When the weather would not allow walking outside, on occasion Eugene would walk around and around inside the home, carrying his infant son Bob with him. Being held, carried, close, secure—this was strength and great joy for the little boy. The two Reardon boys both noticed that their father was so attentive to their mother, sending love letters to her when he traveled and never leaving the house—even to go out to mow the lawn—without finding and kissing her.

On Monday mornings, Pastor Reardon's weekly day of rest from ministerial duties, Eugene usually was in the Walnut Street basement helping Pearl wash the family clothes. Their love for each other enveloped the household and made the boys feel tenderness, caring, and security. Years later Bob's own son Gene would experience his dad passing on this sense of loving and reassuring acceptance. Robert Reardon "could be warm and affectionate," says Gene. "When we went on trips, I used to sit on my knees in the back seat and hug him while he drove. He never pushed me away. It was a feeling of blissful security." Daughter Kathy is so pleased that "Dad was generous with hugs. I remember being cradled asleep in his arms so many, many times and carried up to bed to be tucked in."

As a small boy, Bob Reardon lived in a church community of dreamers who had a great vision about a newly purified, unified, and global church reaching out at any cost to sound the trumpet of reformation before the Lord's soon return. The dream rooted in a movement that embodied the concerns that had first been those of its primary pioneer, Daniel S. Warner (1842-1895). In 1881 he had stood up in a country meeting house in Beaver Dam, Indiana, and declared himself free from all human institutions, creeds, and unsanctified practices in church and personal life. One of the earliest centers of the resulting church reform movement was a campground near Beaver Dam on the shore of Yellow Lake. Bob Reardon's Aunt Edith and Aunt Marion bought a cottage there just after World War I. It would be the scene of many formative memories for the impressionable little boy.

Young Bob was first brought to Yellow Lake as a baby when his father and prominent church leader F. G. Smith were on their year-long mission journey around the world. While still living in Chicago prior to 1920, the Reardons made an annual pilgrimage to these Indiana church grounds, getting off the train at Claypool and finishing the trip by a horse-drawn cart. When Bob was three years old, his Aunts Edith and Marion came to Anderson from Chicago to be married by Pastor Reardon in his home, with Aunt Edith marrying Raymond Mills and Aunt Marion marrying Forrest Higgins. In preparation, Pearl cleaned the house on Walnut Street with great care and scrubbed Bob to within an inch of his life. Unfortunately, just before Rev. Reardon was to begin the ceremony, Bob appeared in the house after having spent some unplanned time outside in a mud puddle or two. The ceremony was halted abruptly until he was "restored" to relative decency.

The tale of this unpleasant episode was told many times in family reunions over the years to come. The scene was usually the Higgins farm near the campgrounds at Yellow Lake in northern Indiana. "Uncle Forrest" was "an incredible character" and a leader with Aunt Marion in the Akron, Indiana, Church of God congregation. He was a great storyteller and together with Marion they hosted the whole Pearl (Horman) Reardon family every Thanksgiving. Robert Reardon recalls fondly how his Uncle Forrest would attach the handle of their ice cream machine to the back wheel of his Model A Ford, start the engine, put it in gear, and thus marvelously spin a sweet treat for all! His humorous comments abounded, like this observation on life: "Since the earth is three-fourths water, I assume that God meant for us to spend three-fourths of our time fishing!" About 1980, Robert and Geraldine Reardon would themselves buy a cottage on the church campgrounds at Yellow Lake, keeping alive the family heritage in this area.

The Park Place Church congregation back in Anderson prospered under Rev. E. A. Reardon's leadership, averaging about eight hundred people in Sunday morning services. Church of God people in Anderson in the 1920s were "separate" people. They were come-outers from the accommodations and divisions of the larger Christian community and deliberately distinct from many of the ways of the world outside the church. Most families in Park Place Church of God derived their livings and otherwise oriented their lives around the Gospel Trumpet Company or its little Anderson Bible Training School that had been founded by the company in 1917. If someone on the sidewalk was smoking, Pearl Reardon would quietly say to Bob, "that is not one of *our people*."

One distinction of Church of God people was the strong belief in divine healing. Some insisted that going to doctors and having faith in God were not compatible practices. When there was sickness in a church family, Rev. Reardon was called, usually before and probably instead of a doctor. He always carried a small vial of olive oil that could be clipped into his pocket like a fountain pen. It was applied to symbolize the powerful presence of the Holy Spirit in time of physical distress.

Rev. Reardon certainly believed in divine healing, although he did not claim a special gift of healing like E. E. Byrum, who by the 1920s was called upon regularly to pray for the sick, often traveling hundreds of miles to a bedside. Eugene Reardon, however, did not argue against the legitimacy of doctors as did many church leaders. Once his son Bob fell in the kitchen of their Anderson home and injured his head. Blood was running from an eye. Before his father could get home to pray for healing, his mother Pearl applied a typical home remedy of the time, a spider web spread directly on the cut. The bleeding stopped and infection was avoided, although Bob would always carry a little scar. The Reardon family was drug free—no medicine of any kind was kept in the house. A good supply of faith was always available as necessary.

Glaring social realities were never far from the Reardon home in the 1920s and 1930s. The city of Anderson and Indiana in general were influenced heavily at the time by the Klu Klux Klan. From the perspective of the Church of God movement, the KKK members were surely *not* "our people"! Large numbers of Black believers came to the Anderson Camp Meeting each year. They slept, ate, and fellowshipped freely on the grounds with no apparent discrimination. Bob Reardon recalls that "this stirred up the townspeople, who protested to E. E. Byrum and others, but were not violent about it as long as this 'insanity' was confined to the campground for one week a year" (*The Way It Was* 13). At the Yellow Lake campground in northern Indiana, an old center of the Church of God movement, the summer festival of preachers included the voices of persons black and white, men and women. It was believed that such social distinctions as gender and race are transcended in the church by the grace of God. The church is not to be *more of* but *other than* the world.

Beyond the relative absence of the typical racial discrimination of the time, there was to be no card playing, drinking, smoking, games on Sunday, premarital sex, or use of slang like "gee whiz," "darn right," or "you bet"—language too close to cursing or worse, blasphemy. Anyway, Christians do not "bet." Many sermons warned women of the evils of bobbed hair, painted faces, and short skirts. Women, recalls Robert Reardon, were "supposed to look like Russian peasants—plain, unadorned, fully covered" (*The Way It Was* 7). Little Bob had to repent often for playing marbles "for keeps"—"gambling," said his mother, "pure and simple."

It should be said, however, that the Reardon household was hardly provincial, destructively judgmental, or culturally deprived, despite its relative isolation, poverty, and strong religious convictions. The same can be said for the "family" of the Church of God generally as it lived on the east side of Anderson, Indiana. For instance, Mona and Dorothy, daughters of John Morrison who was the president of Anderson College beginning in 1925, recall vividly the "really fun" times of their growing up years. There were wonderful parties in the big Gospel Trumpet home, the location of the new school, and on snowy winter days there also was wild sled riding down the hill behind it.

One day in 1939, Geraldine Hurst, a freshman on campus with a preaching gift and one day to be Robert Reardon's wife, decided to have an expense-free thrill. She went head first into the fourth floor opening of the enclosed tubular fire escape of "Old Main," flew downward, in seconds shot out the bottom, and landed at the feet of President Morrison! While he was not amused, her punishment was not severe—it was her first and probably her only offense. Recalls Dorothy Morrison, "Everybody was poor, but we hardly noticed. We were like a big family and had so much fun. Daddy [President Morrison] was a believer and a dreamer with a good sense of what could and should be." Pastor Eugene Reardon was also a believer and a dreamer. The close friendship of Pastor Reardon and President Morrison would be crucial for young Bob Reardon's future.

Diverted to Denver

Life for Park Place Church of God was mostly good in Anderson, Indiana, but all was not well in the Reardon household. Eugene was pastoring the "mother" church in what was considered by Church of God people the spiritual center of the world and he was functioning as a key player in much that was going on in the reform movement worldwide through its Anderson-based ministries. At the same time, the Reardons became deeply concerned about their older son Willard. He had begun suffering from a lung condition causing "a wasting away in flesh and energy," as his father put it. It appeared to be tuberculosis. One day Willard had slipped

Pearl Reardon, about 1936.

secretly down to the nearby White River to go swimming alone at a popular spot for local youth. This may have led to a lung infection that, whatever it was, kept lingering. The source was never clear, but the situation was becoming serious.

Otherwise, most things proceeded rather normally. The family gathered daily for the discipline of worship and the boys continued to tithe their weekly allowance to the church (they had their own envelopes). Bob's mind would sometimes wander as his Aunt Sarah's prayers would "begin in the Garden of Eden and end on the Isle of Patmos!" Through it all, however, Willard's illness persisted and Eugene and Pearl

Rev. Eugene A. Reardon, Denver, Colorado, about 1932.

came to agree that God was directing a family move to a different climate as a way of addressing this problem. Discussion began quietly with the congregation in North Denver, Colorado, a church that needed a pastor. Then in July, 1926, after the Anderson Camp Meeting, the Reardon's 1925 Studebaker was loaded, tearful good-byes were said, and the beloved pastor and his family headed west to a new pastoral responsibility and hopefully better days for Willard's health.

As Bob Reardon later said of Denver in the 1920s, "the air was as crystal and clean as the driven snow" (*The Way It Was* 25). Hopefully, this would be just what Willard needed. On the way west, the Reardons had Willard examined at the State Sanitarium in Norton, Kansas, through the contact of church friends in Hill City, Kansas, with whom they stayed. They were told that the xray showed a serious case of "T.B." This troubling but hardly surprising news was received, the parents gave thanks for the kindness of the doctor who refused any payment, and the family continued on its long journey. The Colorado state campmeeting of the Church of God was in progress in Berkley Park when the Reardons arrived in August. A divine healing service that week saw Willard and others respond to an invitation for prayer. He was anointed for healing and ministers laid hands on him and prayed earnestly in faith. Willard remembers this as "a stirring time, a great sense of loving community." Something happened there that in a very short time greatly reduced the heavy flow of mucus that had plagued him. An amazing healing seemed to have begun.

Brother M. A. Monday came to the Reardon tent at the Berkley Park camp meeting site and announced that God wanted to heal Willard fully. He and the Reardons gathered in a circle in the tent and Rev. Monday prayed a wonderful prayer in this regard. No fire fell from heaven, but Willard continued to eat better and gain weight. The family soon enjoyed a time away in a lovely mountain town that offered healthful diversions. Fresh xrays were taken at a local hospital and no trace could be found even of the scar tissue in Willard's lungs! The problem that had prompted the Reardon move to Denver in the first place appeared to be gone—and clearly gone only by the grace of God. It would never return in Willard's lifetime. His younger brother Bob was quite impressed by all of this, and rightly so. Rev. Eugene Reardon reported the following to the church at large through the *Gospel Trumpet* (Feb. 3, 1927, 3): "God did the rest. Immediately the dull, heavy load of oppression left his

[Willard's] breast and he began to have a good appetite. Thereafter we found him in the very front of the bread-line at the camp cafeteria."

Eugene Reardon pastored the North Denver Church of God for seven years beginning in 1926. It was located at 34th Avenue and Vallejo Street. The Reardons lived at 4627 Moncrief. The church had fallen on hard times prior to the arrival of the Reardons. Young people on the back pews were eating ice cream and speaking disrespectfully during worship services. Attendance was down and morale was poor. Bob Reardon remembers his father telling his mother that it might take five years to put the Denver congregation back on its feet. The ice cream eating at the wrong time and the general disrespect were gone in only one week, but the challenge of congregational recovery was not so easy.

One young lad in this congregation was Harold Phillips, who later would be a college friend of Bob's back on the Anderson, Indiana, campus and then much later a colleague in national church life. For now, they were just boys in Denver with no awareness of such a future. They worshipped in a challenging setting. The church was located in a strong Italian-Catholic community and housed in a gothic-style building previously abandoned by the Presbyterians. The impressive pipe organ had been removed by the new Church of God occupants because they viewed it as an extravagant sign of sectarian opulence. Stereotypes were common on all sides. Although this church would grow during the seven years that Eugene Reardon was the pastor, not one ethnic neighborhood family would be won to the church. It was a difficult field of service.

Young Bob Reardon was put in the third grade at Edison Grade School, a very good school that was academically superior to the Park Place public school he had been attending previously back in Anderson, Indiana. He found himself behind, in part because previously his mother had "pushed me up a grade," so that now all of his new classmates were a year older. "I had a pretty hard time adjusting," he recalls. It also was not easy to adjust socially to the local youth of Italian ancestry who tended to dominate the scene and had never heard of the Church of God movement—and would not have been impressed if they had.

One semester Bob brought home all "Ds." This greatly troubled his school-teacher father, who joined his wife in surrounding Bob with home support and encouragement. Bob was assigned a different psalm to read in family worship each day. Even so, he felt the terror of being behind and on occasion having to go to the blackboard to do math or read a paragraph that was beyond his readiness. He sometimes struggled with his self-image.

A physical examination once yielded the fact that one of Bob's shoulders was a little higher than the other. For days his parents did not know why he seemed so depressed. Much later he told an Anderson College chapel audience (September 5, 1978): "The news of my deformity hit me hard—I thought everyone else's shoulders were absolutely perfect and I alone was deformed for life!" He again was humiliated when his seventh-grade teacher made him stand in front of the class and ask his peers to tell him how he could become a better student. This left a permanent social scar and also sensitized him to the delicate feelings of struggling students, a sensitivity that would be appreciated by hundreds of college students later in his life. He also risked a physical scar or two while a youngster. In April, 1975, then President Robert Reardon told the Anderson College students in chapel that in his Denver boyhood days he got involved in some actual fighting, concluding: "That's how I got prepared to be the president of Anderson College!"

Bob did find some heroes while in Denver, including giants of faith in the biblical record, stalwarts of the international mission of the church, and public figures like Charles Lindbergh who flew non-stop to Paris and then rode in an open car on parade in downtown Denver, Colorado. The Reardons were among the admiring thousands lining his way. Bob also heard Al Smith speak from a truck in downtown Denver when Smith was running for the presidency of the United States. Church of God people of that time, however, could hardly accept Smith as a genuine hero since he was a Roman Catholic who presumably would be controlled by the Pope if ever President. He also was against Prohibition, an unacceptable moral and political stance in the eyes of most church people.

While Bob was hunting for heroes, his older brother Willard was discovering his mechanical ability. Still a teenager, he removed the motor from the family car and repaired it in the basement of the home, making a workbench by placing a board over his mother's washtubs. Bob may not have had his brother's level of mechanical ability, but he surely had a boyhood fascination with cars, learning to know every model on the road and the year each was made. More important for his future, he seemed to have an instinctive social intelligence, the ability to read well the motives, thinking, and concerns of his peers. Years later he would be a college president who was a shrewd judge of character and an astute reader of the issues before him and his campus back in Anderson, Indiana. But that was still a very long way off.

Bob Reardon also would be an effective storyteller. He once told the following humorous story about his early life in Denver (*The Way It Was* 54).

> Elitch's Gardens was known for its magnificent dahlias and its terrifying roller coaster. Since mother was interested in the former, and my brother and I in the latter, we schemed to entice her into this den of iniquity one week while father was away. After patiently observing the flowers, we guided mother to the roller coaster. After a lengthy pleading and assurances of pleasures and safety, mother agreed to go, with the provision that we go together and that she choose the seat. We were pleased when she chose the first seat. I can still recall the long ascent to the top of the first incline—highest, they said, west of the Mississippi. Mother's fears were put to rest as we ascended upward with a fantastic view of the city and the Rocky Mountains to the west.
>
> Then for a moment we hung over the abyss, followed by a real gut-wrenching dive downward, passengers screaming, holding on for dear life. On and on we went, skyrocketing upward, plunging downward on this hair-raising ride. I looked at mother. Her hairpins had come loose, her hair was streaming out behind, and she was crying to the Almighty for mercy! We led her, somewhat shaken, to a quiet place after the ride finally was over. There she swore to God that never, no never, would she ever put herself into such a contraption of the devil again. She never repeated this experience to father.

Later, when he was in high school back in Anderson, Indiana, Bob became known for telling stories well—stories with a range of relationships to the exact facts involved. He also created anxiety for his parents on occasion. Once he and a friend sneaked into a Sunday afternoon movie—behavior considered wholly unfitting for a Christian young man. When his mother learned of this erratic behavior, she feared that Bob had ruined his father's reputation as a Christian pastor and damaged "the cause" (the mission of the Church of God movement). Somehow they all survived relatively unscathed.

With the storytelling skill went Bob's natural sense of humor, diplomatically used in later years before meetings of college faculties, trustees, student chapels, and sessions of the General Assembly of the Church of God movement. This skill would help him handle many tense situations yet to come; sometimes it also got him into trouble early in life. For instance, one year there was an Easter pageant at the Denver church. Sister Ingram tried to become an angel by dressing in a white bathrobe with makeshift wings attached. When young Bob saw her appear in front of the congregation, he laughed out loud and, "with the speed of light, mother had me shoved under the pew!" (*The Way It Was* 39). Less funny at the time was his throwing a snowball that hit a neighbor man who was painting his house. The man was angry, caught Bob, and actually painted his face white. It took Bob's mother and a generous use of turpentine to get him cleaned up. Then came the embarrassing moment of mandatory apologizing to the man so that all consciences could be clear.

Areas of home support for Bob, other than his mother's amazing patience, were his father's discipline, academic tutoring, and the world of music. The Reardon family bonded by singing and playing instruments together. There may have been no radio in the home, but there was an upright piano that mother Pearl played, sometimes to accompany Willard on his coronet. Soon after the family's arrival in Denver, Bob began taking piano lessons from Sister Carson of the church. Mandatory recitals came along and nearly scared Bob to death, but his lifelong love affair with music was born. A special interest in classical music was stimulated when he first heard the great organ in the Civic Auditorium in Denver. He admits, "I never was the same again and determined that someday I would play a pipe organ" (*The Way It Was* 30). Indeed, he would. He also played in other ways. Their dad taught Bob and Willard how to throw a baseball, swing a bat, ride a bike, swim, drive a car, and ice-skate at Berkley Park.

Rev. E. A. Reardon became State Missionary Secretary of the Church of God in Colorado, a state made up of the relatively large Denver congregation he pastored and several smaller works scattered widely. Soon he was organizing chapters of "Missionary Volunteers" in the congregations and successfully promoting the following resolution at the Colorado ministerial assembly that convened at Olathe on the Western slope:

Whereas, On account of a shortage of funds, our foreign missionaries have had to suffer a cut of from 10 to 20 percent in their necessary allowances, therefore be it *Resolved,* That we as ministers of Colorado call upon our people to raise their budget allowances for foreign missions from 10 to 20 percent and thus share the sacrifices of the missionaries.

He then reported widely through the *Gospel Trumpet* (Feb. 10, 1927) that "I spoke to the brethren on the subject of missions; and, of course, since they are good brethren, they were heartily in favor of a forward move." Rev. Reardon, partly because of his own earlier missionary experience in Egypt, had a global heart and did not shrink from forward moves. He was a good model for his boys.

Pastor Reardon, once a school teacher when young, was also a strong advocate of education. He remained close to President John Morrison of Anderson College, who earlier had pastored in Colorado and had been a parishioner of Eugene Reardon's back in Anderson, Indiana. Reardon received an honorary doctorate from the school in 1929. During one of his illnesses, Morrison came to Denver and stayed for a month with the Reardons. These two men were very close friends and corresponded on occasion about school, church, and personal matters. A Reardon letter from Denver to President Morrison in Anderson, dated August 22, 1932, included this:

When are you coming to Denver again? We are having lovely weather, lots of sunshine and such perfectly cool nights in which to sleep. Be assured the latchstring is out whenever you wish to come. We are happy in the service of the Lord and trust that we shall be faithful to the end. Times are hard here as well as in the East, but we are planning on sending Willard back to university soon. We feel that he would be better in school than at home doing nothing, even though we should have to borrow the money to send him. He got along fine last year and is anxious to return.

The university in question was the University of Colorado in Boulder. Willard was well recovered from his earlier illness and pursuing his interest in electrical engineering. When the family bought its used 1927 Nash, within a week Willard had the engine out of the car and in the basement grinding the valves. It was the beginning of his education and eventually his career.

Meanwhile, key events were transpiring back at Park Place Church of God in Anderson, Indiana. Albert F. Gray, the pastor who followed Reardon, had been a trustee of Anderson College before coming to the Anderson pastorate in 1926. Less than a year after his arrival he was elected president of the Missionary Board of the Church of God, a large responsibility to which he gave major attention. For three years the congregation broadcast its Sunday morning services over Anderson radio station WHBU, but in general the church was not prospering. This was in part because of the economic woes of the Depression, in part Gray's preoccupations outside the congregation, and in part his personal style, hardly a warm and relational person like Rev. Eugene Reardon. Gray, although sincere and committed inside, was externally somewhat formal, even aloof. Reports Robert Reardon of Gray, "If you saw him walking down the street, you might think he was the Chief Justice of the Supreme Court." A planned educational unit for the church had to be deferred for monetary reasons. Numerous congregational members were out of work, some even having to move away.

In 1933 Gray decided that he also would move on, returning to the West Coast area to pastor in Seattle. A pastoral search committee of Park Place Church was named. It did not include the strongest leaders in the church and soon struggled for direction. John Morrison and A. T. Rowe stepped in and got a petition going among the church members. It suggested that E. A. Reardon be invited back as pastor. This petition got some five hundred signatures and helped determine the future. Morrison wrote a personal letter to his dear friend Rev. Reardon, encouraging him to consider the possibility of returning. He did consider the idea and soon actually brought his family back to Anderson. The Denver sojourn, occasioned primarily by Willard's illness, had ended. It was time to be "Hoosiers" again.

At Home Again in Indiana

Living again in Anderson, Indiana, Willard Reardon continued his engineering education at nearby Purdue University. Now a young man of fourteen entering the tenth grade in school, his younger brother Bob finally managed to overcome the academic problems that he had faced throughout his Denver years. He felt right at home as a Hoosier. Bob not only had lived in

Anderson before, but had visited with his family every summer of their years in Denver. The family made the annual journey to the Anderson Camp Meeting, always memorable and difficult trips by car. The dirt roads in Kansas were rough and nearly impassible if it rained. There were no motels along the twelve hundred miles and the few existing hotels were usually beyond the means of the Reardons, so they stayed with "the saints." Whatever it had taken, they had done it.

Now back in Indiana, the Hoosier saints of Park Place Church of God in Anderson were pastored again by E. A. Reardon. This new pastor could be fun-

Rev. Eugene A. Reardon, about 1936.

loving, but there was a formality about him that certainly was seen in the seriousness with which he took the task of preparing and delivering sermons. Sometimes the needed solitude was compromised. Carol Olson, a neighbor girl on Walnut Street where the Reardons lived, liked to get in a car tire and roll about the yards and street. She recalls one day when her loud and childish play was interrupted by "Auntie" Reardon (the pastor's wife). The noise just had to stop so that God's proclamation could be prepared. Brother Reardon was working on Sunday's sermon.

The people of Park Place Church of God had much in common, but they did not always share the same perspective on a range of matters. One difference was over the possibility of a pipe organ for the church. Bob Reardon had returned to Anderson as a young man who could play the piano quite well. He began studying with Dr. Paul Breitweiser and still dreamed of great organs. Naturally he was enthusiastic when the idea of installing an organ at Park Place Church first came up in family conversation. His father broached the idea with the church trustees, got a mixed response, but at least an agreement that it could happen if special money were found. The church's youth, prominently including Bob Reardon, began fundraising and soon a rebuilt organ was installed above the baptistery. Meanwhile, Bob had been practicing on the organ of First Christian Church in Anderson and studying with Mallory Bransford, a graduate of Oberlin Conservatory in Ohio. Bransford likely is the main reason why Bob later would decide to spend the summer of 1938 studying organ at Oberlin. This was a real love of his and Oberlin was one of the best locations nationally for quality organ instruction—and also for graduate-level ministerial education, a fact later to be pivotal in Bob's life.

Young Bob Reardon was growing up in a pastor's home, sometimes resisting but never resenting it, pushing against some of the constraints of the church, but never turning away from the faith itself. He learned to know quite well most of the prominent leaders of the Church of God movement. Often he played in the F. G. Smith home. Frequent visitors in the Reardon home were people like Joseph T. Wilson, John A. Morrison, Russell Olt, Frederick G. Smith, Enoch E. Byrum, Charles E. Brown, Andrew L. Byers, and others. These were names revered across the church, people bigger than life. But young Bob knew them first as good neighbors, nurturing elders, very human people different from each other, yet with much in common since, as Bob later recalled it, they all "were passionately committed to a great dream." None of them became rich. All of them "poured their lives, without personal regard, into the bloodstream of the Church of God movement" (*The Early Morning Light* 11).

Young Bob knew these prominent church people as his extended family and later confessed with deep appreciation that "they have shaped my life and everything good that has happened to me" (*The Early Morning Light* 11). Late in life he would recall on occasion exactly where these legendary leaders of the Church of God lived and how he used to deliver the daily newspaper to most of them. He thought of the Park Place community on the east side of Anderson in the 1920s and 1930s as a "very enclosed community" where most of the people worked at the Gospel Trumpet Company, went there to work when the siren signaled the beginning of a new work day, and worshipped together on Sunday at Park Place Church. These people knew who they were. They were part of the great Church of God movement, a vibrant witness to the wider church world, while the people downtown were "the world."

Bob grew up feeling loved and safe in a wonderful environment—separate and strange as it may have seemed to the general public. In spite of the politics and occasional trivialities of some church people and practices, both the North Denver and Park Place congregations were essentially healthy, loving, and nurturing settings in which children and youth could flourish. Bob Reardon certainly did. In Anderson, for instance, he got permission to drive his special friend Mona Morrison around in the family's new 1936 Studebaker. He loved cars and for a while thought he loved her too. She and he were sweethearts for years, although later their marriages would not be to each other. Even so, sixty years later they would still be friends and laypersons together in Park Place Church of God, the congregation in Anderson, Indiana, that they both loved and knew from childhood.

The young Bob Reardon carried the *Anderson Daily Bulletin* newspaper to 220 homes and the downtown drugstores, enabling him to have his own money, provide for his own personal needs and wants, buy the kind of clothes his parents could not afford, tithe to the church, and in effect run his own little business. He had one problem, however. It was a "chronic grouch" on College Drive who regularly complained that something was wrong with his paper— late, wet, in the wrong place. He threatened to report Bob to his manager. Bob says he replied modestly to the man "with the limited vocabulary imposed upon me because I was the local preacher's son." Things began to change for the better one Sunday. David Gaulke, Bob's Sunday school teacher, explained to his young students about the hurtfulness of bad attitudes. Sometimes we just do not know the heavy burdens being carried by other people. Responsible Christians have to find ways to bring reconciliation. Here was Bob's response as later published in David Liverett's *Bridges of Reconciliation* (102):

> I knew what I had to do. In the next few weeks, I made sure the paper was delivered properly…. When I went to collect, I found my smile and made some conversation. The ice between us began to thaw. One day I had the courage to ask how it was to live alone. He surprised me by saying that he had a wife…. I can still remember the day when he said that she wanted to meet me and I was led into her bedroom. On the bed lay a frail, wasted, invalid dying of cancer, nursed by her devoted husband. In that moment I found my enemy, I understood, the wall came down, and we became friends.

Also on this newspaper route, Bob Reardon developed a very special friendship. Charles Naylor was a major player in the life of the Church of God movement, writing several of its most loved songs, including "Spirit Holy," "He Wants His Way in Thee," "Are You Adorning the Doctrine?", "Be an Overcomer," "Wholehearted Service," and "I'm On the Winning Side." He also was bedridden because of two serious accidents, one in 1908 and one in 1909. Upon returning to Anderson from Denver, Bob regularly visited with Naylor in the process of delivering his newspaper six days a week. Naylor's house on Eighth and Chestnut Streets featured facilities for his disability, a shortwave radio by which he listened to international news broadcasts, and newspapers like the *New York Times*, all indicating an alert and well informed Christian man. This was unusual for that time and community. Reardon later called Naylor a true intellectual whose mind ranged easily across politics, religion, literature, and world events, exactly what Robert Reardon himself one day would champion as the genius of the "liberal arts" on the Anderson campus. Naylor also was lonely and chose to befriend the pleasant young man who came to his side regularly. Bob was fascinated by Naylor's special radio, transcribing machine, literature, and stories. He realized that this older churchman truly enjoyed him and treated him with respect. It resulted in a mutual affection.

Particularly impressive to Bob was the occasion once a year when his pastor father would invite Naylor to preach at Park Place Church. The pastor would help to carry the handicapped man onto the platform. Naylor died in 1950 and was buried in relative obscurity within the very large Maplewood Cemetery next to the Anderson campus. In Reardon's view, Naylor was a giant among Church of God people, a giant who, for various reasons, ended up virtually shunned by many in his own church community. Decades later in 2003, honoring this treasured man of now-distant memory, the elderly Robert Reardon would spearhead a drive resulting in a large crowd of church leaders gathering around what had been the modest grave of Naylor in Maplewood Cemetery, singing some of his songs, and dedicating an impressive new stone marker to replace the little one that had been there for decades. It would be an act of loving gratitude. This giant of a man would no longer lie like a virtually forgotten pauper. Robert Reardon would see to it that honor was given where he considered it due. This would become a habit of his lifetime.

College and Full Spiritual Commitment

The Church of God movement experienced by Bob Reardon in his youth was a strongly revivalistic tradition in which the conversion "experience" made the believer a real church member. Preachers spoke of a "know so" religion. A true believer could testify to the dramatic time and place of the Christian conversion that reoriented one's life by God's transforming grace. Reared in a devout Christian home, Bob was taught confession to God and stood through many invitation songs sung at the end of evangelistic preaching. He was not drawn to a public altar himself until his high school years. He had taken his turn praying during family worship, considered himself a Christian, and was baptized at age ten. Attending services of worship was typical for him. Something less usual among Christians was the practice of footwashing, an "ordinance" considered crucial among Church of God people in the 1920s. Bob found this practice an uncomfortable experience of questionable meaning until as a teenager he once saw John Morrison, the local and esteemed college president, humbly wash a janitor's feet. There was obvious meaning here that he would never forget.

The typical pattern during Bob's growing-up years was for a congregation of the Church of God to have two "revivals" per year, many lasting two weeks each. Pastor Eugene Reardon was not the fiery evangelist type, but he imported various revival preachers who were. This tended to satisfy the desire of his people for such variety. One fiery evangelist was J. W. Lykins, a southern orator who told dramatic stories of the terrible things that happened to people who rejected altar calls to "get saved." Another was Harvey Pinyoun, a dynamic young preacher from Canada. He came to preach at the North Denver church after Bob's Aunt Marion heard him preach in Akron, Indiana, and encouraged Rev. Reardon to give him an opportunity.

During the resulting Denver revival, Bob, age twelve at the time, fell into conversation with Pinyoun in the basement office of Pastor Reardon. He was pressed by this evangelist. The man asked Bob personal questions about his spiritual state. Was he saved? "I guess so," Bob answered. But Pinyoun countered, "You need to say a more definite 'yes' to God." So they got down on their knees at the pastor's old couch and prayed. When Bob finally got up, his heart was "filled with sunshine" and "light as a feather." This defining spiritual moment was supplemented by one more during Bob's later high school years back in Anderson, Indiana.

Robert H. Reardon,
Anderson High School, 1935.

The ground had been laid for the next spiritual experience when young T. Franklin Miller, still a college student himself, was leading the programming of the youth group of Park Place Church of God. Bob Reardon and his special friend Mark Bright were always present. One evening the group became quite loud and even disrespectful of its leader and Miller finally interrupted and told them he had had enough and would not be back to work with them. Bob Reardon stood up, apologized for himself and the whole group, and promised a much better future if Miller would stay. He did, things improved, and Miller soon realized that Reardon was a natural leader in this group and likely would be in others as well. The additional and very special spiritual moment then came for this young leader on a Friday night during a revival at Park Place Church. The guest preacher, W. C. Gray of South Bend, Indiana, gave an invitation after the preaching. Bob and several of his friends went to the altar. It was another time of Bob saying an increasingly clear "yes" to God.

The group of Park Place Church young people at the time was large and all went to Anderson High School downtown. Since his earliest years in Anderson as a child, Bob had known well Dorothy and Mona Morrison, daughters of John and Eunice Morrison, first man and lady of the college. These church youth experienced some negative attitudes in school toward Church of God people, those "peculiar specimens" from across the White River on the east side of town. Sometimes they were disgraced for being associated with the Church of God movement, even on occasion by subtle comments of teachers. Bob, Dorothy, Mona, and others from "the East side" walked to the high school—quite a distance. Although Mona was an outstanding student and pianist, she hated high school in general. After the 1930s, however, public attitudes toward the east-siders softened some. The youngest Morrison daughter, Vivian Jean, was even the high school prom queen, although she had to promise her father that she would not dance at the big prom event over which she would reign. It was a workable compromise in an awkward circumstance.

There were the "B" boys at Anderson High School, Everett Beck, Melvin "Buck" Thornburg, Mark Bright, Bob Reardon's closest friend, and Bob himself. Many memorable events are recounted involving these men. For instance, walking home from high school with his friends one winter day, Bob, used to ice skating on lakes in Denver, Colorado, decided to test the ice on the White River just blocks from his home. Although he was sure he knew what he was doing, suddenly the ice gave way and he fell through. Help came quickly from his friend Mark Bright who crawled to him on an unbroken section of the ice and saved the day. Bob then ran home in great discomfort to his shocked mother. No permanent harm was done. God was not done with this gifted and sometimes rash young man.

Bob Reardon thought of Paul Byrum, Tom McMahan, David Martin, and Mona Morrison as the "smart ones." He had never been a particularly good student himself and hardly appeared to others as premier college material. Even so, as a high school senior Bob finally made the honor roll, graduated in 1936, and was identified in the school yearbook as "academic" (as opposed to "vocational"), "Science Math 3," and "History Club 3." That fall he would go on to do well in college and have ahead of him an outstanding career of thirty-six years in higher education. All of this, of course, could hardly even be imagined when Bob was just leaving high school.

In the fall of 1936 Bob Reardon entered Anderson College as a freshman. It was a small and unaccredited place, hardly something to brag about among his high school friends. But it was the church's school and his parents wanted him there, at least for the first two years. They said that they would help him go elsewhere after that if he really wanted to. However, after two or three months as a freshman, he fell in love with the little Anderson campus and its people and never thought of going anywhere else. He lived at home, kept enjoying his mother's cooking, and opted for the comforts of his own room and bed instead of the austerity of the school's Old Main just blocks away.

Bob continued from his high school years his close personal relationship with Mona Morrison. She and her sister Dorothy were also students at the local college where their dad was president. Often Bob played the organ and Mona the piano for Sunday evening services at Park Place Church. Afterwards, she reports, "we went to the old Eastside Jersey Dairy and had huge ice cream cones. We never exactly made it straight home!" But Bob dated more girls than Mona. As his future wife Geraldine Hurst recalled much later, "Bob was very popular on campus. He was a skilled musician, athletic, and had religious depth. Many women in Park Place Church hoped it finally would be their daughters whom he would marry." Dorothy Morrison recalls Bob as a "handsome blonde teenager, the golden-haired hero." He added a public flair to his good looks and good connections, like being the beloved pastor's son.

Bob's brother Willard had taken another educational route, the University of Colorado while the family was in Denver and then Purdue University when they moved back to Indiana. He graduated from the engineering program of Purdue in 1936 and began his career with General Electric, being located in Fort Wayne, Indiana, from 1936 to 1954 and then in Erie, Pennsylvania, from 1954 until his retirement in 1974. Willard married in 1938, had three children born in Fort Wayne, and became associated in satisfying ways with Methodist and Presbyterian congregations—more convenient and compatible than the particular congregations of the Church of God that happened to be nearby. Therefore, over the years Willard was not as committed to direct association with the Church of God movement as was his father and brother Bob, although in retirement he would happily rejoin the Park Place Church in Anderson where his father Eugene had pastored and his brother Bob was a longtime member.

By contrast with Willard's educational path, Bob always knew that it would be Anderson College for him, at least for the first two years as his parents urged. In the 1930s the Anderson campus was still not accredited, had poor facilities, and was thought of locally as mostly a "preacher factory" for Church of God students. A large concrete block building called "Old Main" is about all that there was. Nearly everything, including student and faculty housing, chapel, the classrooms, and the maintenance shop, was under that one big roof. The economic depression was barely beginning to lift as Bob Reardon became a college student. Optimism was a rare thing. Faculty members were each receiving salaries of only about $500 per year, if they could collect. Otherwise, there was a bartering system functioning to circumvent the lack of cash.

Beyond the money crisis, a major confrontation with conservative elements of the Church of God movement was fresh in everyone's memory. The agitators had wanted a change of administration and a return to the original Bible Training School that was said to have been compromised when the liberal arts curriculum was introduced in the late 1920s. But school leaders had held their ground with passion and patience, something that deeply moved Bob Reardon in the 1930s and something he himself would continue in later decades. Sometimes staying on course is as difficult as it is important.

President John Morrison and Dean Russell Olt had been dedicated to the cause of the kind of Christian higher education they judged essential to make intelligent participants in Christ's great mission. According to Robert Reardon, this "inspired us, lifted our sights, and saved us from self-pity" (*The Way It Was* 74). In the 1930s the school administrators could easily have given up the dream of the school continuing at all, but they would not accept closing as an acceptable option. They would stay the course in spite of everything. This course, this dream, took deep root in the heart of Robert Reardon and for decades to come he would try to be faithful to it. Later he would understand in more detail that Russell Byrum, prominent teacher on the Anderson campus in the 1920s and author of the influential book *Christian Theology* in 1925, had been a personal victim in 1929 of the school's resistance to the excessive conservatism that elements of the church attempted to force on the campus. Byrum had been accused of teaching unacceptable viewpoints and, although cleared of the charge, had resigned to spare the school any more embarrassment. It was a big loss.

During summers in his college years in the late 1930s, Bob Reardon worked as a carpenter for Russell Byrum, framing houses and putting on cedar siding. The theologian now was a builder of homes rather than an influential shaper of ideas and beliefs. Even so, he still held to high standards and affected the lives of many who one day would be leaders of campus and church—including young Bob Reardon. Other key people slipped in and out of Bob's life. One was Harold Phillips whom he had known back in Denver, Colorado. In June, 1937, Bob had just completed his paper route for the day, went home to the parsonage on Walnut Street, and discovered a wedding in progress in the house. His father was officiating at the wedding of Harold Phillips and Ethel Mott. Home, ministry, and college were always connected closely for Bob Reardon.

Dean Russell Olt certainly kept the small campus on course academically. He had helped assemble a superb group of faculty members, including Amy Lopez, Carl Kardatzke, Earl Martin, and Otto Linn. From them shined the ideal of faith, learning, and sacrificial service. Olt, both dean and an outstanding teacher of psychology, was rigorous and often intimidating for students. Bob Reardon's turn to find this out came in relation to a term paper that he tried to disguise and use a second time. The dean recognized the ruse and delivered an "F" and a strong lecture on honesty. This stern lesson was received humbly and then was supplemented by the mandatory chapel sessions that "called us back again and again to our Christian roots and helped us to engraft ourselves into that great tree of life" (*The Way It Was* 78-79).

Reardon learned early as a student that no magnificent buildings, libraries, faculty credentials, or accreditations can replace the loss of the "heavenly vision." But in 1936 he was not always this reflective about the big issues. He actually did a little suffering in chapel. When Dean Olt presided, without any warning he often would name some student to pray in front of all the faculty and students. On one such day Reardon was so frightened that he might be called on that "I got up, rushed out, and did not return until this part of the worship was over." He confessed: "Another time when the Dean nailed me, I floundered around hopelessly and wound up with 'O Lord, er, ah, help us be walking billboards for Thee,'" to which his student friend Val Clear brought forth a loud snort! (*The Way It Was* 79).

Bob sowed a few "wild oats" outside of chapel and also was a student leader in more constructive ways. Gale Hetrick, later the executive of the Church of God in Michigan, wrote to Reardon on the occasion of his retirement as President (1983) and recalled that in the fall term of 1938 he had seen Bob "swinging down a hall in Old Main dressed smartly in a zoot suit, one of those long double-breasted coats with balloon trousers and small at the ankles." On the less than admirable side, young Reardon and his friends Carol Helvey and Val Clear, "convinced that Jesus had not turned the water into Welch's grape juice," visited a tavern in nearby Noblesville "to prove to ourselves that drinking was no sin" (*The Way It Was* 83). Judgment came in the form of Bob's throwing up on the way home.

Another confession by Robert Reardon was made to the Anderson College chapel audience convened on February 22, 1977. He recalled that, when a college student himself, he, Val Clear, "and some other of our nefarious

The Booster Club, Anderson College, 1940. Front row, left to right: Robert Reardon, Fred Schminke, faculty advisor, Warren Edmondson, Val Clear and Gerald Erickson. Second row, left to right: Lloyd Hargett, Carol Helvey, Jack Van Dyke and Irvin Shrout. Last row, left to right: Leslie Ratzlaff, Glen Renner, John Sayre, Charles Young, Alfred Brown, Robert Gray and Ray Keith.

friends on campus" decided to go to Indianapolis to a burlesque show. It was at a seedy old place, "one of the creepiest theaters in the city." Everything about the show was "a complete statement of vulgarity." These Anderson College students soon walked out into that cold night just before Christmas, carrying with them a fresh load of shame. Reardon recalls, "We realized that in front of us was a Salvation Army band, fingers freezing, playing and proclaiming the gospel of Jesus Christ right outside this theater." Given the guilt, "all of us opened our pockets and poured everything we had into the kettle!" But that was not all for Bob. When he got back to his home in Anderson late that night, his pastor father was still up reading and Bob lied to him about where he had been.

On the more positive side of things, in 1936 Bob, David Houghton, and Mitt Williams organized the Booster Club, the first social club on the Anderson campus. They wrote a constitution that called for eternal fidelity to Anderson College, admitted a group of their buddies, the presumed cream of the student crop, had black sweaters made with a large orange "A" on them, and started strutting about the campus. The Boosters sold candy, planned social events like an annual formal, held early morning hikes out to Jackson's Crossing, and claimed to champion good causes, especially "boosting" the college however they could. Reardon was the club's president in 1938 and, according to *Signatures* alumni magazine (Winter 2003, 17), he was the one "who actually heisted, or adopted, the Booster tune from a Nelson Eddy song that was featured in a Hollywood movie." For the lyrics of this song, see Appendix D.

Reardon's college academic program centered in his two majors, English and psychology, with a minor in history added on. This curriculum, along with the mandatory liberal arts program that had survived earlier church criticism, opened for him the worlds of the arts and letters, history, and both the physical and social sciences. The composite provided an excellent personal and professional foundation. Key to Reardon's future were three outstanding teachers about whom he would speak with great affection for decades to come. One was the education professor Carl Kardatzke. Sometimes this man would say to the students in class, "You are welcome to miss my class any day if you can think of anything more important to do!" This attitude encouraged Bob about the Christian life. It was to be a walk determined by positive and important things. He began to think in a new way about the Christian faith, rejecting preoccupation with the "thou shalt nots" so often emphasized in church life in the 1920s and 1930s.

Another of his teachers was Miss Amy Lopez, a sophisticated Jamaican who had studied at Oxford in England, held a graduate degree from Columbia University, and challenged the students at Anderson College to write daily and enjoy great poetry. She was, as Bob Reardon characterizes her, "a strong, sweet, and fascinating human being." Mona Morrison refers to her as "absolutely a queen." Geraldine Hurst, Reardon's future wife, was an English major during her two years on campus (1939-1941) and describes Miss Lopez as "knowledgeable, stately, the woman who taught us to love literature and write creatively." Later, this beloved professor would offer the prayer as Bob Reardon was being ordained to the Christian ministry on June 1, 1941, in Park Place Church of God in Anderson. On that key occasion, Amy Lopez prayed for young Bob Reardon to realize constantly that he must serve in love and put primacy on the things of the Spirit. Eloquently, she called for a special anointing of the Spirit so that "ministry shall be marked by the power of the gospel. . .and serve with the sweetness of divine grace."

The third teacher of particular influence on Bob Reardon was Dean Russell Olt himself. He was demanding, made Bob want to excel, and sensitized him to social responsibility in relation to issues like racial justice. Olt was a pacifist and supported unions in the local auto industry as agents of fairness. He and the other faculty members widened Bob's world and helped him to move away from the narrowness of so much of the church life of his boyhood—although that narrowness in many cases was much less evident in Bob's own home than it was generally among the churches.

Bob Reardon's spiritual life also continued to grow in the midst of this academic stimulation. In addition to his two earlier and significant religious experiences (under Harvey Pinyoun in Denver and W. C. Gray in Anderson), there came a third in his senior year in college. He did not know what he was going to do with his life and this disturbed him. Should it be business, music, or what? He had earlier crowded to the back of his mind the idea of Christian ministry, but he sensed that the "Hound of Heaven" may be urging him toward the most honorable of all callings—being a full-time minister of Jesus Christ. One Sunday afternoon under a big tree on the Anderson campus, T. Franklin Miller and Bob Reardon had a long talk. Bob was feeling a call to Christian ministry, was quite unsure of himself in this regard, and asked many questions of his trusted older friend. Was he fit for ministry? How can one be sure about God's will? These were important minutes together.

One evening soon after, with Miller's help in mind and some of his questions still very much unanswered, substantial progress on Bob's spiritual journey was made while he was doing homework in the living room of his Walnut Street home. He closed the book he had been reading and told God that he really needed to know about his future. The thought then came to him that he felt sure had originated with God. It was, "Are you available for whatever I want you to do?" He answered this divine inquiry with a simple but profound "Yes!" Then a feeling of deep peace came into his heart. There may have been no lightning blazing from the sky, but this was a foundational moment in his religious journey. It was like John Wesley's "strangely warmed heart" at his Aldersgate experience in 1738. In all of the years to follow, Bob Reardon would look back on this divine question and his humble answer as a major turning point in his life. That "Yes" would keep him on a divinely appointed course. He now could live with the fact that the particulars of his coming ministerial service were still unknown. God would direct and he would follow.

Late in life Reardon reflected on this key experience of his full spiritual commitment. He explained that "my spiritual pilgrimage is not a story of a rebel far from home leading a desolate life eating in a pigpen." Instead, "my sins had to do with playing marbles for keeps, an occasional ten cent shot in a drugstore slot machine, or misspending school money on candy or a racy magazine like *Uncle Billy's Whizbang*." He had answered "yes" to God, and later reported this result in Barry Callen's book *The Wisdom of the Saints* (221):

> Through the years I have come back to this place of surrender many times. It is an altar that has brought me to opportunities of service I never dreamed of, resources beyond imagination, and the fulfillment of God's promise to walk beside us as friend and guide.

The year 1940 was outstanding for young Bob Reardon in several ways. He graduated from Anderson College, got accepted into Oberlin Graduate School of Theology in Ohio, became engaged to marry Geraldine Hurst, and got his pilot's license. The flight training had been part of a program at Anderson College funded by the government. One day, knowing that Wendell Willkie would be campaigning for the presidency of the United States in his hometown of Elwood, Indiana, Bob contacted his good friend Mark Bright, then a student at DePauw University, and invited him to fly with him to the big event happening only a few miles from Anderson. This was Mark's first airplane ride ever and he was enthusiastic about the experience. They circled over the great crowd in Elwood and then Mark was especially dazzled as Bob showed off his new skills with the airplane—rather daring spins and rolls. Soon Mark, truly inspired with flight, became a Navy fighter pilot flying off the aircraft carrier Yorktown against the Japanese. He did not return home again, a significant personal loss for Bob Reardon.

Geraldine Hurst was from the Princeton, Indiana, Church of God congregation. Her father was a boiler inspector for the Southern Railroad. After her mother's early death when Jerry was only eleven years old, her father remarried. His new wife had a daughter, Lucille Strawn. In 1945 she would become a student at Anderson College and later functioned for many years as the Registrar of the Anderson campus, dying in 2003. The Hurst family came to Anderson Camp Meeting on the railroad each summer. Jerry found this so exciting, always remembering those times when the trainman would call out, "Anderson!" as they rolled into town.

Geraldine Hurst was converted to new life in Jesus Christ in the old tabernacle in Anderson. She soon began traveling among the churches in the immediate Princeton area, first to give her personal testimony of salvation and then as an evangelist. Her popularity as a gifted young speaker grew quickly. After her high school graduation in 1936, Jerry functioned for two years as an evangelist and had occasion to speak in Anderson College chapel and in a revival meeting in nearby Noblesville. Bob Reardon and his friend Mark Denton went to hear her preach. At that time (and this would surely change), Bob was "not strong for women preachers," but he was really impressed with this one!

Soon Bob went to the 1938 International Youth Convention of the Church of God in Milwaukee where Jerry Hurst was a featured speaker. He actually met her there for the first time and tried to get a date with her, but she declined, apparently having heard some negative rumor about him—which likely was true. But she did join the Anderson College student body in 1939. Later, following their eventual marriage, he would tease her, insisting that she came to Anderson as a student only to be close to him. She recalled: "There could be a little truth there, but not entirely."

Now that Jerry was on campus, Bob had daily opportunities to build a positive relationship with her. According to Jerry: "We had long talks. He helped me to think through my faith so that I could come to a more reasoned and intelligent belief. In my home setting, one just believed what was preached and didn't question." By the Christmas in 1939, Bob was hopelessly in love with this "beautiful, blue-eyed, blonde-haired creature" (*The Way It Was* 81). She had completely overcome her earlier hesitancy about him, to the point that in May, 1940, they sat under a great ash tree on campus, confessed their mutual love, and soon after announced their engagement to be married. Bob was too poor to buy her a ring, something generally frowned on anyway by the church as prideful adornment, but a watch was purchased and long treasured by her.

The actual marriage would have to wait a year. Bob was off to seminary in Ohio in the fall of 1940 while Jerry spent her second year on campus in Anderson. He quickly realized that he had to protect his considerable interests in her since she was beautiful, was named "best all-round woman on campus" for 1940-1941, and several other young men appeared clearly interested. On occasion Bob would hitchhike home from Oberlin to Anderson to see her and, of course, to be seen with her. In November of 1979, Robert Reardon, then president of Anderson College, recalled for the students in chapel a time when he hitchhiked the two hundred miles on a cold and snowy December day. With his usual touch of humor, he said that he had begun the process by standing on the edge of the northern Ohio town with his thumb out, but unsuccessfully for a long time. Standing calmly in the snow with a suitcase, he thought he was "a fairly decent looking human being," although drivers looked at him as they went by "as though you're something that fell out of the backend of the garbage truck." He added, for the inevitable amusement of college students, "After a while I began making comments about the ancestors of the people that drove by me!"

Geraldine Hurst was special, well worth all of Bob's inconvenience. She was the student speaker at a campus Religious Emphasis service when an Anderson freshman, Robert Nicholson, experienced a "true conversion" that stabilized his spiritual life and allowed him to focus better on his future vocation—which in 1958, ironically, would come to involve Bob Reardon in a dramatic way (President and Dean of Anderson College!). Of course, nothing like that could be foreseen in 1941. Meanwhile, much was going on in Bob's life over in Ohio and he was anxious for Jerry to join him as his future was unfolding.

The time finally arrived. On a beautiful Sunday morning in August, 1941, Robert and Geraldine were married as part of the regular Sunday morning service of Park Place Church of God in Anderson, Indiana, where his father was pastor. Bob realized that he had little more to offer his bride than his father had had to offer Bob's mother, Pearl, thirty-three years earlier back in the Faith Missionary Home in Chicago. Even so, God was in this marriage and Jerry was wonderful and willing to risk the unknowns of the future with young Bob. The marriage knot was tied and they would face the future together.

During the marriage ceremony, when a thousand pairs of eyes were closed in the sanctuary during the benedictory prayer being offered by his father, Bob slipped on to Jerry's finger a very modest ring. It was done in this clandestine way since most of the married women in the church did not wear rings by choice and Bob's own mother had been cautious about the idea of a ring. She particularly had frowned on his buying for Jerry anything that had a stone in it or was flashy gold in color. Pearl had agreed reluctantly to Bob purchasing a plain band. He had been "liberated" from the narrowness of such sensibilities, but most others in the church were not. Soon he would learn to balance carefully many issues of this kind as he and his new bride set off into the great unknowns of their common future. Although off to Ohio together for Bob to complete his seminary education, in a few years they would be back home in Indiana, but only by way of a significant stay in Pennsylvania.

CHAPTER Three

Road to the Presidency

A ll leaders of the Church of God movement did not share the same dream for the future of the young Anderson Bible Training School that had been started as part of the Gospel Trumpet Publishing Company in Anderson, Indiana, in 1917. The little school was barely three years old when the Reardons first moved to Anderson in 1920. Joseph T. Wilson was the school's founding Principal in 1917 and by 1919 Rev. John A. Morrison had arrived in Anderson from a Colorado pastorate to stand with him in this new ministry. By 1925 the school became independent of the Gospel Trumpet Company, Morrison was named the first president, and Russell Olt joined Morrison as the school's new dean.

Bob Reardon was a little boy just beginning school in 1925. The Bible School was a special concern of his pastor father. Rev. Eugene Reardon knew nearly all of the students by name and ministered directly to most of them. Early in life, Bob absorbed the dream for the school's future that was so alive in President Morrison, Dean Olt, his own father, and others of his immediate acquaintance. In the decades to follow, he would find his way into this school's life and determine to keep the fulfillment of this dream on course. It was a long road into Christian ministry that finally led Robert Reardon to the presidency of Anderson College and School of Theology in 1958.

The Maturing Anderson Campus

During a late afternoon in the winter of 1933, when Bob Reardon was fourteen and the nation was in the midst of the economic harshness of the Depression, President John A. Morrison and his pastor and close friend E. A. Reardon walked eastward from Anderson out the old railroad traction line to Jackson's Crossing at the bridge that spanned the White River. It was approximately one very cold mile from the campus. Their spirits were low. The air temperature matched the chill of the times. Student enrollment, school income, and faculty salaries all were down. Campus relations with the church were strained and campus accreditation was still little more than a distant gleam in Dean Olt's eye.

President Morrison and Pastor Reardon were quietly plodding along over the frozen ground on their way back home. They passed the old tabernacle that housed the big worship services of the annual Anderson Camp Meetings and then saw the twinkling lights of Old Main gently piercing the winter darkness. They stopped and stared. Reardon placed his reassuring hand on the burdened president's shoulder and said, "See those lights, J. A? By the grace of God, we'll never let them go out!" In fact, they never would, although many difficult days lay ahead. Reardon's friendship and support were timely. One act of campus appreciation later extended to Pastor Reardon was that the 1944 school yearbook, *Echoes*, was dedicated to him. The campus owed him much and knew it.

Dramatic world events brought new circumstances. In June of 1946 President Morrison explained to the Board of Trustees of Anderson College that World War II had caused the regional accrediting body for higher education, the North Central Association, to discourage schools from making application for initial accreditation. But now this had changed and the backlog that had developed during the war accounted for the unusual number of twenty-six schools that had applied during 1945-1946 alone. Anderson, in this long list, had moved forward immediately and was one of only seven to be successful— a real milestone in school history! Morrison had visionary plans for the expansion of the newly accredited campus, but the strain of it all made an untimely and very unwelcome appearance in his quite fragile body. Arthritis brought him great discomfort and at times considerable loss of mobility and even depression. It became necessary for Earl Martin to function as Acting President from June 1946 to April 1947.

Finally making his reappearance in college chapel on April 23, 1947, was President Morrison. He came to attend a brief ceremony marking his official return to executive duties. Although on crutches, he also managed to be on the commencement platform to introduce the speaker, D. Elton Trueblood. By July of 1947, Robert H. Reardon had arrived from his pastorate in Pennsylvania to bring welcome help as the new presidential assistant. A dark year was ending in Morrison's life; a major beginning was unfolding in Reardon's life.

There were big institutional challenges just ahead in 1947 and now fresh administrative help on the scene. There had been a long road followed by Robert Reardon from his own college days in Anderson (1936-1940) to this return to his alma mater as an administrative leader by the president's side. As time eventually would show, God had been in it all. It had begun with Reardon's seminary education in Ohio.

Seminarian at Oberlin

In the summer of 1938 Robert Reardon journeyed to northern Ohio to study the pipe organ with Arthur Crowley at the Oberlin Conservatory. He lived with Dan Martin and his wife Esther, Church of God friends from Anderson and now seminarians at Oberlin School of Theology. Dan was the son of Earl Martin, an Anderson campus leader. Through the Martins, Reardon got acquainted at the Kipton Community Church located five miles from and where Dan was student pastor. Reardon enrolled in three college classes and had a marvelous summer experience. During this summer, Gene W. Newberry visited Oberlin while traveling as a student recruiter for Anderson College. He spent the night with Reardon and then was shown around the Oberlin seminary campus. The next year Newberry would return there as a seminarian, as would Reardon himself in 1940 and soon a series of others from the Church of God movement. Most of these young leaders eventually would return to be key church and campus leaders in Anderson, Indiana.

In 1938-1939 while a junior back at Anderson College, Reardon listened to W. E. Monk talk at Park Place Church of God about the many congregations without pastors. He wondered whether one day he could and even should himself meet the need of one such church. Maybe "I might be able to serve some small, remote congregation out there in desperate circumstances" (*The Way It Was* 87). This is just about how it would work out, first in Ohio and then in Pennsylvania. But first came his seminary preparation. The Church of God would not establish its own seminary in Anderson until 1950, so Reardon's choice of schools was not difficult. He returned to Oberlin in 1940 for a seminary education. He was only twenty-one and knew that he was not yet ready to assume full pastoral responsibilities without further education.

Oberlin Graduate School of Theology was a significant educational center on a campus with a rich heritage in the holiness movement, particularly in the person of its first president, Asa Mahan (1799-1889) and in that of its second president, Charles Grandison Finney (1792-1875). It was on this campus in 1841 that the first women in the history of the United States received the Bachelor of Arts degree. Also it was here in the mid-1800s that the underground railroad was active on behalf of slaves fleeing the South. At one time during the Civil War it is reported that all members of the Oberlin faculty were in jail in Elyria, Ohio, for smuggling American slaves into Canada. "It is altogether likely," observes Reardon, "that the place of women and blacks in our [Church of God] movement in its early days may have been encouraged by views assimilated by Daniel Warner at Oberlin" (*The Early Morning Light* 14). Warner, primary pioneer of the Church of God movement, had been a student at Oberlin decades before Reardon's arrival.

Warner's relatively brief involvement with Oberlin was in the nineteenth century. Now Oberlin again was impacting the life of the Church of God movement. In the late 1930s and especially in the 1940s, a series of college graduates from this movement, most graduates of Anderson College in Indiana, began pursuing their seminary educations at the graduate level, with Oberlin usually the school of choice. About fifteen became Oberlin graduates and came to have influence on the reform movement far beyond what this modest number might suggest. Several, including James Massey, Gene Newberry, Hollis Pistole, John Smith, and Robert Reardon returned to the Anderson campus and helped shape its future in major ways. The first Church of God persons to attend Oberlin in the twentieth century had been Anna Koglin, Dan Martin, and Gene Newberry in the 1930s, with Koglin returning to Anderson College to teach German and Greek and Newberry soon to return in theology and later becoming dean of the new Anderson seminary that would be founded in 1950.

It was here at Oberlin, for the first time in his experience, that Robert Reardon found himself immersed in classrooms filled with students from a wide range of Christian denominations and expressing differing beliefs and practices. His direct educational expenses were funded primarily by his functioning as organist in Fairchild Chapel. This was a wonderful role for him for more than financial reasons. He loved the organ in particular and music in general. Also, key faculty members would lead chapel worship services and, in their preparation process, they usually would consult with him about appropriate music. These were great opportunities to build relationships with scholar-teachers who enjoyed national and even worldwide reputations.

One special faculty member at Oberlin was Dr. Walter Marshall Horton, professor of theology. A graduate of Harvard and Union Theological Seminary, Horton also had studied at the Sorbonne and the Universities of Strasbourg and Marburg before earning his Ph. D. in philosophy from Columbia. Reardon's dear friend James Earl Massey, also to be a student of this same theology professor later than Reardon, describes Horton as "one of the most honored liberals at work in the church, university, and theological scene. I found him to be a scholar who did his work with the whole church in view, eager to help the church recover her ecumenical spirit and task" *(Aspects of My Pilgrimage* 196). Reardon experienced Horton much the same way. He thought of him as a wise "saint" who opened the wider world of Christian theology. This theological opening was not a doctrinaire "liberalism" failing to appreciate the text of Scripture and the recent contributions of the neo-orthodoxy of Karl Barth, but it was helpfully "liberalizing" in relation to various fundamentalisms often characteristic of most conservatives, including most of the Church of God movement at the time.

Horton's significance in the classroom spilled over into his eventually supervising Reardon's thesis, written for a Master of Sacred Theology program after he had finished his basic Bachelor of Divinity degree. In 1955, when Reardon was attending the first World Conference of the Church of God convened in Fritzlar, Germany, Horton, then living for the summer in Geneva, Switzerland, invited him to come and visit. Bob would never forget being shown all the local Geneva sights by his beloved teacher, including John Calvin's rich reformation heritage. Such gracious influence impacted the Church of God movement generally through Horton's relationship with Reardon and the other young Church of God minister-scholars, especially through the several soon to return to lead the Anderson College and School of Theology campus into their future. As church historian Merle Strege observes, Horton's theology was "compelling and attractive" to this group of first-generation seminary students of the Church of God. It was a "liberal" theology, while also being respectful of the church, open to the language of spiritual "experience," and concerned deeply for the unity of Christians.

Dr. Horton's orientation to pietistic and ecumenical concerns was not identical to the typical kind of emphases in the Church of God movement on these mutually valued subjects, but his instincts and spirit were highly compatible. He connected constructively with these sons and daughters of the reformation movement, leaving them, as Strege puts it, "far more open to theological sources and ideas originating outside the Church of God" (*I Saw the Church* 245). This openness was reflective of the attitudes of key leaders of the Church of God movement like John Morrison and especially Russell Olt and E. A. Reardon, Robert's father. These committed but progressive men understood the burden of the movement to involve (1) being open to all truth as God reveals it to searching hearts willing to be guided by the Holy Spirit and (2) refusing to be bound by restrictive churchly institutions and traditions. They predisposed Reardon's generation of seminarians to be open to the wider world of the church. This predisposition was nurtured at Oberlin.

After marrying Geraldine ("Jerry") Hurst on August 24, 1941, in Park Place Church of God in Anderson, Indiana, Robert Reardon and his new bride moved into a comfortable apartment on the Oberlin campus. Jerry became both a college student there and an employee at the campus switchboard. While still preaching on occasion, she now was ready to be primarily a wife and mother. She was lovely, graceful, and hospitable—great qualities for supporting her husband's emerging ministry. While at Oberlin, the nature of Robert's coming ministry was tested. Would it be pastoral ministry or not? The test grew out of the fact that the world was at war and young men could not avoid addressing their own relationships to this massive conflict.

Pearl Harbor had galvanized the nation. With his graduation from seminary coming in June, 1943, and knowing that most of his close male friends already either had been drafted or had enlisted in some branch of the military, Bob Reardon talked at length with Jerry about what his relationship to the war should be. His high school friend Mark Bright, now a navy fighter pilot, visited Oberlin for a few days and they talked much about the war and Bob's potential role in it. Bob was not a pacifist, strictly speaking, although he thought of himself as a "semi-pacifist." Listening to Adolf Hitler on the radio, hearing about the horrible injustice being done to European Jews, and realizing that the Navy needed more chaplains, Bob became convinced that he had to do something to help confront this "monstrous evil." He read Hitler's *Mein Kampf* and was left "with a rock in my stomach." By nature he was drawn to where the action was, and now it was the world at war.

Jerry said it had to be Bob's decision primarily. The decision finally was made that Bob would go to war as a military chaplain. The couple obviously was uncomfortable about what this would mean for them and they were a little

Geraldine and Robert Reardon, wedding day in August, 1941.

Robert and Geraldine Reardon's wedding, Park Place Church of God,
August, 1941, with Rev. Eugene A. Reardon officiating.

uneasy about how this war involvement related to Jesus, the Prince of Peace. Regardless, Bob sought entrance into the American military as a Navy chaplain. With his seminary degree pending, he qualified educationally and there were openings. He drove to Cleveland to enlist. Finally, however, he was rejected because of medical treatment he had taken earlier at the Cleveland Clinic for asthma and allergy problems. While this was a keen disappointment, he looked for God's hand in it and turned his energies elsewhere, especially toward the pastoral ministry. Later he would look back on his rejection by the military as "a major turning point in my life. I accepted the decision as the hand of God in my affairs and went on" (*The Way It Was* 96).

Although not becoming directly involved in the world conflict, World War II kept striking close to home for Robert Reardon. His dear friend Mark Bright was lost in the Pacific. One of his student friends at Oberlin was Timothy Hirazawa, a pastor from Tokyo, Japan. When Pearl Harbor was bombed in 1941, he sat on the floor in the Reardon's apartment, obviously embarrassed and saying, "Please excuse my country!" In 1943 Hirazawa was returned home to Japan under painful circumstances. Reardon by then had agreed to support his friend's oldest son in any American college when the time came, but it never did. Once home, Hirazawa was conscripted by the Japanese military, sent to China to serve, and never returned home alive. The war was bringing so much pain.

Coming from the home of an exceptional pastor and himself a practical man, Robert Reardon did not take the advice of some Oberlin faculty members who were sure that it was best for young seminarians to stay away from pulpits until they were more ready—they likely would only deepen bad habits, it was said, by preaching and counseling prematurely. Instead, during his first seminary year at Oberlin, and while he was still single, Reardon found his way into pastoral ministry. With the help of Rev. Warren Roark of the Church of God in Canton, Ohio, he joined Warren Edmondson, with whom he lived in Bosworth Hall, in co-pastoring a little rural church outside Loudonville, Ohio—a church forty-five miles south of Oberlin that no one else wanted and that agreed to pay them a total of $5.00 per week.

On their first visit, they went by bus, could not locate the church, and learned that it met three miles out of town up in the hills at Walter VanScroder's house. Warren and Bob shared the "salary" and grew in the experience. Bob later recalled that it was one thing to study theological greats like Karl Barth and Walter Rauschenbusch during the week, but it was quite another thing to get back to earth with an actual sermon every Sunday preached to real people with real needs. He often thanked God for the forbearance of the people in the little congregation near Loudonville. The group grew and even managed to move into a building of its own in a little more accessible location.

During this year a special opportunity came to seminarian and young pastor Robert Reardon. F. G. Smith, beloved Church of God writer, former Editor of the *Gospel Trumpet*, and personal acquaintance of the Reardons in Anderson, Indiana, since Bob's boyhood days, was now pastoring in Akron, Ohio. It was there that a young man named Norman Beard was converted to Jesus Christ in 1944. Later he would become a key staff person under President Reardon at Anderson College. It also was there in Akron that young J. H. Edwards was mentored in Christian ministry without benefit of a college education. J. H. was the father of James L. Edwards, later to be mentored himself as a campus administrator by Robert Reardon and then still later would himself become President of Anderson University seven years after Reardon's retirement. In the little town of Newton Falls not far from Akron, a new Church of God congregation was just beginning. Lillie McCutcheon, its outstanding pastor for decades to come, held F. G. Smith in high esteem. From her congregation would emerge Barry L. Callen, one day to be a seminary dean in the Robert Reardon administration in Anderson. Beard, Edwards, and Callen eventually would mean much to Reardon in the future. Northeast Ohio was a strong center of emerging leaders for the Church of God movement.

F. G. Smith invited Bob Reardon to come to Akron one weekend in 1942 to preach for him. Bob was pleased to go to this exceptional church and be with this influential pastor. Traveling by bus, he had an embarrassing experience on the way that he told Smith about—to Smith's amusement. Here is how Reardon later reported it (*The Way It Was* 93):

> I fell into conversation with an attractive, handsomely dressed man and his bejeweled wife. "What did I do?" he asked me. "I'm a minister in the Church of God, but of course we are non-pentecostal, don't speak in tongues; we frown on that sort of thing." "What do you do?" I asked. He replied, "I'm a minister." "What church?" "The Assembly of God," he replied. It was a long ride to Akron in which to contemplate my ineptitude.

As his first year of seminary education was ending at Oberlin, Robert Reardon's formal ordination to Christian ministry occurred on June 1, 1941, and his wedding plans were being made for later in the summer of 1941. He needed a job in the meantime and Warren Edmondson was willing to handle the Loudonville church on his own, freeing Bob to find something else. While hitchhiking one day from Ashland, Kentucky, he got a ride with the personnel manager of the U. S. Steel Mill in Lorain, Ohio. After visiting for a while, the man offered him a job, one that was dirty and even dangerous, but paid well. Bob jumped at the chance, was sure God had provided, and became a brakeman on the narrow-gage railroad pulling red-hot ingots in the Lorain mill. He soon had his baptism into the real world, listening to the "colorful" talk of the steel workers, joining the union, contemplating the fountain of sparks flying into the night sky

Robert and Geraldine Reardon
as college sweethearts in the 1930s.

from the great blast furnace, thanking God for the income if not for all of the experience, and dreaming of the day in August when he would be freed of the factory scene and marry the beautiful Geraldine Hurst.

Pastoring was in Reardon's heart, not steel mills. By the middle of the summer he rode his bicycle five miles west from Oberlin one Sunday morning to attend the Kipton Community Church. Bob had attended this church back in 1938 when he had spent the summer at Oberlin studying organ and living with Dan and Esther Martin. Dan was then pastoring this congregation while he was a seminarian. Bob had made some friendships in the church then and now was just visiting. He discovered, however, that they were in the process of looking for a part-time pastor, so he offered his services and got the position for fifteen dollars per week and a plot of land for a garden. Preaching regularly there in the Kipton church would sharpen his communication skills considerably and give constant real-people perspective to the rest of his seminary studies. The congregation grew under his leadership to about 150 people, a good country church with a gifted young minister in this little Ohio town.

After his wedding in August, 1941, Reardon settled back on the Oberlin campus with his bride and continued his preaching at Kipton on weekends. He made a trip home to Anderson in 1942, hitchhiking because of gas rationing made necessary by the war. Once home, he persuaded President John Morrison of Anderson College to come to Ohio and hold a series of special services at the Kipton congregation while spending a week with the Reardons. They were living in a little "quad" apartment on the Oberlin campus. Bob arranged for a private room for Morrison on the quad. It turned out to be a wonderful week, with Jerry and Bob entertaining the distinguished college president, a close family friend of the Reardon family, and under whom both Bob and Jerry had been students. They journeyed each evening to Kipton for services and during the days met Oberlin's president and various faculty members, visited classes and chapel, and walked the same grounds as had Charles Finney and Daniel Warner, primary pioneer of the Church of God movement who had himself been a student on this campus in the nineteenth century.

Although the Reardon and Morrison families had been close since the 1920s and Bob had been in the Morrison home often, particularly when he was dating the President's daughter, Mona, this Oberlin week together gave opportunity for the President and the young Reardon to become acquainted as adults. They talked long hours. Likely this was when Morrison for the first time began to think of young Bob as a minister, serious student, and reflective church leader, not just as a family friend, former college student, pianist, organist, and occasional choir director in Anderson. He even began to speculate about a possible role for Bob in the future of Anderson College—something that actually would materialize just a few years later.

Morrison also was learning what a seminary was all about—something else that would be crucial in a few years on the Anderson campus. A very astute person, as Reardon later characterized him, Morrison realized that the Church of God movement would be losing key young leadership to other churches if their graduate educations were received at Oberlin and elsewhere outside the movement. Bright young people could easily lose their loyalty to the reformation movement and be drawn back into denominationalism where the opportunities for leadership presented themselves. Neither Reardon nor Morrison knew during this week in 1942 that the years just ahead would be ones of great physical struggle and depression for President Morrison personally and, partly for that reason, that a long and dramatic period of Reardon's leadership back in his Indiana hometown would loom just over the horizon.

Robert Reardon graduated from Oberlin in 1943 with the standard Bachelor of Divinity degree. Years later, when Oberlin merged with Vanderbilt University, Reardon's records were examined and Vanderbilt determined that he had met requirements for their Doctor of Ministry degree and thus granted it to him. This was based on additional work that Bob did at Oberlin beyond the B.D., including his thesis supervised by Dr. Horton and titled "The Doctrine of the Church and the Christian Life in the Church of God Reformation Movement." He wrote this in longhand and then it was typed by his wife Geraldine. Horton was ecumenically minded and most supportive of this exploration into a little-known church reform movement that featured a burden for the unity of the church in modern times. The findings of the study were hardly dramatic for Horton, but they were received as alarming by an element of conservatives in the Church of God movement. Key material from this thesis is found in Appendix E.

Pastoring in Pennsylvania

In 1943, after graduation from Oberlin and with military chaplaincy no longer a viable option, Geraldine and Robert Reardon were open to remaining with the Kipton congregation full-time if it were willing to end its independent status and identify itself formally with the Church of God movement. There was, however, evident hesitation to do this among the church's leaders, so the young couple looked elsewhere for their own ministry. They were committed without question to the Church of God movement. Finally, they were called to a full-time pastorate at the little congregation of the Church of God in Brookhaven, Pennsylvania, in a borough of Chester near Philadelphia. It was the only call to service that Bob had when he completed his seminary training at Oberlin. It would be a venture of faith. God had seemed to open this door. They would walk through it wherever it led.

The Brookhaven church would turn out to be a challenging and

The Brookhaven Church of God in Chester, Pennsylvania,
sixth anniversary, February, 1945. Pastor Robert Reardon is second
from the left in the back row and is holding his daughter Becky.

satisfying four years of ministry for the Reardons. The congregation was young and small and worshipped in a one-room frame building at a location where the Presbyterians, Baptists, and Pentecostals already had failed. There was no toilet in this box of a structure. It did have a curtain that was pulled across the sanctuary on Sunday mornings to divide the two adult Sunday school classes. If a person was not pleased with the teacher's lesson, the other teacher could be listened to through the curtain even if not quite visible. The children and youth went to the parsonage to meet. It was a small home on the property next door into which Robert and Geraldine had moved.

The young Rev. Reardon's image of pastoral work had been shaped significantly by the distinguished service of his own father. Preaching was viewed as a major responsibility and Robert determined to be the best pulpit man in the community. He was relatively inexperienced, of course, but he worked very hard at the preaching task. He traveled regularly to Crozer Seminary to use its fine library. To him, churches rarely grow with a weak

Pastor and Mrs. Robert Reardon, with daughter Becky, Chester, Pennsylvania, 1943.

ministerial presence in the pulpit. He considered it his responsibility to think, plan, and lead; he did so as a new pastor and later also as a college president.

The Reardons were at the Brookhaven church for four years, during which time they organized a program of personal evangelism in the community, made some lasting friendships, mentored some new church leaders, and saw some real growth. As Reardon says of himself, "I have a German disposition, so I am an organizer."

Accordingly, they got a choir started, with Jerry in the lead. On occasion Jerry would preach for her husband, a role for which she was clearly gifted and experienced. A pattern of worship services was begun in a local "project" of low-income housing set up by the government, with Pastor Reardon usually preaching there before the regular service at his church. Some of these project people began coming to the Brookhaven church itself. As the church grew, it became obvious that a new facility was necessary. Reardon led the way in sacrificial giving. He sold his fine Oldsmobile that he had bought in Anderson, Indiana, replaced it with an older and cheaper car, and gave the dollar difference to the congregation to launch a building fund. This generous leadership inspired others to join in the effort. He had learned how to motivate people for important causes. This would be a key skill to be used often by him in the years ahead.

Meanwhile, God's will for the future of the Reardons was still unclear to them. Having been turned down by the military for the chaplaincy role while still back at Oberlin Seminary and now having success as a young pastor, Rev. Reardon was nonetheless unsettled and needed a question answered. What about service as a foreign missionary? This kept suggesting itself to him, encouraged in part by Adam W. Miller back in Anderson, Indiana, who himself had been a missionary to Japan earlier. Now that the big world war had finally ended, doors were again opening to Christian missionaries in the Far East.

Was the missionary pull being felt merely that Reardon felt a little left out and not where the action was since he did not participate directly in the war and was still not "out there" as the world tried to rebuild itself? Was it just sentimentalism in light of his father's step of faith in going to Egypt decades earlier? He and Jerry spoke of this often and finally went together to New York City to attend a large ecumenical gathering of Christian missionaries, many of whom had earlier been run out of their fields of service in China and Japan and now were planning to return. As these people talked, the Reardons listened to test the kind of life it would be and their suitability for it. Once back home with their young children and after more thought and prayer, the idea of their potential foreign service slowly evaporated. Apparently they were not being called to this service after all.

The first of the four Reardon children, Rebecca Ann (Becky), had been conceived in Oberlin, Ohio, and born in October, 1943, in Wilmington, Delaware, not far from the Brookhaven church. Soon born there also were the other two daughters, Constance Ruth (Connie) two years later and then Mary Kathleen (Kathy) two years after Connie. Their son Robert Eugene (Gene) would be born later when they had relocated back in Anderson, Indiana (see Appendix H). Bob and Jerry were committed Christian parents. Beyond parenting in their own home, the Reardons were influential otherwise in a mentoring role. For instance, they altered the life direction of one key leader of the future, causing him to remain with the Church of God movement.

The parents of Maurice Caldwell had deep roots in the Church of God movement and were married by Rev. Eugene A. Reardon in Park Place Church of God in Anderson, Indiana. Maurice, however, had become discouraged about the movement after experiencing in California what he perceived to be some fanaticism. He became associated with the Methodist Church while studying in a college in Missouri as part of his training in the U. S. Naval Reserve, ending up at Drew University in Madison, New Jersey, to complete his seminary education and further deepen his Methodist ties. Then Pastor Reardon began inviting him on occasion to spend weekends with his family in nearby Pennsylvania. Rather than the turn-off of fanaticism, Maurice found the Reardon family and congregation to be bright, dynamic, and truly attractive. Geraldine Reardon was "a fabulous cook," reports Maurice, and the little girls "were adorable."

Reardon became Caldwell's mentor, thinking of him as "a bright young man with a good Church of God background who was being swallowed by the Methodists." The pastor and seminarian talked at length, resulting in Maurice recommitting himself to the Church of God movement and accepting the leadership of a congregation of the movement in Palmerton, Pennsylvania. The relationship of Robert and Maurice would be a close one for decades to come. For example, in 1950 Maurice was one of the key planners for the International Youth Convention of the Church of God that convened in Toronto, Canada. There he met Dondeena Fleenor, whom he married later that year. The officiating minister at their wedding in Park Place Church of God in Anderson, Indiana, was Robert Reardon.

Five years after the Reardons left the Brookhaven church in 1947 to return to Anderson, the congregation in Gloucester City, New Jersey, needed a pastor and sought the help of Robert Reardon whose reputation for wisdom still lingered out East. He pointed the church to the youth pastor of the Grand Avenue Church of God in the Bronx who was in his first year in seminary in New York. On the strength of Reardon's trust in a young leader with clear ministerial potential, Donald Collins became the new pastor in New Jersey, the first of his many leadership roles in the Church of God during the decades to follow. It all happened, Collins later said, because "the reservoir of trust that Bob had earned he risked passing on to me." Such passing on of trust and influence would be multiplied scores of times as the years would come and go. Reardon continued to watch, encourage, and recommend young people called of God to ministry in the church. Meanwhile, he had his own burdens to bear.

One especially dramatic and unwelcome event occurred in the extended Reardon family during the Brookhaven years (1943-1947). Bob's father Eugene had retired from full-time pastoral work in June, 1945, leaving his long pastorate at Park Place Church in Anderson, Indiana. The church was strong and debt free at that time. Gertrude Little was the Director of Christian Education and Professor Paul Breitweiser of Anderson College was the Director of Music. Rev. E. A. Reardon had announced in 1943 that he would retire in 1945 and then spend a year in mission service abroad. President John Morrison of Anderson College, a leading layperson in the Park Place congregation, wrote to Rev. Dale Oldham, then pastoring in Dayton, Ohio, to tell him of this news

*Robert Reardon and his family being greeted
at the door of Park Place Church of God
in Anderson, Indiana, by Pastor Dale Oldham.*

and of the possibility that he soon would be called to the pastorate of Park Place Church.

Oldham was very happy with his ministry circumstance in Dayton, Ohio, and did not want to live at Church of God "headquarters" as an Andersonian. Some vocal leaders like Rev. Earl Slacum of nearby Muncie, Indiana, already were aggressively criticizing the Anderson ministry agencies for supposed doctrinal deviations, worldliness, and exercising centralized power at the expense of the ordinary minister. Oldham saw such criticism as likely to be ongoing, "one of Christendom's favorite indoor sports" (*Giants Along My Path* 229). Such criticism was viewed by Oldham as a churchly "game" and Oldham preferred to stay on the sidelines. But Park Place Church did call Oldham and he reluctantly consented, finally judging that it was God's call. Installed on September 9, 1945, with controversy threatening to split the Church of God movement nationally, the Oldhams began a long, challenging, and rewarding pastorate in Anderson, Indiana.

Meanwhile, Rev. Eugene and Pearl Reardon had retired and were serving for a year on special assignment troubleshooting the missionary work of the Church of God in Kenya, East Africa. He had pioneered the work in Egypt as a young minister in 1907-1908, had been a charter member of the Missionary Board of the Church of God in 1914, and had never lost his global vision. Apparently some of the mission personnel in Kenya had come to feel that others were running the big mission station too much like their private preserve. As an older and highly respected man, the Board sent the wise Reardon to assess and confront the circumstance.

The eventual report from Rev. Reardon was frank and respectful—typical of him. He urged the board members to be careful with his report so as to "preserve the good name of our missionaries, whatever their mistakes may have been." After all, "it is thrilling to have had just a little share in the blessed fellowship of those brave and noble pioneer missionaries who blazed the trails through infested swamps and thickest jungle, bearing untold hardships to bring the glorious light of the gospel of Christ to Africa." When Eugene and Pearl Reardon had completed successfully their overseas assignment and filed the report, they flew home on September 30, 1946. Their two sons, Willard and Robert, were waiting for them at the airport in New York City.

Willard Reardon, on a business trip in the northeast, met his brother Bob at Grand Central Station. They toured around for the day and then in the late afternoon met their parents at the airport. It was a joyous reunion. When Bob left the city, taking his parents with him to Brookhaven, Willard said goodbye and, with no prior warning, would soon learn that he had seen his father alive for the last time. The next day Bob and his beloved father took a long walk by the river in Brookhaven. Bob updated the older man on some of what he had missed in American church life while gone, especially the anti-Anderson turmoil inspired largely by Rev. Earl Slacum and others. In fact, the younger Reardon's Oberlin thesis was being quoted by Slacum to help prove that his concerns were well documented. E. A. Reardon himself tended to represent the "liberal" trend of the Church of God movement dating back to the 1920s and his 1929 address on Christian unity to the General Ministerial Assembly. That Wednesday evening Eugene Reardon spoke in the prayer service at the Brookhaven church and then developed considerable stomach pain during the night. Home remedies were tried and failed. Finally, he underwent emergency surgery and unexpectedly died in the process. It was October 3, 1946, a dark day in the Reardon family.

The stunned Robert Reardon called Adam Miller in Anderson, a dear friend of Eugene Reardon. Within three days there was a large funeral in Park Place Church of God honoring the life and ministry of a man deeply loved by so many. It was said that the church had lost a great and good soul. Unfortunately, President John Morrison, who had just lost his best friend, was unable to attend the funeral for health reasons. He had been through nearly four years of virtual incapacitation from severe arthritis and resulting bouts of depression. He wanted very much to return to his presidential duties and serve out his remaining eleven years before retirement age, but probably could not manage it without real help. This circumstance was the door that soon would open to Robert Reardon.

After the funeral service celebrating the outstanding life and ministry of Rev. Eugene A. Reardon, his son Robert went to the Morrison home to share his grief with them, dear friends of many years. In their living room on that Sunday afternoon, October 6, 1946, the president asked that young Reardon return to the campus as the speaker for the next Religious Emphasis Week. Then he went even further, raising the idea of Robert joining his staff as the presidential assistant. He was open to helping the president in this way, but hesitated, noting that he was hardly qualified. Morrison persisted, even suggesting that as president he had an obligation to bring someone along who could gain the experience necessary to allow the trustees later to look favorably on him as the potential next president of the College. Reardon agreed to the speaking assignment, but leaving the pastorate for a life of college teaching and administration was a lot for the young church leader to ponder. The two men separated, grieving their great loss, with the question of the future left open.

Eleven Years of Grooming

On the drive back to Pennsylvania from the funeral of his father, there was much time for Robert and Geraldine Reardon to think and pray about the issue that had been laid before them. Was Bob's divine calling in the direction of President Morrison's proposal? Should he leave the pastorate and assist his old friend and his beloved alma mater, devoting his life to college teaching and administration? There were aspects of his life to date that suggested preparation in this direction. There also was the biblical model of shouldering new responsibility from a previous prophet. This model was raised in an October 20 letter to Robert Reardon from his esteemed professor at Oberlin seminary, Dr. Walter Horton. Eugene Reardon was identified by Horton as a man "who rode the winds and has left a son who also rides the winds." The father had "gone out like a rocket, leaving a trail of fire like Elijah, with the future up to the young Elisha." A great servant of God was gone. What great thing was his son now left to do?

There certainly was a rich legacy on which to stand. Never did Robert Reardon recall thinking of his family as poor in any sense. Yes, he had grown up during the Depression of the 1930s when things were hard for most people that he knew. Money was scarce, he usually wore hand-me-down clothes, and his pastor father talked little of money and much of selfless servanthood as the expected Christian norm. As Eugene Reardon always said, he had received from his churches a modest "allowance," God's gracious provision for necessary living expenses, but never had he received a "salary" like the secular world gives its hirlings. Bob and his brother

Robert and Geraldine Reardon and family playing a fun game together.

Bill (Willard) did get a modest allowance of their own as boys, twenty-five cents a week, but soon Bob had found ways to supplement this with a little skill and strategy—key elements of an effective executive, as the future would show quite clearly. As Reardon later explained: "I was the best marble-shooter in the neighborhood and shot the other boys out of their hoard, which filled several cigar boxes. This was the currency I used to trade for things I wanted, and I became a very good businessperson early on" (*The Way It Was* 34).

Robert Reardon's life preparation for a possible role in college administration, beyond a good business sense, was a developed pattern of discipline. As a young boy living in Denver, Colorado, in the 1920s, his brother Bill was involved in some military training as part of the regular programming at Southside High School. Then their father Eugene decided that his son Bob would benefit from military-like discipline and signed him up as a "Highlander Boy." This was a part-time academy of weekly drills and instruction in marching, camping, and competition designed to instill discipline, patriotism, and a code of honor. The boys occasionally marched in the city park past admiring and applauding parents. Bob's first time away from home was a week-long camp in the Colorado mountains with tents, campfires, and vigorous singing. He managed to absorb this military mentality despite considerable homesickness. Later he recalled with some sadness "how nearly absent from our church was the 'peace witness' so central among the Mennonites" (*The Way It Was* 50). What was very much present and crucial for Bob's professional future was respect for discipline, a code of honor, and a sense of ceremony.

The Reardon roots were deep in the soil of the Anderson campus. Rev. Eugene Reardon had been a great campus friend since the school's beginning in 1917. Now in the 1940s the younger Rev. Reardon, an appreciative alumnus, had his own deep love for the school and a great respect for President Morrison in particular. A fork in the road had been reached professionally for this educated and now experienced and successful young pastor. He called on his friend T. Franklin Miller to come to the Brookhaven congregation and preach an eight-day revival for him. Miller came, thoroughly enjoyed his stay in the Reardon home, and was greatly impressed by the quality work of this young pastor who had led the congregation in an extensive time of detailed preparation for the special meeting. The people had been trained in how to visit church prospects and then make them welcome and comfortable at the church. Miller, already was an experienced evangelist, had never seen such good pastoral work. Before the meeting was over, Reardon broached with Miller the issue of the Morrison invitation for him to return to Anderson College as presidential assistant. He asked for prayer. These good friends sought divine wisdom together.

Having thought and prayed much about President Morrison's offer, Reardon recalls that he and Jerry "opened our hearts to God about it and, as we did, the decision to return to the College became clear and compelling." In the language of that time, they developed "a burden for the work of the school." He returned to Anderson to be the guest preacher for Religious Emphasis Week and talked further with Morrison about the future. It was decided. By July, 1947, the Reardons were back in Anderson to stay, initially living in the old house of the Reardon family at 914 Walnut Street. Later they and Robert and Dorothy Nicholson built homes next to each other on Seventh Street. Along with good friends Val and Evelyn Clear, the Reardons made regular visits to Petty's Auction on Saturday nights to furnish their modest living quarters. Just opposite the Seventh Street home of the Reardons was that of longtime friend T. Franklin Miller. The four Reardon children played often with Tom and Sue Miller and with Paul and Gary Nicholson.

Robert Reardon had come back to Anderson ready to assume whatever responsibilities President Morrison had in mind for him. Reflecting later on this big move from Pennsylvania in 1947, he said, "My coming back to Anderson was clearly God working in my life." At the time of his retirement in 1983, he observed this about 1947: "I was 26 years old, too full of zeal for the College I loved to care what my salary was, endowed with a lovely wife, three precious little girls, and too inexperienced to know what formidable obstacles lay in the road ahead." His wife Jerry said that for her it was like a "homecoming" since she had loved her two college years in Anderson and knew so many people there.

Among the many things the young Robert Reardon brought back to Anderson with him was a sense of humor and the ability to adapt as necessary. One story he sometimes told, probably original with Gene Newberry, involved an old prospector and a brash young cowpoke who decided to have a little fun with the old man. He asked him, "Do you know how to dance?" The old man didn't, so the young man taught him by peppering the ground around the man's feet with his six shooters. The prospector did indeed dance—around his mule, under his mule, over his mule. The cowboy had his fun and turned his horse to ride off. As soon as he turned his head, the old timer yelled, "Hey, Bud." He turned back around and was looking down the barrel of a Winchester. The prospector asked, "Did you ever kiss a mule?" The cowboy replied humbly, "No, but I've always wanted to!" After telling such a story, Reardon would move quickly to make some significant point that was key to the moment.

Connie fondly reports the following about her beloved father: "My dad is a man full of laughter. I have wonderful memories of being tucked in bed and hearing Dad laughing with friends that he and Mom had invited over. He delights in making people laugh. He often has helped me see the humor in a stressful situation." Reardon's son Gene puts it this way:

> Dad was generally a serious man, but he loved to laugh and he loved unsophisticated, earthy humor. I recall Dad watching the old comedy show "Red Skelton" and laughing almost to the point of hysteria as Red came out in a boxing ring as "KO Pectate." I recall only one really crazy thing that he ever did. He came home early one evening and went up in the access and made weird noises to scare us all (I probably was about five). That was really

Mealtime prayer at the Reardon home. Left to right:
Gene, Becky, Robert (father), Kathy, Connie, and Geraldine (mother).

strange and out of character for him, but it was fun. Dad is not a silly man. It isn't that he is cold or stiff; he just doesn't have a childish nature.

Connie further recalls how hardworking her dad always has been: "When I was a child, Dad often was gone on College business or preaching on weekends to make extra money to support the family." Reardon had come to his new role in Anderson with no formal contract; he had not even asked in advance what his salary would be. That first year it turned out to be $2,080 or $40 per week.

Beyond making extra money, Robert Reardon also was out among the churches nurturing relationships and recruiting college students. For instance, in 1956 he called Pastor Paul Tanner of the First Church of God in Milwaukee, Wisconsin. As Paul recalls it, Reardon indicated that likely he would be the next president of Anderson College and was anxious to make his acquaintance and relate to his church and its youth. Tanner invited him for a series of services, being "honored to have someone of his stature willing to be a guest in our home and preach in my church." It was the beginning of a wonderful relationship that now has spanned nearly five decades. Soon a series of young people from that Wisconsin congregation did attend Anderson College under the presidency of Robert Reardon that began in 1958.

The first office occupied by Reardon in 1947 was a small and modestly furnished room on the first floor of Old Main. With a twinkle in his eye, he admits that he always kept his door open that first year, both for the convenience of the faculty, staff, and his forty student advisees and to keep available the view across the hall to the Registrar's Office "where there were attractive office girls who brightened each day!" Apart from advising students and appreciating beauty where he happened to see it, Robert Reardon had been given quite an extensive and open-ended set of

President John Morrison passed the presidential responsibility to Robert Reardon, 1958.

duties. At the time of his retirement in 1983, Reardon reported that President Morrison had said to him (*Anderson College Reflections* 10):

> I want you to do everything you can to help me. We need just about everything. Recruit students, raise money, strengthen our public relations in the city and in the church, and keep a sharp eye out for troublemakers. Keep your eyes and ears open and come share with me whenever you can. By the way, we'll have "Assistant to the President" printed on the glass door of your office and the Dean will be assigning you nine hours of teaching in the religion department.

Reardon began functioning on many fronts, including the teaching of classes in the fields of pastoral work and introductory Bible. One early Bible class taught by Reardon was comprised mostly of athletes—the College had just launched a football program to stimulate enrollment and public visibility. They seemed to be doing little but meeting a requirement by merely being in the room. One day a student athlete, more athlete than student, asked the young professor, "What is this circumcision that Paul is always talking about?" Reardon ventured an appropriately delicate response to a very unacademic and even cynical question.

With the new crowd of football players and some six hundred GIs on campus, mature beyond their years and anxious to get on with their lives now that the big war was over, there were some interesting social dynamics. Many young couples had babies to care for as well as books to read and grueling football practices to attend. One day Reardon's office door was closed as he talked with an advisee. Lettered for him on the frosted glass of the door was "Assistant to the President." Two of his GI advisees, annoyed at the slowness of his response to their knock, put their hands over all but the first three letters of "Assistant" and then ran away laughing. Campus leaders need to have warm hearts, tough skins, and flexible senses of humor. Reardon had or at least was in the process of developing all of these.

Ministerial education was close to Reardon's heart. Student Richard Swank (B.S. 1949, B.Th. 1950) recalls a class in preaching in 1950. Professor Reardon was very encouraging of his young students. Week after week in this class he "shared from his own education and experiences in his typical style of precise and pointed phrases, always with depth and often with humor." Students were tense on the day of the final exam. Quite unexpectedly, Reardon announced that he had learned enough about them from the whole semester and did not need to give one more exam. Instead, he led them across campus to his home on Seventh Street where he and his wife Geraldine entertained them. Swank and the others would never forget that day! Recalls Swank, "It showed the warmth, the caring, the grace of a husband and wife, deeply in love, ministering together."

President Morrison shared candidly his personal wisdom and opened all his office files to the welcome new Assistant. Jerry Reardon later called it a "father-son relationship." Reardon, now with the president on a daily basis and part of the inner administrative circle, drew on his 1942 exposure of President Morrison to Oberlin Graduate School of Theology to press for the launching of such a seminary in Anderson. They talked often about this possibility, with Gene W. Newberry, Harold L. Phillips, Adam W. Miller, and T. Franklin Miller joining Reardon in being very supportive of the idea. All of these men had themselves attended a seminary and were strong for the idea of graduate-level ministerial education becoming reality on the Anderson campus. They had suffered the nation-wide disruption the Church of God movement in the 1940s and felt that a better educated ministry could help to avoid such a sad and fruitless thing in the future.

Reardon further explained to Morrison his view that the growing numbers of educated laypersons in Church of God congregations would be retained better if they had educated pastors with professional credentials. Both of these college leaders knew that the young Church of God people then going to seminary elsewhere were being tempted toward the ministries of other church bodies. Soon the president was on board with this vision of a new seminary and the Board of Trustees was easily convinced. The new Anderson School of Theology came into being in 1950 with thirty-two graduate students enrolled. Reardon was a charter member of the graduate faculty, with his friend Eugene Newberry being the only full-time professor at first. Reardon wrote the resolution of establishment for the Board's action, joined Harold Phillips and others in sharing many personal books to get a seminary library started, and taught pastoral work and preaching in the new seminary's curriculum. Soon Reardon also would be key in attracting the 1961 grant from the Lilly Endowment that enabled adding full-time faculty positions in the seminary.

By 1955 it was generally assumed that Robert Reardon was being groomed by Dr. Morrison for the school's second presidency upon his own retirement. Reardon's administrative title was changed in 1952 to "Executive Vice-President," primarily because Reardon was attending a range of off-campus meetings on the president's behalf and Morrison felt that "Assistant to the President" was hardly an adequate title for the official representative of the campus. With the title elevation also came professional development.

A former classmate of Reardon's at Oberlin played the enabling role. Now a national leader in higher education based at the University of Michigan, this man invited his Anderson friend to come to the Michigan campus for the summer to study a range of subjects related to higher education administration. Reardon knew he would benefit and so he accepted. This was an important step in an ongoing although very unofficial process that seemed pointed toward the presidential office at Anderson College one day being occupied by Robert Reardon. Important also was the fact that in the 1947-1957 period, Reardon was gone frequently on weekends to preach for Church of God congregations around the country. This church networking was vital for the school's well being and worked toward Reardon himself becoming familiar to and appreciated by scores of ministers.

In 1956 President Morrison made it clear that he would retire in 1958. The Board of Trustees named a search committee in the spring of 1956, with Harold E. Achor as chair. The plan was to name a President-Elect in 1957 and then have the new leader serve transitionally during 1957-1958 under

The Reardon family, October, 1958,
the presidential inauguration day of Robert Reardon.
Left to right: Becky, Geraldine, Robert and Connie,
with Gene and Kathy in the front.

Morrison's mentoring and supervision. Robert Reardon was not interviewed or even contacted by the search committee, possibly because its members already knew him and his work so well. It seemed relatively clear what would happen in leadership transition. Reardon had been in all of the Board meetings for nearly a decade, had been very close to the full operation of the presidential office, and seemed primed for the position. There was no obvious competition and it was an open secret that Morrison favored him as his successor. Of significance in the arena of institutional goals and programs, in 1955 the Board had established a President's Study and Planning Commission to conceive a ten-year vision for campus development. Robert Reardon, then Executive Vice-President, had been named Commission leader. He drew on the consulting help of Dr. Ralph Noyer, Dean Emeritus of nearby Ball State Teachers College (now University) and the active participation of the several executives of the national ministry agencies of the Church of God movement housed adjacent to the campus. Reardon had the Board's attention and earned its confidence.

Robert Reardon appeared to be a natural networker, a visionary thinker, and a likely executive leader for the future of the campus. In 2002 he reflected back on his apparent leadership virtues in 1957 and noted these: a solid family life; the good name of his father; energy; friends across the church; social intelligence; ideas "outside the box"; the courage to pursue these new ideas; and a sense of humor to smooth the way. Already to his credit in 1957 were his leadership of the President's Study and Planning Commission, his beginning Vocation Days and the Laymen Lecture series—significant steps for improved student recruitment and church relations, his close ties to the earliest years of the School of Theology, his key role in founding both the Business and Professional Fellows and Sponsors organizations (local and national), and his successful fundraising for the Wilson Library building, new on campus in 1957. Also to his credit was his obvious ability to judge the gifts and potential of people. For instance, he had been observing with great appreciation the work of music faculty member Robert Nicholson. In addition, for some time young Norman Beard had been assisting Reardon with student recruitment and personnel services. Both men would be key to the future of the campus.

Left to right (standing): Wilbur Schield, Robert H. Reardon, and Russell Olt.
Seated: John A. Morrison, Charles E. Wilson, and Linfield Myers.

Obviously, Reardon already had demonstrated presidential skills and instincts and he had nurtured many relationships on and off campus that would be critical to his future executive leadership. Formalizing his rather obvious presidential candidacy appeared almost inevitable to most observers. He had worked closely with President Morrison for eleven years and judged it "a priceless experience." Morrison was one of the great personalities of the Church of God movement, a humble and generous man with humor, good political instincts, and the will to fight for what he believed. His influence on the younger Reardon was considerable—as was the similarity of their human and executive gifts.

When the Board of Trustees met in the spring of 1957, the last item on the long agenda was a report from the presidential search committee. An executive session was called. The formal report to the Board spoke of twelve persons having been "nominated," although Reardon recalls no one wanting the job since the campus had been in conflict with the church and there were significant financial problems. The campus had suffered a financial loss in President Morrison's last year in office, with income falling well short of necessary expenses. The unanimous agreement of the search committee was that Executive Vice-President Reardon was clearly the right candidate. It was decided. The staff was summoned back into the historic meeting. Reports Reardon (*Some Anderson College Reflections* 18):

> Before I knew it, the chairman, the venerable Dr. E. E. Perry, called for a motion to adjourn. With some timidity, I raised my hand and asked if it would be inappropriate for me to know what had transpired while I was out of the room. At this there was an embarrassed silence. Then Dr. Perry, with a gracious apology, announced my election as the second President of Anderson College. Members of the Board seemed generally pleased.

The choice had been so natural that the Board forgot to report it to the man elected! Now informed and despite the institutional problems, Robert Reardon made immediately clear to the Board that he was prepared and willing to serve.

Having been named President-Elect of Anderson College in 1957, Reardon used that summer to engage in a crucial educational opportunity. The head of the Business School of Harvard University had received foundation money to convene a group of new college and university presidents to study the challenges and dynamics of higher education administration. They would be using the case-study method he was pioneering. Jerry and Robert Reardon were accepted into the group selected to participate. It proved to be a truly significant and enjoyable experience. The new presidents of the Universities of Tennessee and Washington, the incoming president of Oberlin, Reardon's own seminary alma mater, and about twenty others comprised the group. The young Anderson executive, not yet officially in office, felt particularly comfortable with the group since he already had ten years of administrative exposure and most of the others were coming straight from the ranks of their respective faculties.

Once back in Anderson, Reardon's transition to executive leadership was close to ideal. President Morrison spent many hours with the President-Elect discussing institutional problems and allowing him to make key decisions that he would have to live with when his own official presidency began in 1958. The transition of leadership was peaceful, well informed, and unhurried. The General Assembly of the Church of God concurred in the Board's election of Reardon by officially ratifying him. Reardon recorded in his

Robert H. Reardon, 1955.

private journal that only forty-two persons opposed the ratification and "they may have been some of my former students!" He added with more serious intent: "God help me never to betray this sacred trust. It is a wonderful and sobering responsibility." By the time he officially assumed the presidential office on June 17, 1958, he had been involved in the planning of seven different occasions for honoring the retiring President John Morrison.

Just before assuming the presidential office, Reardon began his third term as secretary of the Indiana Association of Church-Related and Independent Colleges, a role that allowed him to know personally all of the higher education presidents in Indiana. Then a signal honor came to him. DePauw University, an old and strong Methodist university founded in Greencastle, Indiana, in 1837, decided to honor Anderson's young leader, Robert Reardon, with an honorary Doctor of Humane Letters degree. This came about through the initiative of a former Church of God man who had become a Methodist minister and then a member of the board of trustees of DePauw. The honor was bestowed in the midst of an outstanding occasion, with Reardon sitting on the platform with the Prime Minister Harold Macmillan of England, who also was receiving an honorary doctoral degree.

It had been a long way from Robert Reardon's birth in a communal missionary home in Chicago in 1919 to his being thirty-nine years old, honored by a prestigious institution, sitting as an equal with one of the world's political leaders, and assuming the presidency of the college where once he had been a student. But so it was.

Standing on Strong Shoulders

Robert Reardon wrote a significant entry in his private journal in March, 1956. It was both an expression of his admiration for President John Morrison and a statement of what he hoped for the future in light of the example of his beloved mentor and his own divine call and gifts. He wrote:

> As I reflect on this great man [Morrison], I try to see what has made him such a force for good. Perhaps his vision of greatness, his unswerving devotion to a cause, personal charm, warm commonness, his ability to lay his finger quickly on the heart of any issue or problem, seeing nearly at once its entire ramifications, his ability to bring people together in a great task and inspire them, his ability to delegate but not abrogate responsibility, and, of course, his wit and platform ability have played a central role in his success.

After Morrison's death in 1965, Reardon wrote about him again, this time in his Annual Report to the General Assembly of the Church of God. He said of his predecessor and mentor:

> Without his dedication and superb educational statesmanship through the years, the Anderson College we know today would never have been brought into being and, as the years come and go, we will come to understand how great a debt we owe this solitary man.... When we were with him, all the good things in

our lives seemed to emerge. We became more understanding, more tolerant, more redemptive in our attitudes, and his rich humor left us a legacy of laughter more priceless than a king's ransom in jewels.

The twenty-five years of the presidency of Robert Reardon (1958-1983) would yield ample evidence of the very qualities that he so admired in

Robert Reardon (right) with John Morrison.

Morrison. Of key importance for Reardon's administrative future were the strong shoulders of President Morrison on which he would stand with pride and conscious continuity. Reardon was very aware of following in the presidential footsteps of a great and respected friend—he could not replace him, only follow the same general trail he had blazed so well. The school's lot had been cast with the church. In that there would be no wavering.

The new president intended to keep the school on a steady course regardless of the changing circumstances. He said this to the alumni as his presidency began (*Alumni News*, July-August, 1958):

Are we on the threshold of a bright golden age where vast new buildings will spring up overnight, funds will pour in Niagara-like, faculty salaries double, utopian relationships exist among students, and defeat become unknown on the gridiron? Obviously, no. The Olt-Morrison years were never anything but struggle. The struggles will continue.

While there surely were many struggles still ahead, Reardon's presidency began with some favorable circumstances. There were no major internal conflicts on campus in 1957-1958 and the transfer of presidential power was peaceful and welcomed. As historian John W. V. Smith put it, Reardon's appointment as President "was no surprise and the transition produced no upheavals" (*The Quest for Holiness and Unity* 365). There also was relative peace on the national church front after the considerable turmoil of the 1940s. A boom was coming in student populations as the country placed major new emphasis on higher education. Fresh money was becoming available to private higher education from corporate and government sources. Wise choices and hard work could make some great things happen in this emerging environment.

Of additional assistance was the fact that the President's Study and Planning Commission of the 1950s had been led by Reardon and had generated a series of six key institutional needs that the new president now announced as primary objectives of his new administration. The road needing traveled appeared clear to nearly everyone, and it was a very challenging road indeed. The goals were to:

1. Exalt the spiritual and train for responsible Christian citizenship.
2. Improve instruction.
3. Attract qualified students.
4. Raise faculty salaries.
5. Build and conserve the physical plant.
6. Increase financial aid for students.

In many ways the circumstance in 1958 had changed little from that of 1947 when Robert Reardon had first arrived back on campus to assist President Morrison. He then had been asked to do all he could to help the President with a small college that needed almost everything. Beginning with his own presidency in 1958, Reardon would lead in major strides forward on virtually all fronts. Many doors were opening, but it would take courage, wisdom, and an increased flow of monetary resources to successfully walk through them.

Different leadership faces were appearing on the Anderson campus as the early presidency of Robert Reardon faced soberly and successfully the deaths of several people who had been much of the heart and soul of the campus—Dean Russell Olt (1958), Professor Ruthven Byrum (1958), soon to be followed in 1959 by the death of Professor Carl Kardatzke, head of the Education Department and college Vice-President, and in 1960 by the death of John Kane, Vice-President for Church Relations. President Reardon

Robert H. Reardon and Robert A. Nicholson, special friends and effective colleagues.

lamented these great losses and, natural leader that he was, accepted the resulting leadership vacuum as an opportunity to bring forward new voices, vision, and energy for a new day.

Of primary importance was the elevation of Professor Robert A. Nicholson from being the recently appointed Chair of the Department of Music to assuming the Deanship of the College. For the quarter of a century to follow, Nicholson would be the strong and wise second man of the institution, a vital asset to the Reardon administration. Other important names to follow over the years included the administrative appointments of Cleda Anderson, Norman Beard, Barry Callen, James Massey, Adam Miller, Ronald Moore, and others, but no one who quite rivaled his appointment of Dean Robert A. Nicholson in eventual significance to the institution as a whole.

So much was new on campus. Darlene Miller joined the campus community in 1958 as a freshman student from Florida. She quickly realized that she was not the only new person on campus. Beyond her freshman colleagues were a new president and dean. She thought, "What a neat thing!" It was a new day and they were all starting together. She observed President Reardon and admits to having thought to herself, "How poised and handsome he is!" Reardon and Nicholson were young and energetic, good models for a new generation. Nearing her time of college graduation in 1962 and having been a student employee in the campus library, the new administration asked Miller to launch an instructional media program, later to become the Instructional Materials Center. She did that and in the process was so impressed at how the new president and dean seemed to have great confidence in each other. Apparently it was both a new day and a very good day in the life of the campus.

Reardon had known Nicholson even before each returned to the Anderson campus in the late 1940s. They first met in New York City where Nicholson was beginning work on a doctoral program in 1946 and while Reardon was still pastoring the Brookhaven congregation in Pennsylvania. Soon both the Nicholson and Reardon families would be back in Anderson, Indiana, where both had attended college. In fact, they soon would be living next door to each other on Seventh Street not far from the campus. Reardon says that he "has always been attracted to bright and dedicated people," and thus to Robert Nicholson. Between 1947 and 1958 he "watched Nick's stature blossom." Geraldine Reardon and Dorothy Nicholson became "like sisters," reports Jerry. They would hang their washings on neighboring clotheslines and picnic together as families.

Nicholson was an energetic young music professor who was very productive and able to handle multiple assignments. While completing his doctorate in the early 1950s, he turned the program wheels for Vocation Days (with Reardon doing the visioning and program promotion). In 1953 he was first elected to the Publication Board of the Church of God and completed the big task of being Editor of the 1953 edition of the church's hymnal. Then he directed the complex project that led to the film "Heaven to Earth" as a key part of the seventy-fifth anniversary of the Church of God movement in 1955, arranging himself the film's musical score. All the while he taught and directed the College choir. Reardon watched as Nicholson handled skillfully a difficult personnel situation among his music colleagues that helped lead to his becoming Chair of the Music Department.

As Reardon became President, it was his choice to have Nicholson become Dean of the College, replacing Dean Olt who was near death with cancer. So they began together the long tenure of a significant administrative team, a marvelous match of two men to rival that of the previous team of John Morrison and Russell Olt. The new team was similar in working style. Just as

Morrison had allowed Olt considerable freedom to lead the faculty and the academic affairs of the campus as he judged best, so did Reardon free Nicholson. It was the model of administration with which Reardon was familiar on this campus and one with which he was comfortable.

The president sat in faculty meetings, but the dean always presided. The two men had great mutual respect and confidence and were close personal friends. When Reardon was away and judgment was needed, the dean could be counted on to know the president's mind and was free to act if necessary, knowing that the president would support his decision, whatever it was. Rarely was there any conflict between them. Says Shirell Fox, assistant to both Presidents Morrison and Reardon, "no institution could have had a more beautiful relationship between two strong leaders."

When Robert Nicholson himself was the president beginning in 1983, he observed that back in 1958 the new President Reardon had a strong sense of leadership, fortunate for a man of thirty-nine becoming president alongside a new dean of thirty-four as they replaced the senior Morrison and Olt, ages sixty-five and sixty-three respectively. He also observed that Reardon's sense of personal leadership was weaker when it came to the academic side of the campus enterprise. This arena he gladly trusted to his new dean, rarely giving him any mandates for the administration of academics. Reardon's instincts were exceptional, as were Nicholson's skills of academic administration. In the vigorous 1960s, for instance, when a range of building projects were launched on campus, typically the president was chief promoter and fundraiser while his trusted dean worked on clarifying the needed programs justifying the buildings and how the programs could be served best by the design of the structures.

There was much more happening than the new president's appointment of key professors and administrators in the period 1958-1960. Very early in his presidency, Robert Reardon faced the need of securing a personal secretary for himself. A young woman from Birmingham, Alabama, had been coming to the Anderson Camp Meeting for some years and helping the campus with an alumni activity. Reardon met Virginia Johnson in Alabama while on a church assignment, was impressed, and invited her to be his presidential secretary at a salary much below what she already was making. She accepted and served his office faithfully from 1960 until his retirement in 1983. Years later he described her as "very supportive of me, very circumspect with her ability to hold confidences, quickly recognizing my weaknesses and learning what she could do to help me." After some years on the job, Virginia met and married the president's brother, Willard, occasionally causing some confusion and amusement as a stranger would learn that Mrs. Reardon in the president's office was really not the president's wife! At Reardon's retirement in 1983, Virginia wrote to him and tried to express her feelings. She was deeply grateful, had felt taken into his family, and observed: "I still wonder how in the world I have been so lucky! You were right when you told me that many wonderful things were 'coming down the pike.' My years here are my happiest years."

During his retirement years, Reardon looked back and observed that "the best thing I did as President was to put together a group of campus leaders who were the brightest and strongest of any campus in Indiana." He had followed the advice given to him by a local Anderson banker, Linfield Myers, who was a great friend of the campus. Said Myers to Reardon about 1956 on the assumption that soon he would be the campus president, "never hire anybody who is not smarter than you are!" This is exactly what Reardon consciously did over the years. He was secure enough personally to do just that. Observing humorously that if he did otherwise he would wake up one day finding himself "knee-deep in midgets," he gathered around him gifted and dedicated people smarter than himself in their areas of responsibility. He surely did hold people accountable, but never did he look over their shoulders on a daily basis and insist that everything come across his desk. He was a shrewd judge of people, naming the best and then setting them free to do their best. It proved to be a winning formula.

Geraldine Reardon was equally successful in her own way. Eunice Morrison, she said, had been such a "strong and gracious first lady" that Jerry wondered if she were up to this high standard. She was reassured by the thought that she did not need to "replace" the woman who would always be the original first lady of the campus. Instead, she would just be herself. The Reardon's lived in a relatively small home on Seventh Street. In that modest setting, Jerry saw her role as the president's wife being to keep an ordered home that would be a place of peace for her busy husband. Being a wife, mother, and homemaker came first and was very time consuming. Entertaining for Jerry "was a joy." She saw her ministry as "encouragement, openness, hospitality, and availability." She was an invaluable presidential companion.

Reardon began his presidency by putting in place a great dean and an excellent personal secretary, while enjoying a very supportive home life. But all was not ideal. All of the change coupled with the lack of financial resources necessary to make possible a rapid accomplishment of the campus goals inevitably brought tensions. One source of early problem for President Reardon was the fact that the campus faculty was very underpaid in the 1950s. The modest compensation that did exist was at two levels only, very modest at $3,800 annually for those without doctorates and slightly higher at $4,800 for those with them. This salary system was designed by Dean Olt primarily as leverage for faculty members to complete their doctorates as the campus was seeking accreditation in the 1940s. However, it no longer would remain unchallenged by a restive faculty.

Professor Val Clear went so far as to openly favor faculty unionizing like the big auto industries locally. The new Reardon-Nicholson administration was sympathetic to the faculty's concern, but was opposed to unionizing—hardly the way to foster warm relationships in the church's school. In the new administration's view, recent years of campus finances made virtually impossible any early action toward immediate change in salary levels. Trust and patience on the part of the faculty would be necessary. Patience was thin; trust had to be earned. It soon was for the most part.

Robert Reardon (left) serving students at Vocation Days outside Old Main.

CHAPTER Four

Love for Students, Faculty, and City

··

hen Rev. Eugene A. Reardon, father of Robert Reardon, died in
1946, many highly complimentary things were said about him in
various publications across the Church of God movement. They
included his being "a man of great courage, of firm convictions," "the prince
of pastors," and the beloved pastor "with a warm heart and a balanced
intellect" who truly loved Anderson College and knew numerous students by
their first names. The October 1946 issue of the college's *Alumni News* was
dedicated to his memory, carried the above generous judgments about him,
and prophetically observed this about his son: "Already Bob is manifesting in
his ministry many of the qualities of his father, and no doubt as the years come
and go we shall see more of the elder Reardon in this fine young minister of the
gospel." How right this was!

Robert loved his father and drank deeply of his idealism, breadth of
mind, warmth of heart, and global perspective. He would always carry with
him and treasure a memorable mental icon of his dad. One morning very early
Bob came into the dining room where his father was sitting by the window in
his favorite chair in the Walnut Street home in Anderson, Indiana. Brother
Reardon was reading the Bible and deep in prayerful meditation. The early
morning sun was shining on the humble and wise pastor, with a virtual halo
seeming to glow on his head. This was a significant symbol to Bob of a special
servant of God in whose steps he would hope to follow. A special beneficiary of
his service would be coming generations of young people who would cherish the
Anderson campus as their alma mater and Robert Reardon as their president.

A Pastoral Relationship with Students

In his own early schooling, especially in the Denver, Colorado, years (grades three through nine), Bob Reardon had struggled personally with the issues of self-identity and academic success. So, as a pastor and for decades as a college teacher and president, he "tried to show genuine affection for people and encourage them to believe in themselves and to support them in their quest" (*The Way It Was* 28). He also supported staff persons whom he appointed to serve with him. As their president, never did he micro-manage these people, but rather he gave them room to use their gifts and always recognized that the good things that happened in his twenty-five years as chief executive officer of the Anderson campus were not all his doing by any means. He admits readily to having been a very effective college and seminary president. By this, however, he means the success of himself *and those key people who served faithfully with him*. The point of all this effective serving was the education of students who chose the Anderson campus. It was education that included mind and spirit, character and vocation.

President Robert Reardon was well aware of the standard wisdom in contemporary American higher education. Presidents are not to be paternal in relation to college students, acting like a young adult's second parent. Reardon nonetheless determined not to function as though no strict moral standards were to prevail on campus and the personal lives of students were not the legitimate concern of teachers and administrators. In fact, he looked at his own relationship with students through pastoral eyes. His consistent intent was to love, serve, and seek to guide the passing generations of students in distinctively Christian ways—and to do so without apology. He gladly affirmed the title of the book chronicling the first seventy-five years of campus history. Using a phrase in the campus alma mater, it was called *Guide of Soul and Mind* (Barry L. Callen, 1992). Campus mission in Anderson highlighted the mind, to be sure, but always in relation to the soul.

As Reardon began his administration in 1958, he made clear his view of the question, "Does a college violate a student when it moves into the arena of character formation?" As far as this new college president was concerned, "the secularization of education has produced a generation of leaders who are intellectual giants but spiritual dwarfs" (*Alumni News*, September 1958). That mistake was not going to happen on Reardon's watch! He recalled vividly

President John Morrison speaking to students on the Anderson campus during the Depression of the 1930s. While the school hung by a financial thread, Morrison said: "I would rather be alive today than at any other time in human history!" He articulated in inspiring ways the proper relationship between education and religion.

Reardon determined to follow in this tradition, speaking often in college chapel as president, seeking to connect student interests and the school's goals. He took such communication occasions seriously and led them exceptionally well. For instance, few graduates of the 1960s and 1970s were not impressed by the president's personal tradition at the annual Christmas chapel of telling the "Uncle Barney" story. This simple but moving seasonal tale had originally appeared as "Let's Go Neighboring" in a 1954 issue of *Guideposts* (see Appendix A for the full text of the original story). In the skilled story-telling hands of President Reardon, it spoke powerfully to students, faculty, and staff by combining sentimentality, traditional family values, and a moving call for Christian compassion—all keynotes of the president's own heart and understanding of the central mission of Anderson College.

Influence usually is rooted in recognition and respect. Reardon surely was widely recognized and certainly respected and even beloved by most students. Dan, his own nephew, son of his brother Willard, visited Anderson in the early 1960s as a student of the University of Illinois. He listened to his Uncle Bob, "a good salesman who really believed in Anderson College," and decided to finish his education in Anderson. In fact, various students and others not of the President's personal family affectionately called him "Uncle Bob."

It was Reardon's long experience on the Anderson campus that gave him broad perspective on the changing generations of students. At the end of the 1940s, when he first carried major leadership responsibility on campus under President Morrison, the student body was dominated by eager and serious war veterans. Then had come the expansionist and relatively quiet 1950s, a momentary pause before the turbulent 1960s with its rebellious, impatient, even revolutionary students. Reardon expressed hope to the General Assembly of the Church of God as the 1970s opened that maybe the campus could recover "something of the quiet thoughtfulness and balanced judgment which are marks of civil and refined people" (*Annual Reports*, 1972). He knew, however, that peace comes only with justice, so he reported proudly in 1972 that the number of African-American students enrolled at Anderson had increased dramatically from 39 in 1967-1968 to 122 in 1971-1972. A significant segment of the constituency of the Church of God movement in North America was African-American, so it seemed that Anderson, the main college campus of the movement, should position itself to serve such youth effectively.

Robert Reardon was open to all aspects of student life. Beginning in 1945, Kenneth Hall and Mel Goerz tried to get a student newspaper going. During 1946-1947, when President Morrison was ill and away from his office and Earl Martin was Acting President, they succeeded in gaining from the administration permission to publish, but within "a tough set of requirements to be met related to circulation, printing costs, and advertising policies." They met them and got the *Andersonian* going just as Robert Reardon was arriving on campus as Assistant to the President. Hall recalls that Reardon "was always friendly and supportive." Over the years to follow Reardon would be an advocate of students and their legitimate voice, although he also would insist on some clear guidelines to protect the institution from what easily could steer it in a direction other than its historic course. When important matters were in question, Reardon was a man known for staying the course.

The mission of the Anderson campus was challenged in at least two different ways in the first decade and a half of the Reardon presidency. The second of these ways was prompted particularly by the Viet Nam War and is recalled below. But first came the more ironic and quite subtle distractions of institutional success. Between the beginning of his presidency in 1958 and the middle of the following decade, the Anderson campus under Robert Reardon increasingly became busy, varied, and full of pride in its progress, with quality performance the intended end product of whatever was being attempted. So much was this the case that, in a report to the Board of Trustees in 1965, Reardon said that the church's growing pride in the campus was verging on being so great that pride itself could become a threat to institutional integrity. He elaborated:

> There was a day when most of us went out into the church. . .and much of our energy was spent carrying on a battle with the "saints." One of the most difficult things we have had to adjust to in the last decade has been the general love, trust, and acceptance with which the institution has been accepted by the church.... However, beneath that smile I think I sometimes detect a pride in

size, status, and an over enthusiasm for what education can do. The college now must change its stance. It must abhor the prospect of becoming a denominational status symbol.

A steady state for institutional mission would also be tested vigorously in the struggles of the civil rights movement and the Viet Nam War, both of which would bring social turmoil to the American scene generally and to the world of higher education especially. Flexibility would be demanded by dramatically changing times, as President Reardon said clearly to the constituencies of Anderson College (*Anderson College News*, special issue, 1964): "Many sacred academic cows will be slaughtered in the field.... Colleges which are either unable or unwilling to change, modify, and face the new day with courage and imagination will be left behind like the village gas station deserted beneath the new interstate highway. *Anderson College has no such destiny in mind!*" There would have to be change, but only within carefully identified limits if institutional mission were to be maintained with integrity. Reardon wrote this personal reflection in Nairobi, Kenya, in 1988, five years after his retirement from the presidency:

> During the Viet Nam War many college presidents ran, gave in, capitulated to extreme student demands. The more radical student activists in Anderson knew that I would listen, but would not permit unreasonable demands. I wrote a long letter to parents at this time spelling out the way the game was played at Anderson College. We did not fall apart in Anderson during those hectic days.

The letter in question had come from the President's desk in July, 1969. To send such a letter was a risky move in the view of some campus administrators since its timing was just when students were deciding whether or not to return to campus in the fall—and their presence was crucial for the school's financial stability. Even so, Reardon opted for institutional integrity whatever the enrollment cost might be. He told the students and their families that Anderson College was a special place with clear standards. If they did not agree and fit, it might be better if they did not return! Reardon had just told campus trustees that "there is something apocalyptic about these times." Campus life across the nation had been "politicized, radicalized, and in many cases immobilized." Returning students now were being told by the letter that

President Reardon intended to strengthen the common life on campus by keeping it on its historic course in the midst of national chaos. Whatever the enrollment fallout, this campus would stay true to itself.

There were traditional Christian standards of conduct that would be maintained, announced the president, including a rejection of discrimination based on color, race, or creed. One key sentence of the 1969 letter read: "Students advocating racial separatism, non-negotiable demands supported by threats of violence, or hostility toward Christian teaching on brotherhood should seek their education elsewhere." There also was the traditional feature of campus life, mandatory chapel/convocation, that was convened twice weekly for all students and faculty and was always partly or wholly religious in nature. It was a reflection of the school's core heritage and an administrative instrument of ongoing community building in the face of constant pressures toward campus fragmentation and secularization. In the 1960s many students mounted a considerable effort to have chapel turned into a voluntary school program, a change that many church-related colleges were agreeing to do in these years. But no basic change would occur on the Anderson campus.

The Reardon administration held the line in the face of student efforts to deemphasize or even eliminate the regular chapels. The number of excused absences per semester was increased and there was obvious sensitivity to the student call for a greater breadth of programming—including the beginning of "multiple" chapels, two or three with different emphases occurring simultaneously in differing locations. Even so, there was to be no change in the mandatory and significantly religious nature of most chapel/convocation sessions. The breadth of programming, overtly religious and otherwise, was significant and would not have existed without the President's blessing. It was an intentional reflection of his educational vision. Chapel was too central to institutional mission in Robert Reardon's view for any major change to be allowed.

Changes in location of chapel sessions certainly did come along. After Park Place Church built its magnificent new building opposite the campus in 1960, the classic old structure of the church at Eighth and College was passed to College hands for chapel use and as a music hall. This old building, of course, was filled with personal memories for President Reardon. Some years later there was a fire at the old church and chapel shifted to what now is called Byrum Hall and then to the new Park Place Church sanctuary. Many years later, in 1983-1984 when Reardon Auditorium was built in large part to better house the regular college chapel/convocations and be the home of the Anderson Symphony Orchestra, it was natural and wholly appropriate to place the Reardon name on this magnificent building. A celebration of worship and the arts was a fitting honor for the church-musician president who held the line on the significance and continuance of mandatory chapel and insisted on quality music and meaningful relations with the local city.

Good perspective on President Reardon's relationships with students demands more than awareness of student protests and determined presidential standard keeping, as noted above. It must include awareness of the president's strong commitment to the freeing aspects of the "liberal arts" curriculum that tend to give students an informed and independent mind and voice. In this regard, Reardon was very direct in writing to alumni (*Anderson College News*, October, 1964):

> This college cannot keep an honest student protected from those ideas which challenge the validity of faith. In the Anderson College library one can find every major critic of the Christian faith in the last 2,000 years. We would not have it otherwise. Unless a student is led to struggle with these giant beasts and dragons of the intellectual world, faith remains inarticulate, untried, and soft.... We expect, however, to have at hand those wise, mature, and seasoned instructors who can give understanding and support to faith along the way.

He added even more when speaking to the General Assembly of the Church of God at the end of the turbulent 1960s. John Foster Dulles once had said, wisely in Reardon's view, that "the Christian Liberal Arts College is the guardian of the soul of America." The president proceeded to tie this statement to his own Christian faith, concluding: "It is this rich heritage borne down to us through the noble lives of the saints, the prophets, and the martyrs which helps us know who we are and whose we are. I am confident that this is the compelling, underlying, unifying force that draws us together on this [Anderson] campus to carry forward our work as the people of God" (*Annual Reports*, 1969).

Experiencing the 1960s on the Anderson College campus certainly was not as confrontational or disruptive as was sadly true at Harvard, Columbia, or San Francisco State. Even so, reported Reardon to the national leadership of the Church of God movement, "It would also be grossly inaccurate to describe our own campus as a quiet backwater, undisturbed by the great tidal waves and treacherous currents generated by the unresolved social ills of our troubled times." He warned, "Many of our students have lost confidence in the church, in the nation, in things, and in that cornerstone of our modern tower of Babel—the university itself." Reardon determined that, at least at Anderson College, student frustration would be met with understanding. Administrative office doors were kept open and student leaders were involved more deeply in certain of the institution's decision-making processes. Much of the interaction between administration, faculty, and students was constructive. Reardon judged optimistically that, among faculty and students, there was a deep reservoir of affection for the school. He saw this eventual result: "Whatever sparks fly off in the future. . .some of them may light the way ahead" (*Annual Reports*, 1969).

This light that can lead into the future was sparked often by student experiences in the TRI-S program (Student Summer Service), an international exposure and service program beginning on the Anderson campus in 1964. Led through its early years by Norman Beard, who deserves much credit for the program's significant evolution, originally it was the dream of Robert Reardon and became one aspect of campus life about which the president would be most proud. He was anxious to end the all-too-easy pattern of college students spending "four years in never-never land, not once having felt the sharp sting of the real world" (*Anderson College News*, October 1966). Jerry Reardon recalled much later that a highpoint of her husband's whole presidency was the TRI-S trip the Reardons once led to Japan—a great relationship with twelve wonderful students. President Reardon told the campus Board of Trustees in 1965: "Students cannot grow spiritually without activity and involvement. The answers to our questions about God, man, life, death, and human destiny cannot be found in the library alone." From the very origin of TRI-S, the dream of its potential was shared with the president by student leader Larry Brown and the program's administrator, Norman Beard. Thousands of students would come to share the dream over the coming years.

In the last chapel before the summer vacation of 1966, with the TRI-S program then only two years old, more than one hundred students were commissioned to serve instead of vacation. That fall Reardon told alumni that already TRI-S had opened a new world of learning for students. The returning volunteers "have made the campus come alive with the ferment created by first-hand encounter with the great issues of our time.... These TRI-S volunteers have built bridges of understanding out into a world hitherto unknown except as a student comes to know it in books, lectures, and visuals." The President predicted correctly that this program "will mark the beginning of a whole new epoch in the life of this college and will have a renewing effect on the church we seek to serve" (*Anderson College News*, October, 1966).

There were other international and experiential student programs that carried the obvious marks of President Reardon—a continuance of the global vision of his father. For example, when music professor Eugene Miller wrote to congratulate the president at the time of his retirement in 1983, he reflected on how Reardon often had assisted the outstanding music program of the campus. Miller recalled a recent trip of the Male Chorus that he had directed. Reardon personally had made it possible for these men to go into the Soviet Union. The president had traveled with the group for two weeks in Finland, sometimes playing cards with some of them in the back of the bus during long drives. According to Miller's letter, "the men of the Male Chorus hold you [President Reardon] in extremely high regard and affection. Many of the men expressed their delight in getting to sit and talk with you and generally to know you better as a person."

Miller further observed that Reardon's educational vision was fulfilled on this outstanding travel and service occasion—which included significant group interchange with an atheistic Soviet guide—since these college men "will be more prone in the future to deal with the germane issues of life, relationships, and religion and be less apt to be drawn into spinning their wheels on petty details and issues. Perhaps these lessons can be learned only through personal experience." Wrote some friends in loving appreciation of their president who loved music so deeply:

> Robert Reardon, musician.
>> Player of the keyboard,
>>> strong, rich-voiced leader of chapel sings,
>>>> keeper of words to hundreds of hymns. . .
>>>>> nodding and smiling in time and tune to choir,
>>>>>> knowing and understanding music *from the soul*.

President Robert H. Reardon with three of the Anderson College students so loved by him.

Reardon's "pastoral" relationship with students was enriched by such an artistic appreciation and driven by such an educational vision, one that was experience oriented, global in breadth, and intentionally integrating Christian faith with all of learning and life.

Thousands of students made their way into Boyes House in the years following its building in 1968. For Geraldine Reardon it was such a joy to move into this fine presidential home on the edge of the campus. She had grown up in a small Indiana town in a family that did not own a home until after she was in college. Most students came to Boyes House as part of invited groups, but sometimes things got quite personal. In 1972, for instance, David Reames and Greta Blocher were dating and in love. Greta's sister Wanda, while a sophomore earlier, had been hit by a car and killed near the campus. President Reardon had told the story of this tragic death and the family's heroic faith in his 1968 presidential Christmas card (see Appendix B). Now Greta also was a student. She and David were invited one evening to Boyes House for fellowship with President and Mrs. Reardon, presumably for some scheduled occasion with a larger campus group. But that was a ruse of the president and David. There would be no one else. Greta was confused as Jerry graciously escorted her to the kitchen for some little delight. Then Greta became a little bewildered as Robert and Jerry politely excused themselves and left the young couple all alone in the presidential home. Soon Greta and David were seated on a sofa under which David had previously hidden the engagement ring. Marriage was proposed and accepted, allowing the Reardons to return home and offer their sincere congratulations.

Robert Reardon's relationships with students usually were characterized by mutual appreciation, personal warmth, and occasionally even by outlandish humor. He graciously received much respectful kidding from hundreds of student leaders over the years, students who considered him both an honored president and personal friend (see Appendix C for the eloquent and humorous example of Bob Holstein). One Christmas season in the 1970s included the presence on campus of a student, Judy Sowers (Hughes), whose minister father, Rev. Austin Sowers, was desperately ill with cancer in Australia. Reardon encouraged a campus-wide offering that soon sent her across the Pacific Ocean to visit her parents. She was shocked and profoundly grateful for such generosity.

Some of President Reardon's famous presidential Christmas cards carried beautiful photography of campus life and heartwarming stories that he wrote about individual students who in his judgment exemplified the best of campus mission. One such card Reardon sent to his good friend Charles Schulz, the famous cartoonist of "Peanuts" fame. "Sparky" wrote back to "Bob" in January, 1973, to express thanks and report that he had pinned the card to the wall behind his desk in Santa Rosa, California, "because I was much

Charles "Sparky" Schulz, receiving an honorary doctoral degree in 1963, with President Robert H. Reardon (right).

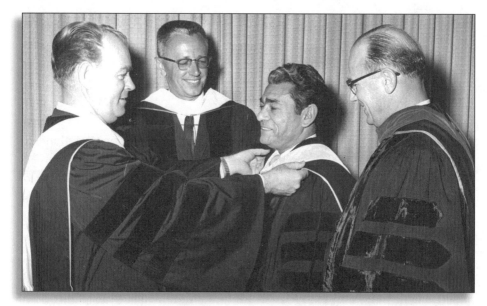

President Robert H. Reardon presenting an honorary doctorate to
Izler Soloman in 1963 as Charles Schulz and Harold Boyer look on.

impressed by the message." Thousands in the campus alumni world shared this sentiment annually as their cards arrived at Christmas.

Geraldine Reardon recalled fondly when Charles "Sparky" Schulz and his wife stayed with the Reardons in Boyes House when they came to Anderson for the dedication of the Krannert Fine Arts Center in 1979—a wing of this building was funded by Schulz in honor of Rev. Marvin L. Forbes whose ministry was a strong influence on the personal and professional lives of Schulz. He came to breakfast at Jerry's table in the morning and presented her with a gold chain that had on it a gold Snoopy. She was so honored to have these and so many other prominent people as house guests—and she always treasured that Snoopy!

Every commencement at the end of the school year featured the President delivering another of his annual messages, what he called his "Charge to Seniors," a printed copy of which was given to the graduates as they departed the big platform with their diplomas. These formal statements, each delivered personally by the president to a graduating class surrounded by some 7,000 people, usually had a touch of humor mixed with a heavy dose of presidential and even fatherly advice about how graduates should recall their college experiences and approach their futures beyond college. For instance, in

June, 1970, he told the graduating class that some of them had been "a pain in the neck" while in college. Even so, they should be crusaders who do not play it safe in the world and do not get "too loud or self-righteous."

In June, 1972, President Reardon admitted to that year's graduating class that the world can be a very hard place, hard on the idealism of the young; still, he insisted, "don't bet on the cynics. Noah's friends did, and look what happened to them!" In his chapel address to the College student body on March 17, 1977, he recalled his many sleepless nights during the student radicalism of the 1960s. He had been determined to keep civility and campus mission on course. But a decade later he now was asking, "Where are the student activists?" Idealism had been swallowed by despair, apathy, and even a greed trying to milk the system for personal gain. This loss of a Christian prophetic voice, uncomfortable as such a voice often is, "troubles me just as much as some of the campus violence troubled me in the 1960s." It was a given for Reardon. To belong to Jesus is hardly to make peace with an unjust status quo!

Reardon loved symbolism, a funny story, a good parable, a timely phrase. He had a genuine affection for college students and in his own person there was a playful side that allowed ample room for fun and teasing—at least when he judged that the time and setting were appropriate. Occasionally he would appear at Christmas chapel dressed in a Santa Claus suit. Once at a hilarious student event and while still fully dressed, he allowed himself to be thrown by students into a swimming pool. The Camarada Club on campus always brought to the president's home a chocolate cake for his birthday. They knew it was his favorite and that Mrs. Reardon would have ice cream to add so that all could have a great time.

The Anderson College commencement address in June of 1978 was delivered by President Reardon himself. He humorously reported to the big crowd that just a few weeks earlier the college men on the third floor of Smith Hall had asked him and Mrs. Reardon to come for a visit. He accepted the invitation "with mild apprehension, knowing that it was near exam time and whatever inclination these men ever had for good housekeeping would have long since vanished." The presidential couple climbed the stairs and entered the third floor, "looking neither to the right nor to the left for fear of encountering strange or unimaginable sights." They were met and led to a room that was "hurriedly swept and garnished for the occasion." Many men gathered into the little room, "a little like circus clowns in a Volkswagon." It turned out to be a fun time with really good conversation. Here is the president's summary of that visit: "I can't tell you what deep affection we have for young men like these—full of mischief (like I once was). Ah, but they are so alive with hope and they are stretching forward for a place in the sun. God bless them!"

Bob Holstein and Robert H. Reardon (right), both dressed as Superman.

Once President Reardon willingly endured with obvious delight a comedy routine that featured embarrassing and amusing imitations of himself. This happened in 1978 on the occasion of the campus celebration of his twentieth year as president. Bob Holstein had graduated five years earlier and now was in medical school. On one of the volatile days when he was a college student, young Bob had taken advantage of the moment by violating President Reardon's high valuing of college chapel. He had "streaked" in front of the gathered student body, running across the front of Park Place Church and right under the pulpit where the president stood. The sudden arrival of what appeared to be public nakedness (but actually was not because of flesh-colored tights) made the President understandably and vocally angry. A much later and humorous recalling of this dramatic incident, and also a Bat Man and

Robin joint appearance by student Holstein and President Reardon, is found in Appendix C.

By the time of the 1978 celebration of the president's twenty years in office, Bob Holstein had matured, survived his probation for the streaking episode, graduated, and gone on to medical school to become a doctor. Reardon had gotten past his anger and both men now took genuine pleasure in clever parodies of the president's distinctive persona—and Holstein was very good at imitating the President and Mark Twain. In fact, Holstein saw Reardon as a contemporary Twain. The scene was the same as the earlier streaking incident, college chapel in the packed Park Place Church of God sanctuary next to the campus. Now, however, the mood was so much lighter than years before. Junior student and ventriloquist Mary Mathis joined the fun with her "dummy" Danny and director M. Eugene Miller dignified this wonderful occasion of presidential honor with music by the Male Chorus that Reardon so enjoyed. The outpouring of student, faculty, and staff affection for their president on this occasion was what most college presidents only dream of (see Appendix F). Jerry Reardon recalled this time as one of the real highlights of her husband's presidency. One reason for its outstanding nature was that, as a complete surprise to the Reardons, their daughter Becky, then a professional entertainer on the West Coast, suddenly appeared on stage to sing in honor of her parents.

Other examples of hilarious student reflection on President Reardon came several years later when he was about to retire in 1983. In the college chapel of April 5, 1983, again in the sanctuary of Park Place Church of God, the beloved president was led to a central seat. Rev. Robert Culp of Ohio recalled his student years at Anderson and especially his memories of President Reardon. Culp had been a basketball star in college, was a slender African-American, and later would be a valued trustee of the campus and the elected Chair of the General Assembly of the Church of God. He said respectfully and humorously to the delight of all on this occasion of presidential honoring, "Robert Reardon had a great impact on me personally. When I first came to Anderson College, I was short, fat, and white!" Only a man greatly loved could be teased in this hilarious manner.

On the same occasion, Rev. James Sparks shared with the crowd a little student history with the beloved president. During his senior year in 1968, Sparks and some friends had decided to express their love for the esteemed president with a midnight invasion of Boyes House, the presidential home. Armed with a huge supply of toilet paper "borrowed" from various campus facilities, they had covered his trees and even mounted the roof and wrapped the chimney before hurrying silently back to their dorm rooms where they had begun "laughing hysterically and pledging silence unto death or commencement, whichever came first." They had not known that, at the very time of their prank, the President was hosting in his home a visiting ambassador from abroad.

Five years later, Reardon was guest speaker at the congregation where Sparks was pastoring. In casual conversation, this little piece of campus history came up. The truth emerged and, said Sparks, "Dr. Reardon's easy smile and warm personality placated me into ratting on my roommate!" "Would he take away my diploma, ripping it off my office wall in public disgrace?" Of course not. The subject easily drifted away with forgiving smiles. Now, on the occasion of Reardon's retirement fifteen years after the toilet paper incident, the deeply appreciative Rev. Sparks recalled the past and concluded his public remarks by observing:

> Greatness is the ability to laugh at ourselves, to learn from our laughter, and to love the learning process. Dr. Robert H. Reardon is truly "great." He experienced the event totally, remembered it accurately, and forgave it completely. Our "T. P. Party" was given that frosty fall night in 1968 with love and respect. This remembrance of it is given in the spring of 1983 with the same sentiments.

Robert Reardon recalls this outstanding day with the following entry in his private journal (April 5, 1983): "It was truly a day to remember. College chapel was packed and a series of people spoke words of deep appreciation for their retiring president. I received a long and very emotional standing ovation. The crowd adjourned to the central campus ravine to plant a tulip tree in honor of Jerry and me. What an overwhelming reward for the thirty-six years I've spent here! It put all the hard times in perspective and confirmed my trust in God's providence." Shortly after this he said the following to the Board of Trustees: "When I made a fool of myself playing Superman or Batman and Robin, the barriers went down and they [the students] opened their hearts to me.... Of all things, I shall miss college students most keenly." They also would miss him.

Faculty: Good People with Relative Freedom

President Robert H. Reardon once observed that it is difficult to really show a college to a visitor. The buildings are obvious, but they are hardly the college since "regardless of the physical surroundings, the world will beat a path to the door of a great teacher" (*Alumni News*, January 1959). He went on to list the key people that he had appointed, relied upon, trusted, and become indebted to for outstanding service to the Anderson campus as part of his administration. The names included Cleda Anderson, Ted Baker, Norman Beard, Barry Callen, Donald Collins, James Edwards, Shirell Fox, Duane Hoak, Virginia Johnson Reardon (his longtime secretary and later wife of his brother Willard), Sena Landey, James Earl Massey, Adam Miller, Ronald Moore, Gene Newberry, Robert Nicholson, Larry Osnes, Paul Sago, and Frederick Shoot. He said, "These key people on my staff are the ones who made the institution work." He thought of them all as especially skilled and dedicated campus administrators, accountable to him, but leaders in their own right.

Over the years, Reardon encouraged ongoing staff development and extended this growth concern to members of the faculty. Those who lead and teach, he believed, must themselves be growing and learning. He says that he never looked over his shoulder at his strong staff, worrying about who might be interested in unseating him as president. Reardon was confident that he was called and gifted to do some things that none of them could do and he was comfortable that each of them could do something better than he could. That is how he wanted it—a strong president surrounded by a strong staff.

A prominent example of staff development came in 1968 when, in a time of increasing secularism in the nation, Reardon managed to secure a grant from the Lilly Endowment to send the entire religion faculties of Anderson College and School of Theology to the Middle East for six weeks of intense archaeological and historical exposure, all in the name of enhancing religious instruction in Indiana. Later the president surprised and delighted Dr. Gustav Jeeninga, Professor of Old Testament and Archaeology, by announcing that he had arranged to secure for him something that he had long wanted but had found impossible to get. Jeeninga had hoped for a real Jewish Torah Scroll for illustrative use in his Bible classes. One day the phone rang. Gus answered to hear the president saying to him, "Gus, could you ask all of your Bible 101 sections in Old Testament to meet together in Decker Hall 133 the next class session? The Rabbi of Bethel Zaddik Hebrew Congregation of Indianapolis will be on campus to speak to the students on the Hebrew Torah. After his lecture, he will present a copy of the Torah for the Anderson College Bible Museum." After Gus hung up, he shouted out loud in his office, "Terrific! I cannot believe it! He did it! He did it!" (Jeeninga, *Doors to Life*, 159).

Another instance when professional growth was enabled by President Reardon was the experience of Dr. Larry Osnes. Coming to the Anderson campus in 1969 as a gifted young professor of political science, soon he was given significant administrative responsibility as Chair of the Department of History/Philosophy/Government. Then he became founding Director of the Center for Public Service launched in 1973 and was appointed Dean for Academic Development on campus. Some years later his highly developed skills were recognized off the Anderson campus and he became a successful leader of higher education in Minnesota and then the college president of one of the Minnesota campuses. He wrote a personal letter to Robert Reardon in April, 1986, wishing him "good rest and relaxation in retirement—and a good thrill now and then!" What he really wanted to convey to Reardon, however, was how wonderfully things had gone for him, concluding: "I have thought about you many times during the past several years.... I am working daily with a group of superb college presidents who are my closest friends and colleagues. I am constantly reminded of your enormous gifts and your distinctive capacity to lead—and I will always be genuinely grateful to you for being willing to help me learn and grow while I was at Anderson College. I have much more to learn—about a lot of things—but your influence on me has been enormous, and I am deeply appreciative." There were several others who felt much the same way.

Having made his first really key appointment in 1958, that of Robert Nicholson to replace the recently deceased Dean Russell Olt, it was quickly clear that the new President and Dean had to face a difficult issue with faculty. It was not the most comfortable way to begin a new administration. The last year of President Morrison's administration had been a bad one financially (a $60,000 budget deficit), so there appeared to be no way to grant faculty salary increases the next year. But faculty members were underpaid and understandably upset about this. There was talk and even action in the direction of faculty unionization like the big automotive industry workers locally. Fortunately, Reardon and Nicholson made their way with faculty, earned the necessary respect, avoided the political environment of unionism, and the next budget was better met so that soon faculty salaries could be increased. Reardon teasingly observed: "It never bothered me at all that Nicholson was up there running faculty meetings. It meant that he was the one who had to take most of the blame from the faculty for things they didn't like!"

Faculty members usually think of themselves as semi-independent professionals, subject to as little supervision as possible. Robert Reardon once defined a faculty member as "someone who thinks otherwise!" Dr. Val Clear, for instance, had been a college classmate of Reardon in the 1930s and had returned in 1941 to begin his long career of teaching sociology on the campus. Clear and Reardon remained close personal friends, although their differing campus roles sometimes put them at odds with each other over various issues. Once Reardon had become President in 1958, Clear chose to think of himself as faculty leader of the new administration's "loyal opposition." He later admitted, "sometimes I was vigorous in my dissent about some administrative stances, sometimes almost contemptuous." Even so, and on the very evenings that he had been a strident voice of opposition to the president in faculty meetings, the Clears and Reardons would be seen having dinner together. Clear wrote a tender letter of appreciation to Reardon on July 22, 1987, saying:

> Ours has been a rare friendship built upon profound respect for each other, a love that does not question, and commitment to common values. This is the fifty-first year of that friendship; not many people have such wealth. That it was built on solid ground was proven by the way in which it survived the compartmentalization created by our relationship at the college, in which I came to be recognized as the main cog in the loyal opposition. At times we both were exasperated with the other in the academic roles we occupied, but the friendship and the respect endured through thirty-three years of that adversarial relationship.

Robert Reardon could tolerate honest and well-meaning opposition and he was very loyal to friends who were well intentioned and shared his basic values.

Commencement, 1974. Left to right:
Robert A. Nicholson, Barry L. Callen, and Robert H. Reardon.

Several key appointments were made by President Reardon after that first flurry of personnel changes at the beginning of his administration in 1958. The intent was to have new people who were strong, not spineless "yes" types that Reardon was never prepared to tolerate. For example, two young men graduated from the Anderson campus in 1966, Ronald W. Moore with a Bachelor of Arts degree in accounting from the college and Barry L. Callen with a Master of Divinity degree from the seminary. Robert Reardon saw leadership potential in both and they were given increasing opportunities to serve the institution. Over the coming years Moore served as Chief Accountant, Treasurer, Director of Development, and finally Senior Vice-President. He originally had come as a student from Florida, at first a very insecure young man who soon matured into a wise and effective campus leader, largely because of the great influence of Dr. Glenn Falls and President Robert Reardon in particular.

Callen served over the coming years as Chair of the Department of Religious Studies, Dean of the School of Theology at age thirty-two, Director of the Center for Pastoral Studies, Editor of Anderson University Press,

Vice-President for Academic Affairs and Dean of the College, and author of the published history of the campus in 1992. He too was first pressed into administrative responsibility by Robert Reardon who showed great faith in him. Callen researched and wrote this present biography of Reardon as an act of respect and appreciation. Moore said the following at his own retirement in 2003: "I've always had profound gratitude for Dr. Reardon. I think he saw things in me that I didn't see myself. I was only able to do what I did at such a young age because I felt so supported" (*Signatures*, Spring 2003). President Reardon had an uncanny and largely intuitive ability to judge people's abilities, motives, and commitments.

Ronald J. Fowler had also graduated with Callen from Anderson School of Theology in 1966 and in the early 1980s would become Chair of the campus Board of Trustees. He too felt great support and confidence from President Reardon, with whom he worked closely. Just after Reardon had told the Board of Trustees about his intention to retire in 1983, the president and Rev. Fowler walked across the campus together. Fowler asked: "Dr. Reardon, what has been the secret of your effective leadership over the years?" The reply was simply this: "Ask the Lord to give you bright people and then be sure they really love the Lord. Then get out of the way and let them do their jobs. Hold them accountable, of course, but stay out of the way!" Over the years, Reardon generally prepared Board agendas himself and chaired its Executive Committee, but he always gave his Board chair thorough background on all issues and listened to his opinions with great respect. This helped Fowler learn to deal with corporate leaders in Akron, Ohio, where he ministered and became a highly respected and influential city leader.

Such a supportive attitude by President Reardon on campus was also experienced by family members in his home. Recalls his son Gene in an email to Barry Callen dated March 2003:

> The rules at home were clear and did not change. The main rules were no disrespect of Dad, Mom, the church, or any authority, no mutiny within the family, no petty complaining. Within those boundaries there was great security. There was freedom and even joy within those limits. There was never any nuance of chaos or inconsistency. In some areas I had a great deal of freedom. I did my own thing, with only arm's length supervision.... When I put

up two large "lawnmowers repair" signs on our fence, Dad was fine with that. Later in life, when I decided to major in psychology, Dad didn't come to me with any criticism or disapproval. I knew where Dad stood on many issues. He didn't need to come to me and give me a lecture.

Faculty respect for campus executives always relies in part on their sensing the freedom to teach and write as they judge best. Especially in a college closely related to a conservative church constituency, there is a delicate balance between academic freedom and institutionalized limitations on such freedom. As the Bible says, truth is crucial and does set free. For truth to be well served, freedom is an important prerequisite. But so is responsibility. President Morrison had put it clearly in 1953. A college should believe in academic freedom,

The Reardon family. Left to right: Kathy, Becky and Connie (in back); Robert, Geraldine and Gene (in front).

although the exercise of such freedom in church-related colleges can "cause college presidents bad dreams." Why? Because someone involved is likely to have difficulty with the inevitable truth that "all social benefits are had at the expense of social restraint" (*Triumphant Living*, 1953). President Reardon affirmed a similar view of this circumstance: "Difficult though it may be, the church college must bear the intellectual initiative, struggling to hold in balance the affirmations and the questions" (*Anderson College News*, May 1976).

This sometimes difficult balance is a way of life for and with faculty members. Reardon came to pride himself in allowing professors significant freedom to teach what and as they saw fit within their areas of specialization,

Commencement, 1976. Left to right: Ronald J. Fowler, Thomas R. McMahan, Barry L. Callen (rear), Senator Sam J. Ervin, Jr., Robert H. Reardon, and Robert A. Nicholson.

although he insisted that there is no such thing as absolute freedom. There also is responsibility and accountability. For him, exalting the spiritual in the Anderson campus setting has never been an option to be viewed casually. Reardon said the following in his 1962 presidential report to the Board of Trustees: "It is better to say that Anderson College does not *have* a religious program, but that it *is* a religious program." Therefore, in his view, there must be some faculty accountability to church-related matters beyond that of the standard accountability to the academy of "objective" scholars.

This stance was put to the test in the 1970s. Young professor Delwin Brown was exceptionally intelligent and creative as a thinker and teacher. In President Reardon's view, however, he was moving "outside the box" theologically and this had to be confronted before it became destructive for Dr. Brown and the campus. Doing so with a measured dignity, one day Reardon took a long walk with Dr. Brown and talked frankly with him. A serious church conflict likely would erupt at some point if the direction of his divergent intellectual commitments continued to be expressed in the classroom. It would be a battle with the school's "ownership" (the Church of God movement) that might not be waged successfully. The president told Dr. Brown that he would not be able to support him if confrontation came with the church. Even many of the more progressive church leaders would be skeptical of certain theological views being taught. There was no administrative threat extended on this occasion, just a plain presentation of the situation and the suggestion that some alternative path might be wise. In fact, the next year Dr. Brown found a good faculty position in a more "liberal" academic setting and there he began a highly productive career more in line with his own theological commitments. The separation was necessary in the president's view and it was done without excessive disruption of valued relationships or the developing academic career of Dr. Brown.

This example is evidence of the lack of the absoluteness of academic freedom as President Reardon understood and practiced it, although it is to be balanced with Reardon's long track record of opposing numerous attempts by elements in the church over the years to curb the academic enterprise unreasonably. Other examples of conflict would arise, especially in relation to Drs. Val Clear and Vern Norris who espoused attitudes toward issues like homosexuality that were in stark contrast to prevailing church and trustee opinion. On the one hand, Reardon wanted very much to protect a faculty member's freedom to speak and teach, intending not to allow "the conservative radicals in the church to run the campus." On the other hand, he also sensed where the center of the church was, what the environment would tolerate, and what he himself judged right and proper. Sometimes controversial issues came close to home. The issue of an individual's sexual identity, for instance, became a very personal one within the president's own family. See the impassioned plea for gracious acceptance of a daughter as expressed in his vision of tolerant love. It is found in the "Memories That Never Die" section of chapter six.

President Reardon fought valiantly several important conflicts, especially the ones he was committed to personally and was confident he eventually could win. He valued community and consensus. Sometimes he had to seek some middle ground where the campus would not fragment, the church relationship would not rupture, and thus the essential church-related nature as well as the academic mission of the campus both could be maintained.

Keeping the Campus on Course

Robert Reardon's own view of the presidential office was quite clear. Describing him as an "engineer," he once said of himself, is less accurate than calling him an "imagineer." Someone has to think, to imagine, while the staff and faculty make things happen directly. The president sets the tone of campus life, establishes confidence and community, and keeps and articulates regularly the vision of campus mission. The president selects strong campus leaders, gives them general guidance, and then gives them room to innovate and work. Observes historian Merle Strege: "Although covered by a velvet glove, his [Reardon's] hand always held the tiller firmly in grasp. Urbane, articulate, and a consummate storyteller, Reardon presided over the college during two and a half decades of unparalleled expansion" (*I Saw the Church* 309).

Reardon certainly was a conservative, holding the line on what he considered essential to the mission and tradition of the Anderson campus; he also was a progressive, risking misunderstanding and even abuse in pursuit of what to him was right, just, and essential for a viable and honorable future. On the occasion of his sixty-second birthday, a group of special friends wrote some poetic verses in his honor. One of them read:

President R. H. Reardon, administrator:
　Keen-witted politician,
　　acknowledged leader wherever you are present.
　　　Participant and guide. . .
　　　　but always a little apart,
　　　　　analyzing, observing, putting in perspective. . .
　　　　　　with a touch of gentle, but pointed humor,
　　　　　　　with faultless intuition, knowing. . .
　　　　　　　　when to push strongly and when to lead quietly.

In handwritten notes of his dated 1988, Reardon offered this self-evaluation:

God has given me an inventive mind, the ability to see things from a different perspective, to come up with new solutions to old problems, and to lead with good organizational ability, inspire subordinates, and marshal the troops for action. I was not an absentee president. I walked the campus with students, kept my office door open, spoke regularly, was available. Staff meetings were full of laughter and good fun. We always took the task seriously, but never ourselves. The walls were very thin—we were a team thinking together.

Reardon's own self-image, rooted in his childhood, was that of a "fixer." Coming to maturity during the Depression years of the 1930s, his family fixed things and made do. Clothes would be recycled after any necessary repair. Food was hardly elegant in their home, but typically it was both adequate and attractively presented. If John Morrison, a man of "forgiveness and good will," nonetheless "had a strong propensity for conflict" (Reardon, *Some Anderson College Reflections* 11), his successor in the presidency, although often keeping things on course in turbulent waters, could sense opportunities and rarely would hesitate to cross challenging frontiers when he thought the present needed alteration. By Reardon's own admission, "in my bones is an inclination to fix things, and this is a difficult stance because many things do not want to be fixed!" In his own view, from the very beginning of his administrative career, Morrison had given him the perfect job—"find whatever needs to be fixed and fix it." From the very beginning of his role as "Assistant to the President" in 1947, Reardon began facing real challenges and seeking creative solutions. There certainly was institutional need on every hand. He worked closely with President Morrison for eleven years, with rarely any friction between them on any matter of significant policy or practice.

In the 1950s there was need to do something fresh to recruit students, promote the new School of Theology, and help pastors with their continuing education. So Reardon took the lead to raise money for an annual "Laymen Lecture Series" that would bring top national people to the campus, attracting to Anderson the Church of God youth counselors and pastors who would bring their youth with them for college exposure. Usually the pastors were housed in local homes. The annual event was called "Vocation Days," happened for the first time in May 1952 when Robert Reardon was identified in the catalog as "Coordinator of Public Relations," and lasted for twenty years. Reardon, the visioner, fixer, and promoter, secured the necessary sponsorship for these lectures from the Laymen Life Insurance Company and its leader, Everett

Hartung. He relied on the gifted young music professor Robert Nicholson to help with the program details. The lecturers brought to campus included Dean Elmer Hormighausen of Princeton Theological Seminary and Reardon's own and beloved former teacher, Dr. Walter Horton of Oberlin Graduate School of Theology.

Doing new things usually meant raising and spending new dollars. Financial responsibility would be a keynote of the Reardon years. He told the Board of Trustees in June of 1972 that the institution would have to learn to live "by the rigid application of a simple formula which vanished from the scene in government years ago." This formula was rediscovered, he said with a little smile, "on an ancient Sumerian tablet, inscribed as the distilled wisdom of a bankrupt merchant." It reads: "Live within your income!" Budget control always would be tight on the Anderson campus, with student enrollments and income projections made conservatively since income relied heavily on actual enrollment levels. The result was an annual pattern of very small budget surpluses. Reardon often said, "Black is beautiful!" This experience of taking seriously the old Sumerian wisdom was the projection of a conservative and disciplined personality, that of Robert Reardon.

Other experiences show additional aspects of the president's complex personality. One aspect is his strong sense of justice. For instance, Reardon had entertained Rev. James Earl Massey as the Religious Emphasis Week speaker for the campus in 1962. The two men connected significantly. In 1968 the president wrote to Massey in Detroit and invited him to join the campus family as its first Campus Pastor and also as a faculty member. Massey pondered, "How as an African-American man would I be received by the majority Caucasian faculty there in the college? My contacts with Robert H. Reardon [and others] had been so open and solid that I felt assured I could relate to them with integrity, freedom, and a sense of oneness" (Massey, *Aspects of My Pilgrimage* 251). It also was helpful that both Reardon and Massey were "Oberlin men" who had studied under many of the same professors.

Attempting to secure housing in Anderson, Indiana, the Massey's encountered racial discrimination. When President Reardon was informed of this, he swung into action, mobilizing forces from the campus and Park Place community. In 1970 the City of Anderson passed a law banning discrimination in housing. Massey applauded Reardon's courageous leadership and felt confirmed in his choice to join Reardon's staff. At the campus commencement ceremony in June, 1970, Massey rejoiced as President Reardon cited Rev. Raymond S. Jackson, Massey's personal mentor, for his exemplary ministry and conferred upon him an honorary doctor's degree. Justice was being done.

President Reardon saw himself as a stabilizing force. He determined to keep the Anderson campus on the correct course. This was especially challenging during those deeply troubled years of the Viet Nam War in the late 1960s and early 1970s. In his own judgment, this was a "dreadful time" dominated by a tragic military conflict that understandably generated massive anger in the world of American higher education. Students across the nation allowed their hair to grow long, clothes to stay dirty, and public protests to multiply and sometimes get violent. Millions of youth felt betrayed by the older generation. The Anderson campus was relatively quiet by national standards, but there was tension and concern. One night President Reardon and his wife Geraldine were sleeping in their home on the edge of the campus. Suddenly a big stone crashed through their window. No one ever knew the exact motive or if the thrower was a college student or not, but the volatile environment of the time allowed almost anything to be possible.

One thing clearly possible in the Anderson setting, partly because of the steady and strong modeling from the president's office, was a witness to rationality and an ongoing search for consensus that was open to student input. For instance, in the late 1960s the annual Candles and Carols Christmas celebration on campus had been shaped by a strong peace witness largely through Dr. F. Dale Bengtson allowing the substantial participation of students in the planning. Merle Strege recalls overhearing President Reardon afterwards expressing deep personal appreciation to Bengtson for the unusual and moving thrust of the program. Bengtson responded, "It was the kids, Bob, it was the kids!"

Some things would not happen in Anderson, Indiana, if President Reardon could help it. The main thing in his mind was that there would be no change in the campus resolve to remain true to its historic nature and mission regardless of the pressure of the times. In his annual report to the Board of Trustees in 1971, he put it this way:

> My main concern is not whether Anderson College will survive; the overriding concern is *what kind of institution* we are becoming or ought to become.... If we are true to our Christian heritage, we

most certainly will find ourselves swimming hard against the current. The great moral and spiritual foundations of this nation and of our society are eroding.... The great unchanging ground upon which we stand as a Christian community is the historic event of the Incarnation and the Bible as the fundamental and essential rootage from which our faith must spring.

Robert Reardon was a serious educator; he also was a Christian minister and committed churchman. In order to make it possible for the really important things to stay on course, the president worked hard at keeping communication channels with students really open. He belonged to the group called "Clergy and Faculty Against the War in Viet Nam." While not a strict pacifist, he did not believe in this particular war, openly spoke against it, and worked to keep the campus on a course that was both civil and prophetic in the midst of a national war mentality. His feelings were in sharp contrast to his view of World War II, a massive conflict that to him had appeared fully justified.

When President Richard Nixon began bombing across the border into Cambodia and many college and university campuses reacted with intense anger, a group of Anderson College students wanted to engage in a "friendly protest." Their president was contacted, agreed, and readily joined them in the symbolic action of planting a Ginkgo tree of peace in the central ravine of the campus. About a thousand students, faculty, and staff persons gathered in a great circle, listened to the wisdom of biblical texts read aloud, sang songs of peace, and, as President Reardon later put it, "prayed for forgiveness and strength to help bind up the wounds of the world."

The life and mission of the campus were on display in these sacred moments of word, song, and symbolic witness. The school's president was visibly present and openly supportive. As the tree was lowered carefully into the hole, representing the ancient tree of life, students filed by to help fill in the hole with dirt, putting their hands lovingly, servingly, riskingly right into the soil. There were no shovels—it was a fully hands-on event. Reardon would never forget "the faces of those wonderful kids, shining with idealism, distressed by the course events had taken, but determined somehow to relate their young lives to the pain and agony of the world."

President Reardon was understandably proud of his many years of executive leadership, offering this post-retirement observation in 1988:

For the twenty-five years of my administration there was strong internal peace on campus. Anderson College people worked together without heavy internal conflicts, fears of financial disaster, or inter-Nicean war. Even during the tensions of the Viet Nam period, the bond of trust held between my office and the students.

He later shared that, in his own self-understanding, he was a good judge of people and gave them the right responsibilities. He was a good communicator, kept alive the proper faith/reason balance, regularly articulated the institutional dream, and "protected the soul of the school." Such were his key roles as he understood the responsibilities of his presidency.

Bringing New Partners On Board

In reference to Anderson, Indiana, one might say that Robert Reardon was a son of the city. Anderson has been his home nearly all of his life. He attended Anderson High School, carried the local newspaper, and learned to know many of the new generation of men and women who would lead the city during his later adult years. Especially in his decades as president of Anderson College and the School of Theology beginning in 1958, he penetrated Anderson's life in very significant ways and did so on behalf of the well being of both the campus and city. He was determined to change the older climate of distance and distrust between the two. The eventual level of his success was considerable, to say the least.

The early decades of the life of the Church of God movement had seen most of its adherents viewing the "sects" (divisive denominations) as the enemy of a united church. After the center of the movement's work moved to Anderson, Indiana, in 1906 with the relocating of the Gospel Trumpet Publishing Company, it proceeded with its church reforming work in relative isolation from the city—they were "not our people." When Robert Reardon graduated from Anderson High School in 1936, most of his peers still thought that it was a disgrace to be a student at nearby Anderson College. Reardon's best friend Mark Bright, for instance, got a full scholarship to DePauw University and happily told his friends about it, but Reardon took the "lesser" route of the local campus with the encouragement of his parents. This was hardly a bragging point in front of Bob's peers. Soon, however, he would fall in love with the Anderson

College campus and do no apologizing for it in the many years to come. Longtime Anderson banker Linfield Myers recalled the following in 1973 (*As I Recall. . .The Wilson-Morrison Years* 89). Note his use of the word "colony":

> Historically, this relationship [between Anderson College and the City of Anderson] had been one of quiet but mutual hostility. When the Gospel Trumpet colony moved to town in 1906, the organizers associated the city with the world, the flesh, and the devil. The city had some uncomplimentary reciprocal thoughts of its own about the newcomers, often considering the invaders from Moundsville, West Virginia, as fugitives from the Middle Ages. Even after the college's accreditation in 1946, there was still a residue of misunderstanding that took additional years to dissolve completely.

The change of climate between city and campus was helped considerably over the years as Anderson College graduates remained in Anderson and became teachers, ministers, accountants, lawyers, etc. It was helped further as President Morrison and Dean Olt built many city friendships through their active personal memberships in the local Kiwanis and Rotary service clubs in the 1940s and 1950s. Morrison was a much-appreciated, magnetic, and humorous personality, a trait that helped in his election as president of the Kiwanis Club and as a member of the Board of the Anderson City Library.

In the 1950s more campus-city help came through the work of Shirell Fox, a local journalist who became the Director of Publicity of Anderson College charged with gaining increased public attention for key campus events, teams, and personalities. President Morrison said to Fox in 1948: "We need to let the city know that we are out here, that we are good people, and that we have an interest in offering them opportunities in higher education." The president wanted to see a news story about Anderson College in the local papers every week. He soon did. When Robert Reardon became president in 1958, Fox was a trusted friend of the same age. He was asked to stay as "Assistant to the President" in charge of publicity and chapel programming. As a direct extension of the president's office, with Reardon chairing the Chapel Committee (Reardon, Fox, Nicholson), the twice weekly chapel sessions, mandatory for all, regularly brought to campus outstanding drama, music, preaching, and lecturers on "secular" subjects. The religious depth and cultural breadth of this programming was a reflection of President Reardon quite directly.

Additional assistance with city relations came when local banker Linfield Myers saw value in a local institution of higher education and helped relate to this campus his close friend Charles E. Wilson, a former Anderson man who had become the chief executive of the General Motors Corporation and then the Secretary of Defense of the United States under President Dwight Eisenhower. The campus was building a new library and Myers told Reardon that it should be named for Wilson. This led to President John Morrison and Robert Reardon, then his Executive Vice-President, journeying to meet the Wilson family in their home in the Detroit area. The result was that the family agreed, was generous, and later came to the dedication event in Anderson that enjoyed major media coverage—a new horizon being crossed by the campus. It was in October, 1957, during the annual Harvest Festival and Homecoming, with Charles Wilson himself giving the main address to a crowd of about 5,000 people. The campus, city, and scores of new campus friends had joined to do something truly significant and genuinely valued by the general public.

Dedication of Wilson Library, 1957. Left to right: Clarence Hatch (Church World Service), Fred Damaske (student), Wilbur Schield (trustee), Ralph Ferguson (city mayor), Linfield Myers (local banker), Robert H. Reardon, John A. Morrison, and Charles E. Wilson.

President-elect Robert Reardon offered the invocation prayer for the impressive new Wilson Library. He was on the leading edge both of his own administration and of a dramatic time of campus expansion. If all of the new potential were to be realized, new partnerships were necessary, some even with former "foes." Shirell Fox, a key arm of the president's office from 1948 to

1985, says that the dedication of Wilson Library joined the celebrations of the retiring Presidents Morrison (1958) and Reardon (1983) and the dedication of the Krannert Fine Arts Center (1979) as the outstanding public highlights of campus life during his years, at least so far as the general public was concerned. Reardon was a central figure in them all.

Over the years President Reardon became very active in the cultural and civic life of Anderson, including membership on the governing boards of the local chapter of the American Red Cross, Anderson Council of Social Agencies, Maplewood Cemetery, St. John's Hospital, Wilson Boys Club, and the YMCA. He took a turn as campaign chair for the United Way and co-chaired the financial process that enabled construction of the new Community Hospital. The much-improved relationship between the Anderson campus and the city was demonstrated vividly in the early 1980s when Reardon Auditorium was being constructed. In 1982-1983 when unemployment was especially high in Anderson, the employees of Delco Remy and Guide Lamp divisions of General Motors gave $1,000,000 to support the big campus project that they saw as also vital to the city—home of the Anderson Symphony Orchestra and the site of many other groups and special events of public interest. Campus and city really needed each other. President Reardon was a credible and respected leader in both arenas.

A president of a private church-related college usually carries major responsibility for fundraising. Robert Reardon once said that he did not see himself as a premier fundraiser. All that he knew how to do was speak forcefully and persuasively about the things in which he believed deeply. He also knew how to build personal relationships that gained strength and credibility over the years. Such speaking and relating proved to be the needed elements of successful fundraising. Reardon managed to open doors to significant support through friendships with the Balls, Brackens, Earnharts, Krannerts, and Lillys. Lilly Endowment, Inc., based in Indianapolis, first became a funding resource for Anderson College in 1956 with a matching grant of $50,000 to help construct Wilson Library. Then came $15,000 for improvement of instruction in 1957 and in 1960 another $25,000 to buy books for the new library. Twenty-eight other grants were received by Anderson College from this one key foundation during the Reardon presidency, including a $500,000 challenge grant in 1973 to assist greatly with a campus endowment campaign. Robert Reardon was a key reason why Anderson College managed to move from a newly accredited and relatively isolated operation in the 1940s to a campus that, by his retirement in 1983, enjoyed great respect and support from several of the largest foundations in the country. He was a believable executive who knew where he was going and could be trusted to actually do whatever he promised.

He also was a compassionate man. In the mid-1970s, President Reardon called Professor Fred Shively to ask if he would be willing to push him around the campus in a wheelchair for the day so that he could become more

Robert Reardon and Carl Erskine, beloved community leaders, Anderson, Indiana.

sensitized to the plight of others and learn what it is like to be dependent on other people. The professor did so with delight and the president handled his discomfort with grace and was greeted all day with enthusiasm and appreciation. Then when Carl Erskine suggested in 1977 that the new track and swimming facilities on the campus be made available to Special Olympics for the handicapped of Madison County. Reardon was open to the new idea, personally witnessed what happened, and was thrilled as he watched the one-on-one relationships between the college volunteer students acting as personal coaches and cheerleaders and the physically and mentally challenged children and teenagers. There was sheer joy on faces as blue and other colored ribbons were received and celebrated. Much like the philosophy of the TRI-S program, spectators became participants and meaning multiplied. The campus has been the site for these local olympics every year since. This has brought warm and treasured relationships between the campus and the handicapped community living in Madison County. National president of Special Olympics, Eunice Kennedy

Shriver, wrote the following to President Reardon in May 1978 about that first year's experience on the Anderson campus:

> Carl Erskine wrote me about the fabulous Madison County Special Olympics Games. He was overwhelmed by Anderson College's total involvement; its commitment of excellent facilities, enthusiastic volunteers, and supportive administration. This phenomenal support could not have been possible without your [Reardon's] cooperation. I want to personally thank you for providing an unforgettable experience for 180 special olympians. Thank you very, very much.

During the twenty-five years of Reardon's administration, the campus was transformed from what had been essentially a one-building little school to one of the most modern and beautiful campuses in the Midwest, with twenty major buildings appearing without significantly burdening the resources of the church or acquiring a crippling institutional debt load. Student enrollments in the undergraduate college increased steadily from 1,111 in 1956-1957 to 1,250 in 1960-1961 and then way up to 1,956 during the 1969-1970 school year. Seminary enrollments grew very dramatically in the last decade of Reardon's presidency and under the deanship of Barry L. Callen, a key presidential appointment. Between 1957 and 1962 four major new buildings

Anderson College Homecoming, 1962. Left to right: Robert Macholtz, Robert Reardon, and James Macholtz, mixing mortar to place the cornerstone of the new O. C. Lewis Gymnasium at Anderson College.

were built on campus: a library (1957); a women's residence hall (1958); the

School of Theology building (1961); and a gymnasium (1962).

Following soon after these structures would also be a new Student Center, men's residence hall, and the science building, Hartung Hall, honoring the generous campus friend Everett Hartung who was a local businessman and Church of God layman. There would be erected on campus in 1970 a new women's residence hall named in honor of Anderson banker and civic leader Linfield Myers. In 1972 a new natatorium was built through the generosity of and named for the prominent Anderson dentist Roland (Rollie) Bennett. Represented in the funding and naming of such facilities was a series of new individuals, corporations, foundations, and government agencies now supportive of this rapid expansion.

The person of Robert Reardon was central throughout these many projects. There are many stories told about his fundraising activities. One is Carl Erskine's recollection of the flight he once took from St. Louis to Indianapolis when Reardon happened to be sitting next to him with a duffle bag on the floor between his feet. They were good friends from Anderson. At one point in the flight the president asked Carl, "What do you think I have in this bag?" Carl suggested the usual, athletic shoes and a towel or two. "No," countered Reardon casually, "what I have here is $750,000!" The zipper was opened to reveal a pile of saving, bank, and check books. He had been working with a couple in St. Louis who had just given him for the school all of their accounts that totaled something approaching one million dollars.

Money was put to good use. The 1970s was a decade of several vigorous initiatives taken by the administrative leadership of the Anderson campus, all intended to broaden the base of student learning and increase the range of off-campus partnerships that were prepared to assist in implementing this expanding educational horizon. Beginning with a $300,000 implementation grant from Lilly Endowment in 1976, there evolved a series of coordinated new program thrusts known as "The Anderson College Plan: Expanding the Base for Learning." Featured was a work-learning component rooted in cooperative campus relationships with business, church, industry, labor, and government.

Coming into being were the Center for Pastoral Studies and the Center for Public Service, with key early leaders being Drs. Barry Callen, Jerry Grubbs, Douglas Nelson, and Larry Osnes. A major new partnership evolved with St. Johns Hospital in Anderson as an associate degree program in nursing was begun, later to become a full bachelors program. Added to the list of professional program accreditations during the 1970s were music in 1974, nursing in 1975, and social work in 1979. Between 1971 and 1978, ten major facility projects were completed at a total cost of 10.6 million dollars. Most of this substantial advance of campus programming, relationships, and facilities was related in part or wholly to the credibility, vision, and initiative of President Robert Reardon.

Such innovation had been symbolized at the opening of the 1970s when the historic "Old Main" building, long the heart of the campus as a whole, had been razed and replaced by the modern and magnificent Decker Hall, named for Philip Greene Decker and Phoebe Katherine Spencer Decker, pioneer Andersonians. The very thought of razing Old Main had made President Reardon reflect: "When I think of the great foresight and phenomenal dedication of our forefathers who worked out under these trees to form the concrete blocks by hand and to build this building themselves, something always stirs inside me." He concluded: "I would like to believe that those of us in the present generation could be inspired by their example to put something here in place of Old Main which will reflect well on our generation" (*Andersonian*, May 11, 1967, 3). Again, the heart and vision of Robert Reardon was usually front and center. It was often costly and personally stressful, but the president proceeded nonetheless, sometimes with boldness, typically with creativity, and always with Dean Robert Nicholson at his side.

The president did much networking and relationship building privately. For instance, he once gave crucial financial advice to two former Anderson College students who were beginning to have significant success in their musical ministries. He said to Bill and Gloria Gaither: "It looks like your music ministry is taking off and is going to be very successful. With success comes resources and the responsibility to be good stewards of these resources. You can nickel and dime yourselves to death or give to something really significant that will be here when you are gone." Reardon concluded with this very candid suggestion: "Let me help you with your extra resources!" Both of the Gaithers later observed, humorously and appreciatively, "And boy did he help us!" By then they had become major donors to the Anderson campus, including being co-chairs of a financial campaign conducted by the school, having a wing of the Krannert Fine Arts Center named in their honor, and Gloria having been awarded an honorary Doctor of Letters degree in 1989. Bill Gaither much later reflected as follows about Reardon's early advice to Gloria and himself: "It is

Left to right: Bill Gaither, Robert Reardon, Gloria Gaither, and Robert Nicholson.

one of the greatest things that has happened to us. We have not raised our standard of living over the years. We still live in the same place in Alexandria, Indiana, where we did when we taught school. When we have had extra money, we have given it to the school. This has helped us keep our lives together. Bob Reardon can be blunt. He certainly was with us—and he was right. We don't regret a dime we've given to Anderson University."

Carl Erskine recalls a humorous moment that also had a very serious dimension to it. Linfield Myers, a local banker and generous friend of Anderson College, had died at age ninety-nine. Erskine went to the funeral home to pay his respects and encountered Reardon there alone. Shortly Reardon would preach the funeral sermon for the near centenarian after whom Myers Hall on campus had been named in 1970. But first he spoke with Carl, a famous professional baseball player and now a successful local banker in his hometown of Anderson, Indiana. Said Reardon, "Carl, let me tell you something important. If you will put Anderson College in your will, you will live forever!"

On the personally costly side for Reardon is an example of local social action. Rev. Donald Collins had been assisted early in his ministry by Robert Reardon. Then in 1969 he had joined the pastoral staff of Park Place Church of God, in part to discover the human hurts in Anderson and mobilize members of the congregation to serve these people in the name of Christ. One neighborhood was chosen where there was an unusually high incidence of urban brokenness and little church presence. Collins explained this choice to the congregation and said that a building was needed in the area for the ministry to proceed. At the close of the service, Robert Reardon met Collins at the church door and said, "Find the building and I will pay the first year's rent myself." He did pay. The president later would bring Collins to the campus as the Campus Pastor.

On the politically stressful side, President Reardon led a highly publicized and completely peaceful protest when the City of Anderson proposed the building of a bridge across the White River at Third Street and the subsequent opening of a major thoroughfare down the middle of the Anderson College campus. The president and his staff saw this as a threat to the integrity and beauty of the campus—a major asset of the city and a considerable physical danger to the student body, most of whom crossed this street on foot multiple times daily. It also would be a big problem for the North American Convention of the Church of God meeting on the campus annually. The city and its mayor, Robert Rock, persisted with their plan—and so did the resistance of President Reardon, many students, and local church leaders. One day in the mid-1970s, Reardon, national church leader William E. Reed, and about one thousand college students marched from the campus to the city building downtown, carrying protest signs and singing "Battle Hymn of the Republic" and "I Shall Not Be Moved." There was a press conference and reports reaching the national television media. The bridge eventually was built and the thoroughfare opened, but with a series of key city concessions to the campus concerns.

Occasionally the City of Anderson turned to Robert Reardon for help since he was politically astute, financially wise, and a committed humanitarian who loved his home city. In 1978, for instance, Reardon chaired the blue ribbon committee studying the status and preferred future of Anderson Community Schools. He became a leader in fundraising campaigns to benefit St. Johns Medical Center, Community Hospital, the Wilson Boys Club, the YMCA, the Chamber of Commerce, and the Red Cross. The typical tension between "town and gown" was relieved considerably by the diplomacy and vital public service provided by Reardon. His political instincts and redemptive spirit were surely seen when Robert Rock, Reardon's former foe on the bridge controversy, ran for Governor of Indiana and Reardon hosted a campaign event for him at Boyes House, the president's home on campus.

President Reardon has loved his ministerial calling and lived it out in an academic community as genuine Christian ministry and service. His "parish" was a campus, his pulpit often the college and seminary chapel lecterns, and his constituencies were dozens of trustees, thousands of students, hundreds of faculty and staff, many thousands of alumni, and a city he loved. All of this happened in the context of the Church of God movement, the particular church body that was his home. To be sure, the church was the scene of an occasional love-hate confrontation, but always it was at the heart of Reardon's vision of what God was about in this world. God is building a people, a redeemed and reconciling people, and, in Reardon's view, the Anderson campus is to be a learning community enriched by that divine presence and mission. It

Robert Reardon (right) assumes the presidency of the Indiana Conference of Higher Education in 1969. Left, Dr. Alan Rankin, President of Indiana State University; center, Dr. John Logan, President of Rose Polytechnic Institute.

also is to be a vital resource to God's people. Following the leading of that divine light, he has given himself freely for decades.

Historian Merle Strege has judged that Robert Reardon was reflective of the classic nineteenth-century Protestant college president in America who was the clergy father figure and moral philosopher. Such presidents were the ones who dreamed the campus dream, integrated for its people the nature of the campus enterprise, and took responsibility for conveying to students how life, faith, and learning should come together for the good of their own futures and their service to society. Since Reardon's ability as a storyteller "is legendary," concludes Strege, what you have in Reardon is "a narrative, Christian, moral philosopher."

Rather than a parish pulpit, Reardon played this role of moral philosopher in his regular college chapel speaking (the chapel was his classroom), his occasional commencement addresses to the home campus, his annual "Charge to Seniors" at all commencement occasions, and his presidential Christmas cards sent widely. His annual telling of the "Uncle Barney" story in student Christmas chapels often moved students deeply (see Appendix A), while his regular reports to the faculty and Board of Trustees usually included vignettes of campus life wrapped in paragraphs of his distinctive presidential wisdom. Reardon was the clergy campus philosopher. James Edwards, one day to be the campus president himself, observes that Reardon "was the dominant personality on campus during my college years [1961-1965]. He was the father figure who brought a sense of sophistication with warmth in the process of his making us pay attention to important ideas. He was more pastor-leader and less administrator-manager." This pastor-leader role was consistently characterized by a love for students, faculty, and city. In addition, Reardon's love extended to the church that was his true home.

Robert H. Reardon with Eleanor Roosevelt, former first lady of the nation, on the Anderson College campus in 1959 for the Model United Nations program.

Robert Reardon at the table's head with ministry executives of the Church of God.

Robert Nicholson (left) and Robert Reardon (right)
honoring pastor and campus trustee Rev. E. J. Morris, Jr.

CHAPTER Five

The Church as Home

··

P resident Robert H. Reardon has had a special love for students, faculty, and the local city of Anderson, Indiana. He was at home both on the campus, in the community, and especially with his private family. His son Gene recalls that there was no real distinction between the public and private Robert Reardon, so that "if there had been a hidden camera in our home, there would have been nothing of surprise. I can't recall anything about my father that was inconsistent with his image as president and church leader. Dad has always been an incredibly consistent person." He was, concludes Gene, "very presidential as a father. He stood in the front of our boat and steered through the troubled waters of life. Dad was the same every day. He had the final say on all matters." The church was also the president's natural home, but sometimes the church resisted any effort at being "steered" by any strong leader, Reardon included, even if the guidance was well intentioned and sorely needed.

Being an effective college president is a politically challenging task, particularly when the institution has serious academic goals and, at the same time, is closely held by a conservative church tradition. Rev. Eugene A. Reardon had impressed the following on his son Robert: "Find something really worthwhile and stick to it—when things go well and when they don't. If you do, with God's help, you be able to make a difference" (Reardon, *Some Anderson College Reflections* 22). Robert Reardon took this advice seriously. He had a deep inner certitude that a ministry of leadership on the Anderson campus is what God wanted him to do, so he stayed there full-time from 1947 to 1983, seeking throughout to hold true to what he believed worthwhile and, with God's help, to make a real difference.

Like his father, Robert Reardon had been a pastor. For him, it was natural to take a pastoral approach to college administration. In fact, his ministerial identity has always been key to his philosophy of leadership. There was no conflict in his mind between Christian faith and the goals of an academic enterprise. Nonetheless, a sometimes conflicted relationship was experienced between the campus and the North American constituency of the

Church of God movement, most leaders of which gathered annually for the big Anderson Camp Meeting (North American Convention) on the Anderson campus and adjacent church grounds. Campus life in general often has been admired and supported by the church. On occasion, a campus person or policy has been contested by some church people. Regardless, for Robert Reardon, the church remained his home.

Held Closely by the Church

The many years of service of Robert Reardon on the Anderson campus (1947-1983) could hardly be characterized as a "job" to him, almost not even a "career." They were filled with ministry, divine calling, passion for the grand task he typically saw at hand. Here is how in March, 2003, Reardon's son Gene recalled his dad: "My impression was always a clear sense that his role as church leader was his essence. He was devoted to the church, college, and seminary with every part of his being. It was abundantly clear that this was not a job for him; it was his calling, what he was meant to do. I can't imagine Dad as anything else."

In fact, other options did present themselves. At one point interest was shown by others in Reardon leaving the campus to become the radio minister of the Church of God movement in North America. Clearly, Reardon was an engaging speaker with a pastoral heart, but he loved the campus and was not comfortable with doing manuscript sermons—he was more of a vivid storyteller in face-to-face occasions. He did not pursue this opportunity, nor did he respond affirmatively to another that had significant personal appeal to him. In 1971 the Pulpit Committee of Park Place Church of God in Anderson, Indiana, approached him about the possibility of his becoming the congregation's senior pastor. This was his beloved home church that sits next to the Anderson campus, serves many of its faculty, staff, and students, and was pastored by his father for many years. He lost sleep over this possibility for himself, but finally wrote to the committee, saying, "unless God makes it very evident to me that I can be released from my present assignment to accept a new one at Park Place Church, I must give you a reluctant negative answer." He received no such release and thus never left.

As Robert Reardon remained close to the Anderson campus over the years, so did the campus remain relatively close to the church with his full support. The college and seminary in Anderson, Indiana, have always maintained a significant relationship with their sponsoring church, the Church of God movement (Anderson). This relationship takes several forms. President John Morrison used to say, half teasingly, that a college trustee's value could be measured in direct proportion to the distance he or she lived from the campus—the farther the better! The context of such a judgment was that, particularly in the early years of the college, church priority was placed on the divine calling and gifting of leaders as opposed to reliance on human intellect and credentials issued by denominational colleges. Trustees of the Anderson campus often were chosen by the church to provide a surveillance function to make sure that the president did not lead the institution astray. For the Reardon presidential years, it was the case that a significant portion of Anderson College's annual budget came in the form of a grant from the church. A large percentage of the student population typically came from homes of the church. Campus life was highly visible to the church, in part because the church constituency was concentrated in Indiana and adjacent states.

When church struggles emerged, they easily focused on the Anderson campus because of its strategic influence and its many contact points with the life of the Church of God movement in North America. Any presidential election by the campus Board of Trustees or the election of a new Dean of the School of Theology has had to be ratified by a formal vote of the General Assembly of the church. Consequently, for the president of this campus, the challenge of church relations has been unavoidable and sometimes uncomfortable. President Reardon said this to the Board of Trustees in 1967:

> Our fundamental commitment is to a high quality liberal arts
> undergraduate college, with its ultimate objectives being identical
> to those of the church—the redemption of the individual and the
> redemption of society. Central in this commitment is primary
> responsibility to the Church of God through ownership, operation,
> and control.

The Anderson campus was held closely by the Church of God movement, a fact of institutional life often key to the school's survival and sometimes working in considerable tension with the school's educational mission. The founder of Anderson Bible Training School in 1917 was Rev. Joseph T. Wilson. The first president, Rev. John A. Morrison, had been a pastor; Rev. Robert H.

Reardon became the second president in 1958. The first of these executive leaders to have attended college, Reardon was a seminary-trained pastor and son of the Church of God movement, deeply committed to its life even when he became involved in conflict with some of its leaders. Helping to keep this in right perspective is Rev. Ronald J. Fowler, a prominent member of the Board of Trustees of the campus during several difficult years of campus-church relations in the late 1970s and 1980s (becoming the Board's Chair in 1981).

Fowler has been the pastor of a large African-American congregation in Akron, Ohio, for many years after his graduation from Anderson School of Theology. He carries the highest regard for President Reardon and recognizes readily the complex balance needed and the awkward political position the campus president sometimes is in when it comes to church relations. Rev. Fowler is anxious that it not be overlooked that President Reardon, even when he was in sharp conflict with some church leaders, was himself a man of "tremendous piety," always a devoted churchman who happened to believe that the love of God and the love of learning can and should be joined in mutually beneficial ways.

Reardon understood that numerous congregations of the Church of God movement were conservative in nature and generally suspicious of an academic institution. They feared that the campus was always on the verge of somehow giving away the most precious truth treasures of the church and subtly spoiling the church's new generation of youth with a wave of faithless new ideas and upsetting innovations. Occasionally this fear would break out in open opposition to some aspect of campus life, especially opposition to the key campus leaders who presumably could be held responsible for anything of concern. Since President Reardon had to be ratified by the General Assembly of the church for each of his five-year terms in the presidential office, five terms in all, at each of these decision points ministers had a formal opportunity to express their periodic displeasure with one thing or another. He survived all such tests, partly because of the widely recognized and appreciated quality of his overall leadership service and partly because he was a great storyteller in the tradition of his Irish heritage. Sometimes a little diplomacy and calculated communication can be very important. Under stress, a humorous story can release tension and refocus the attention of critics.

In a way similar to President John Morrison before him, Reardon told stories that often were earthy, funny, and timed well in relation to an awkward

Left to right: Marcus Morgan, Robert Reardon, T. Franklin Miller,
Mort Crim, Robert Nicholson, and Barry Callen, at the commencement
ceremony of Anderson College and School of Theology, 1975.

moment he faced in the church's General Assembly or elsewhere. He could steady a crisis and relax anxious people with a funny little distraction. It often is said about the Irish in general and Reardon in particular that truth is too important to depend on mere facts. For such fascinating folks as Reardon, it is almost impossible to know where fact ends and fiction begins. In the end, the fine line between them may not be all that important. The fuller truth lies in the tale, in a meaningful story well told, with uncanny timing and an important impact in the moment. Reardon's stories tended to be a little like the parables of Jesus—contextual wisdom in earthy terms, often tinged with the humor of irony and a strong hint of the voice of the divine shining through God's humble servant.

One example of his humorous directness comes from the Anderson University commencement ceremony in May 2003. With about 6,000 people in Warner Auditorium, including the fully-robed graduating class and faculty seated in mass on the cramped and strangely angled plastic seats, and with Dr. Martin C. Jischke, the President of Purdue University, sitting next to him on the platform about the give the commencement address, Robert Reardon rose to offer the invocation. He began with, "Oh Lord, our Lord, how excellent is Thy name in all the earth. Lord of life, by whose boundless grace we live and move and have our being, visit us this day." Then, unexpectedly came this as the next part of the prayer:

> Lord, this place is alive with symbolism. The seats we sit in speak
> to us of the misery which inevitably becomes part of our lot in life.
> Designed by the enemy himself to bring us discomfort and pain,
> they test our endurance as we gather here each year!

Faculty members laughed almost uncontrollably, trying to keep their eyes closed all the while. This President-emeritus, then age eighty-four, could still connect with a crowd, even when he was addressing God!

Reardon functioned for many years with this leadership philosophy: "A president who is uncertain of his mission and does not carry out his leadership role from an inner reservoir of confidence will not last long. He will run when no one is pursuing and become defensive over the slightest test of his authority" (Reardon, *Some Anderson College Reflections* 23). Although he and his Dean, Robert Nicholson, functioned together with a marvelous mutuality, Reardon nonetheless insisted that no institution will prosper and work well if people have to ask, "Who is in charge here?" President Reardon faced some significant skirmishes over a range of issues with alumni, students, faculty, the church, and the administration of the City of Anderson, but he always survived, maintained public clarity on who was finally in charge on campus, and thus kept the campus on what he was confident was the right course.

Thinking of the biblical healing story related to the pool by the Sheep Gate in Jerusalem (John 5:1-9), where new health depended on stepping into the pool at just the right time, Reardon typically chose his strategies with care, often not choosing to step prematurely into troubled churchly waters. On the other hand, when he saw that healing was needed urgently in some aspect of the life of the campus or church, he was known to step right in and take bold actions in faith, even when others on his staff feared to risk action. Timing is usually crucial; conviction and courage are always fundamental.

Conflict did not ever come because Reardon was in any sense anti-church. To the contrary, he considered the church his home. Always he has been a son of the church, an ordained and committed minister of the church, a college and seminary leader seeking to serve the church well, primarily through the avenue of quality higher education. Even so, in his own words and at least in the eyes of some church leaders, he had become "something of a scoundrel." His seminary education at Oberlin had brought to him a personal result that naturally would trouble some of the arch conservatives in the church. He once worded the result this way: "Any narrow view of the Church of God that I once had about this movement being God's only true people on the face of the earth had completely dissolved." Over the years, then, Reardon followed the pioneering trail of his father, Rev. E. A. Reardon, and his presidential predecessor, Dr. John Morrison, in "de-criminalizing Babylon" (Babylon being a biblical symbol sometimes used by prominent Church of God leaders to refer to the apostate Christianity that the reform movement existed to alter in the providence of God).

Robert Reardon understood that it was John Morrison before him who had "kept us from becoming cultish." Morrison's controversial and very close re-election to the campus presidency in 1934 was the big turning point. The "liberal arts" curriculum, still relatively new then, had been under heavy attack. Suspicion was abroad that the campus administration and some faculty members were not fully loyal to "standard" Church of God commitments—at least as many prominent church leaders chose to define those commitments. What Reardon found himself doing in his own campus leadership years was to keep Morrison's "anti-cult ball rolling." If Morrison would have lost that battle in 1934 and the Anderson campus had been positioned as a narrow little Bible school, Reardon is sure that the Church of God movement would have become something very different than it did become after the 1930s. Reardon further assumes, however, that, even if Morrison had lost that pivotal vote in 1934, it is probable that level heads with good sense would have intervened sooner or later and tried to stop the slide into cultism. After all, observes Reardon, "a cultic anti-Babylon position is indefensible." While the battle of the 1930s had not been lost, similar skirmishes would still break out now and then.

At stake in 1934, writes Reardon, "was how the church was to address itself in the future—as a cult, calcified, turned in, windows closed, or as a people twice liberated from the rule of new and sterile creeds.... And we can be grateful for the men and women whose vision of the church was so true that they suffered, fought, and persevered for the principles that we enjoy today" (*The Early Morning Light* 73-74). Reardon determined to stay on the good course set by President Morrison in spite of what new may come along. He had begun this process in the church turmoil of the 1940s when, as a graduate student at Oberlin seminary in Ohio, he completed his thesis titled "The Doctrine of the Church and the Christian Life in the Church of God Movement." Here he identified himself as one "born and reared *within* the group, but who has studied *without*." He proceeded to document what some conservative church leaders feared was happening, significant changes in the movement's attitudes toward the doctrines of sanctification and Christian unity (see Appendix E for detail).

Such significant trending in the life of the Church of God movement was viewed in some church quarters as dangerous apostasy. The newer attitudes featured a backing away from perfectionistic claims for and legalistic measurements of the sanctification experience. They also featured a broadened and more inclusive practice of Christian unity, including a conscious retreating from the early exclusivism that arrogantly described this reform movement as the "last reformation" as seen in the prophecies of the book of Revelation. Reardon had learned gracious tolerance of others in his childhood home and certainly in his college and seminary experience. He greatly admired the unusual skill and warm pastoral heart of conservative pastor Rev. Lillie S. McCutcheon, but vigorously opposed aspects of her use of the Book of Revelation and the narrow attitudes of the Pastor's Fellowship organization with which she was closely associated in the 1970s and 1980s. He judged that on occasion she and her considerable influence with pastors was "used" by the most reactionary of church leaders for purposes he thoroughly opposed.

Robert Reardon (seated) and Adam W. Miller with the model of the new School of Theology building.

Thoughtful and inclusive attitudes and actions were in evidence soon after Robert Reardon returned to the Anderson campus in 1947 to be Assistant to President John Morrison. Reardon strongly favored the launching in 1950 of a new graduate seminary as part of the ministerial education program of the Anderson campus. To him, the School of Theology could enable a better educated ministry, graduating men and women who in turn would help future generations of Church of God ministers and laypersons avoid the smaller, exclusivistic, and bitter perspectives and attitudes seen especially in the turmoil of the 1945-1948 period. For him, and thinking again of that story in John 5, the churchly waters around 1950 offered a good time for visionary leaders to step in and bring healing to the church through better training and seasoned wisdom. "The overriding concern," he said, "was for a responsible, well-educated ministry and the School of Theology seemed the appropriate way for us to go."

In the mid-1970s, when the Anderson seminary had its own facility on campus and was playing a growing role in the church's life, the new Adam W. Miller Chapel was added to the seminary building. Robert Reardon, then President of the college and seminary, insisted that worship and learning are to be closely linked. The new chapel was to be a place where great congregational singing could occur. He was a church musician himself and always sought to combine music and ministry, spiritual life and academic pursuits. Robert was much like his teacher-minister father Eugene, carrying on the tradition of the Church of God movement in inspiring, thoughtful, and winsome ways. He had brought Dr. Barry L. Callen to the seminary's deanship in 1973, a young man with conservative church credentials (from Rev. Lillie McCutcheon's congregation in Newton Falls, Ohio) and superb academic credentials. They proved a winning combination for the graduate school.

As the young presidential assistant in the 1950s, Reardon oversaw the beginning of the Layman Lecture series that annually brought to campus speakers of national reputation from outside the Church of God movement who were impressive and helped liberate church leaders from excessively provincial attitudes. He highlighted this in his later years as a crucial development for the church and campus at that stage of their development. Opening the campus doors to new voices was for Reardon not a deviation from the church unity mission of the movement, but a new tool for staying on course toward its fuller realization. It also is the kind of thing that he judged ought to mark the life of a quality educational institution. Openness to truth wherever found and relishing in cultural richness was instinctive for Robert Reardon.

A major occasion in 1955 afforded Reardon the opportunity to exercise

Anderson School of Theology students and faculty, 1953.
Part-time faculty member Robert Reardon is second from the left (kneeling).

a new voice. He had been asked to come to the first World Conference of the Church of God being convened in Fritzlar, Germany, and be one of the guest preachers on this world platform. This was an honor for a young church leader. He both went and made special preparation for his sermon. With the help of Professor Anna Koglin, a former Oberlin seminary student now on the Anderson College faculty, he readied himself to preach *in German*—no other international guest would be attempting such a thing. He delivered the sermon as planned in this historic church gathering, receiving delighted surprise and great appreciation for his effort to communicate with such local meaning. On numerous other occasions, Reardon demonstrated personal courage by acting on principle, opening risky doors in the face of likely church opposition—at least when he judged the issue important enough.

For instance, he received vigorous criticism from some church leaders when he chose the distinguished president of Notre Dame University to be the Anderson College and School of Theology commencement speaker in 1970. The criticism came largely because large elements within the Church of God movement often had characterized the Roman Catholic Church as being the center of a long pattern of Christian apostasy. President Theodore M. Hesburgh, a true statesman in higher education and valued colleague of Reardon's in Indiana, delivered an outstanding commencement address. Threats were heard from some pastors that they would attempt to have church dollars withheld from the Anderson campus because of this rash action of Reardon's, but nothing materialized. Rather than "rash," the invitation to Father Hesburgh was an act of principle based on a particular vision of quality education and good churchmanship. President Reardon was willing to act in such a way on occasion, seeing an action of this kind as fulfilling the school's highest mission and the church's highest ideal (whether all recognized it as such or not). The campus was obligated to the church, but it also was responsible to show leadership to the church when necessary. Reardon accepted the obligation and also risked exercising the leadership.

For Robert Reardon, a prime way to bring fresh leadership to the church is to graduate new generations of church ministers and laypersons who have both strong Christian commitments and informed minds of their own. Church people too easily tend to assume the role of being unthinking defenders of traditional beliefs and practices; but the church needs "critics" who think their own thoughts before God. President John Morrison made his view quite clear: "Blessed is the one who knows how to doubt, for verily he shall not be sucked in by the fantastic claims of some scientist nor gobbled up by the dogmatic pronouncements of some theologians" (*As I Was Thinking* 1964). Reardon made his own view clear to Anderson College alumni (*Alumni News*, September, 1963). He was not calling for "a parade of bulls through the china shop." There are, however, those who earn the right to speak—and they should. What, then, was his view when Anderson College graduates were said to be openly dissatisfied with some aspect of church life?

> I say, Good! Although no student is justified in taking a four-year subsidy from the church only to become sour and destructive in criticism, yet what a tragedy it would be if the church college graduate became so blind and content that he or she was happy and satisfied with the church—satisfied that it holds the whole truth and nothing but the truth; satisfied with its evangelistic outreach; satisfied with its mission program; satisfied with its social concern and stewardship; satisfied that it is carrying out its mission in yearning for unity with other Christians. What a tragedy this would be, indeed! This would be death!... The younger generation makes content people move on, sleepy people awaken, naïve people think, and satisfied people restless.

If the Anderson campus were to graduate new generations of committed Christians with minds of their own, what core commitments should shape campus life? After a year of intense self-examination prompted in part by criticism received from some leaders within the Church of God movement, in 1981 the campus published an extended statement on the nature of its partnership with the church. Titled "Anderson College: In Partnership with the Church" and written largely by Barry L. Callen, then Dean of the School of Theology, it was developed under the close supervision of President Reardon and very much reflected his own philosophy. It states this about the Anderson campus:

> [Its] curricular design and community life combine the honesty and rigor of academic inquiry and the perspectives and mission emerging from biblical revelation. It lives in an atmosphere of free inquiry, even while it affirms that all knowledge is understood most fully in the light of God's redemptive activity in Jesus Christ as that is interpreted through the historic witness of the Bible and the contemporary ministry of the Holy Spirit.

The "contemporary ministry of the Holy Spirit" includes ongoing critique of the church's life by inspired believers with informed minds of their own. President Reardon was a persistent and very visible model of a loving critic of select aspects of church life—the very church that he loved so much.

Approaching the General Assembly with Care

Robert Reardon told the Anderson College Board of Trustees in June, 1974, that the Anderson campus "takes its life from the body of Christian believers and returns life back to the body. If it ever becomes separated it may continue to function for a time, but eventually it will die." Relating an academic community to the church's life was crucial and not negotiable in this president's view, but on occasion such relating was awkward and uncomfortable. Reardon repeated from his own experience what John F. Kennedy said after his first year in office as President of the United States: "The job is interesting, but the possibilities for trouble are unlimited!" At times Reardon would take amused comfort in recalling this observation of Winston

Churchill: "There is no more exhilarating feeling than to be shot at and missed!" John Morrison, Reardon's presidential mentor, had remarkable political skills that included "the subtle, the persuasive, and at times the hammer and tong approach" (Reardon, *Some Anderson College Reflections* 12). Morrison had a very good student as his successor, a man who surely honed his own political skills over the years. Reardon was politically shot at several times—there were no mortal wounds, but all critical barbs did not miss their intended mark!

President Morrison had shared with his gifted successor a calculated strategy for approaching the annual Anderson Camp Meeting and especially the General Assembly of the Church of God that always meets in this summer context. Taking initiative and staying in motion are very important for the president, according to Morrison. He typically had approached this large church gathering on the campus and adjacent grounds by being sure that the College had going some highly visible project that would impress the crowds with the compelling fact that the school was on the move in some innovative and constructive direction. Assuming it is true that people chase after a bouncing ball and kick it when it stops (a saying of Elmo Funk), Reardon determined to keep the campus ball bouncing—especially in the eyes of the church and its leaders. He knew that, when one acts on principle, being popular with everyone is a vain illusion. But acting as one believes right helps sleep to come at night, even if some segment of the campus clientele is infuriated by a presidential action. The unpopular decision takes courage to make, of course. Reardon once observed that "often the president will need to get his troops together and gird his loins for battle" (*Some Anderson College Reflections* 31).

With particular reference to the General Assembly of the Church of God, and noting again a biblical reference made often, Reardon characterized the wisest relationship in terms of the healing story found in John 5:1-9. The goal identified in this biblical text was to be first into the water when it became turbulent because being first was the way healing was to be found. But Reardon sometimes implemented this message in reverse (*Some Anderson College Reflections* 23):

> Dealing with the General Assembly of the Church of God is like entering the pool at Bethesda, only in reverse. You never want to go in when the waters are troubled if you can manage to stay out.

During these turbulent times only the strongest of swimmers can survive, and this writer, on a few occasions, has been glad to escape with his life.

Rev. Eugene Reardon had paved the way for his son Robert, having been the first Chair of the Assembly in 1917 before Robert was born and on occasion having spoken prophetically to its members.

By 1943 Robert Reardon observed in his Oberlin masters thesis that by then there were three groups evident within the leadership of the Church of God movement. Knowing them well was key to navigating successfully through the unstable world and occasionally turbulent waters of campus-church relations. One was a group going all out to maintain the traditional teachings of the movement, allowing no compromise to the most exclusive of movement self-perceptions. A second group was reacting strongly to the first, even with disgust over its perceived fanaticism. At points it was proceeding with a virtual abandonment of some key movement traditions. The third group, judged by Reardon as the rapidly growing majority in the 1940s, was seeking to salvage from the movement's teaching tradition what had managed to stand the test of time—church membership as spiritual in nature, the Bible as the basis for Christian unity, etc., with no inflated expectations about the "last reformationism" of the reform movement and a mass "coming to the truth" and even to Anderson, Indiana, by a properly chastened denominational world.

This third group assumed that there would never be a super-church associated with Anderson and no narrowly defined theological agreement among all Bible-believing Christians. Increased self-criticism and a toleration of diversity inside and outside the movement of the Church of God was the growing order of the day. Many saw the trending of this third group as fully justified, the real heart of the movement's necessary future visioning, while others viewed it with alarm. Dr. Val Clear, close friend and colleague of Robert Reardon for five decades, was a prominent member of this third group. His 1953 doctoral dissertation at the University of Chicago probed the ongoing dynamics of the reform movement from a sociological perspective. Robert Reardon also became an inspiring leader of the group seeking to salvage the good from the past without being captured by the passing preoccupations of a time now gone. Found in chapter seven of this biography are brief expositions of Reardon's perceptions of "ruts in the road of reform" and "the marks of enduring greatness."

By 1992 Robert Reardon had attended the annual General Assemblies of Church of God for forty-one years. He then was an honored senior member who was asked to offer to that year's Assembly his observations of its life and meaning. His comments featured remembrances of a pivotal event in the 1920s that to him represented truly Christian attitudes and a responding Assembly wisdom. The event was the story of his father who had informed the Assembly straightforwardly that a "sectish spirit" had become alarmingly common among too many of the movement's leaders. Enough members did not appreciate his view to the extent that he was voted out of two key positions in national church life. By the next day the voting outcomes were known and he was given the chance to say something to the Assembly. He spoke humbly into the awkward silence on the floor: "I just have one thing to say to you. The Assembly gave and the Assembly has taken away, blessed be the name of the Assembly." Sometimes losing with grace prepares the way for victory the next time. Experience can be a good teacher. Even for a strong leader, proper and timely humility is a wise virtue.

Eugene Reardon's son Robert proudly reported in 1992 that, given the spirit of his father's character and response in the midst of that defeat in the 1920s, the very next year the Assembly had reinstated him to most of his previous roles. Robert generalized on this by seeing wisdom marking most of the Assembly's life ("charismatic church government"), although the wisdom is rarely obvious in the first year that a controversial issue is addressed. This is why, reversing the sequence in the biblical story of the pool by the Sheep Gate (John 5), one must be careful not to step in when the waters are first troubled. Clear heads are not usually the first ones to speak. Reardon also remembered the counsel of John Morrison on church fights: "Before you engage an issue, be sure that you are right and that you can win!"

Three particular times of clear conflict between the Anderson campus and church leadership are worth noting, especially because they reveal the attitudes and working style of President Robert Reardon. The first, less actual conflict and more the personal prophetic voice of Reardon, came in the Assembly of June 1968. The Chair, Rev. Harold Boyer, recognized Robert Reardon, President of Anderson College and School of Theology, who wished to speak to the Assembly. Reardon referred to Charles Naylor's hymn "The Church's Jubilee" and quoted the verse that includes the words "reaching our hands in fellowship to every blood-washed one." He then recalled for the gathered body of church leaders that the Assembly in 1964 had expressed an "open-door policy" for all races, namely: "We urge each individual [Assembly] member to examine his life patterns in the light of the nature of the gospel and to fully welcome into congregational life fellow members and all persons without regard to race, color, or nationality."

Reardon now strongly reaffirmed this 1964 Assembly stance, but also struggled with the continuing magnitude of the racist problem in the culture generally and even in the church. Therefore, he called on the 1968 Assembly to take more concrete action by calling on all local congregations of the Church of God in the United States and Canada to ratify the following declaration and make such ratification known publicly through whatever means possible:

> Resolved that, in accordance with the teaching of the Scriptures, this congregation of the Church of God welcomes fellow Christians without regard to race, color, or national origin, to participate fully and without any reservation in its fellowship and work. And be it further resolved that the Executive Secretary of the Executive Council of the Church of God is instructed to place the above declaration before each local congregation of the Church of God and to make public those congregations ratifying this declaration.

The President was asking the Assembly to encourage the churches to act, to be willing to declare themselves openly, despite any opposition that might be faced in their communities or even in their own constituencies. He was prepared to show the way.

The phrases "a man of conscience" and "a man of action" both fit Robert Reardon well. There were those in the 1968 Assembly who were not comfortable with the action being called for, although they would not have thought of themselves as "racist." On the Anderson campus where Reardon presided, appropriate action would be taken. Soon there would be an African-American campus pastor, James Earl Massey, who later would also to be Professor of New Testament and Homiletics and Dean of the School of Theology. In addition, there would be an African-American Chair of the campus Board of Trustees, Rev. Ronald J. Fowler. Both of these moves were personal and intentional on Reardon's part. The campus, insisted the president, must model what the gospel of Christ requires and what the church across the nation was being asked to do. He would do all he could, although attracting large numbers of the church's African-American youth to the largely White and relatively small city of Anderson, Indiana, would never be easy.

Robert Reardon already had walked a fine line on matters of social justice that had been boiling in the nation. As protestors marched across the South on behalf of civil rights for persons of color, Dr. Candace Stone of Anderson College did not remain idle. Racial discrimination was a standard part of social life in Anderson, Indiana. Reardon recalls well from his boyhood the Klu Klux Klan parades in downtown Anderson on Saturday nights. As he told the students in chapel in January, 1982, "When I was a boy, people did not think much about it." But Dr. Stone did. In 1955 she organized a local rally on behalf of human rights, "the first rally of any town or city anywhere in the north." None other than Rosa Parks herself traveled to Anderson to talk that night. Present and active with Dr. Stone were Robert Reardon, Milton Buettner, Val Clear, Robert Nicholson, and others from the local campus. Reardon, thinking about this again in 1982, told the students that he was "troubled by the gullibility with which all of us seem to accept conventional wisdom, like the acceptability of racial discrimination."

Anderson College students, faculty, and administrators soon organized a rally supporting Blacks in Birmingham, Alabama. President Reardon led a large march in 1965 from the campus to downtown Anderson, Indiana, on behalf of the civil rights of persons of color, a march that was a positive catalyst for at least two students from the South who were dealing with their own stances in relation to racist home cultures. One was Ronald Moore, later to be Senior Vice-President of the College, and the other was Fred Burnett, later to be a Professor of Biblical Studies on campus. The courageous witness of Reardon on behalf of human justice made a lasting impact on these two men and on many others. The parents of some Anderson College students from the South were displeased by this dramatic and very public action of marching, but Reardon stood firm. The dignity of every human being is a basic assumption of the Christian gospel. Christians must risk acting in accord with biblical teaching.

Also among those who marched in 1965 to downtown Anderson was seminary student Barry L. Callen who would be Dean of Anderson School of Theology eight years later. With him on the march was college student James L. Edwards who twenty-five years later would himself be the president of the Anderson campus. The march's personal impact on Moore, Burnett, Callen,

Robert H. Reardon (front center) leading much of the campus and local Church of God community in a civil rights march to downtown Anderson, Indiana, in 1965. Front row, left to right: Stoney Cooks, President Robert Reardon, and Pastor Hillery Rice.

Edwards, and others was considerable and far-reaching. Edwards reports that this prophetic event "was a really significant time in my life since it was a dramatic statement that our campus was going to be in the real world making an actual difference." President Reardon was an activist in the "real world" on behalf of just causes.

In apparent contrast to this marching stand for justice, in the eyes of some at least, the president was inconsistent when he refused to allow the formation on campus of a Black student organization. He wanted to avoid even more polarization over a cause in which he believed deeply. His model of proper racial reconciliation was integration, not institutionalized separation —which is how he thought about the "Black Union" idea. Justice, peace, and effective protest strategies were hard things to judge and keep in balance. President Reardon was determined somehow to move forward on all these connected fronts, experimenting, risking, speaking out, living with the private pain of sometimes being very misunderstood.

The second instance of campus-church conflict developed initially during the 1971-1972 school year. In the face of low seminary enrollments on the Anderson campus, coupled with rising costs and an apparent need for revitalizing the graduate school curriculum, in 1969 Reardon set in motion a multi-year study to determine what set of relationships, circumstances, and curricular designs would prove the best and most practical path of preparation for future ministers of the Church of God movement. This subject was very personal for President Reardon and he remained close to the study. His central goal was to find and implement ways to appeal to a wider range of students with new degree programs, eliminate duplication of campus faculty resources in ministerial education (college and seminary), draw qualified pastors into the educational process, and take the lead in interdenominational cooperation in seminary education. The president wanted academic degrees more achievable for ministerial candidates who were older and/or bivocational (requiring less than the three years beyond college required for the Master of Divinity degree) and the real-world presence of ministerial practitioners in the educational process.

The result of this study was a series of changes set in motion by the president, including new and shorter degree program structures, the establishment of the Center for Pastoral Studies, the naming of Dr. Barry L. Callen as director of the new Center and dean of the seminary itself, and an affiliation with the Foundation for Religious Studies, an evolving ecumenical consortium of theological schools mostly located in Indianapolis, Indiana. Reardon brought all this to the Board of Trustees for approval. The plan was supported with enthusiasm. Then in June, 1972, the Board brought this idealism and the program innovations to the General Assembly of the Church of God for information and endorsement.

President Reardon naturally was seen as primarily responsible and accountable for all that was being proposed. Much of it was celebrated almost universally, but parts were not. The seminary faculty was sensitive about the apparent devaluing of the standard Master of Divinity degree program. A provocative mass mailing in advance of the Assembly criticized especially the ecumenical dimension with the consortium of seminaries based in Indianapolis. A key sticking point for many church leaders was that one of the seminaries involved in this Foundation for Religious Studies was Roman Catholic, a fact emphasized to inflame sentiment against the plan. Some ministers openly feared that soon there would be priests training Church of God ministers and that future textbooks and teachers would have to be approved by the Vatican! This paved the way for some heated rhetoric on the Assembly floor.

The Board's resolution put before the Assembly asked for a committee to be appointed by the Assembly that would evaluate the success of this new cluster of program innovations in its third year of operation, then reporting back to the Trustees and Assembly. In effect, acceptance of the Board's resolution would imply Assembly approval of the whole range of changes, at least for the trial years. The proposed resolution finally was defeated, being successfully replaced by a resolution from the floor that passed 499-422 (suggesting the sharp division over this matter). This adopted motion called for the new affiliation of Anderson School of Theology with the Foundation in Indianapolis to be dissolved at the earliest possible moment.

Reardon took this defeat hard, thinking that much was at stake and that ridiculous rhetoric and groundless fear had triumphed in the Assembly over practical good sense. He understood himself and his colleagues to "have been foolish enough to ask the right question—'What is the best way to educate ministers for the Church of God?'" True innovation had followed, resisted by some faculty and students who held tightly to traditional programmatic territory, while the Board and administration had dared to think new thoughts and forge new relationships. The president and Board had legal control of campus programs and personnel, of course, but defying the Assembly's expressed will would be self-defeating in the long run. The difficult decision was made to comply with the Assembly's expressed will.

Following his father's lead (his speech to the Assembly and then grace in accepting defeat in the 1920s), President Reardon accepted the Assembly's action with all the grace he could and proceeded to find constructive next steps. Several of the innovations went ahead with wide support—the new degree structures, the new Center for Pastoral Studies, and the new leadership of Dean Barry Callen. Subsequent developments between the Assembly and seminary in 1973 and 1974 soon led Reardon to be able to say that "we lost the battle, but I tried to take this disappointment with grace and soon we came out smelling like a rose." The seminary gained unprecedented attention from the church, experienced a greatly expanded sense of ownership by the church, and soon was enjoying financial assistance from the church without precedent in its twenty-three years of life. Barry Callen, the new School of Theology dean, spoke to the Board of Trustees in 1974 and summarized the circumstance as follows:

The Church of God in general and this Board of Trustees in particular have found it necessary to search relentlessly for the most appropriate and feasible model for educating ministers in a context of excellence, without destroying meaningful bridges to the sponsoring church, and without compromising the integrity of the school itself. This process to date has proven time-consuming, painful, and profitable in ways often unanticipated.

Two years after Callen's statement to the Board and with his active participation, the Commission on Christian Higher Education of the Church of God successfully proposed the following to the 1976 Assembly: "We propose that the General Assembly recognize seminary training as the normal, the ideal level of initial preparation for the future young minister, and that the Assembly continue to authorize an annual appropriation of funds whereby this level of ministerial training can be made available to eligible students who give evidence that they will use their educational experiences for the good of the church." It had been a long road from places like Oberlin, Ohio, in the 1930s and 1940s, where a few Church of God persons like Robert Reardon had experienced seminary education for the first time, to a formal recognition that such graduate education should be made available within the life of the Church of God movement and even be recognized as "normal" and "ideal." All battles were not over, but real ground had been gained. President Reardon had steered the seminary ship through some stormy waters to some welcome new ports.

The third instance of campus-church conflict came in 1979-1980 when the Church of God movement was poised to celebrate its centennial in Anderson, Indiana, with numerous guests present from all over the world. Suddenly the Anderson campus and President Reardon were faced with another church relations struggle that rivaled the one President Morrison had faced in the early 1930s. The spring and early summer of 1980 was an especially volatile and painful period. Reardon addressed the campus Board of Trustees and attributed the problem in significant part to "the rise of neo-fundamentalism across the nation" that had created "an atmosphere of fear and suspicion." The president had no thought of breaking campus relations with the Church of God; nonetheless, he warned the Board: "Just as the Board of Trustees stood firm against the imposition of F. G. Smith's 'standard literature' in the early 1930s, so we must be careful to seek [faculty] persons with Christian commitment who are dedicated to the mission of the College and Seminary, while resisting efforts of the Judaizers to foster educational sectarianism in an institution which has a long tradition of freedom to think and explore." The issues were foundational and the president spoke with deep conviction.

In January, 1979, as the Church of God movement was fast approaching its one-hundredth year, Reardon had written to Dr. Barry L. Callen, Dean of the School of Theology, giving him and the seminary faculty the difficult task of developing a "We Believe" booklet that could help fill the belief-identity vacuum the President sensed was then troubling the Church of God movement. He explained:

> Reformation theology—as articulated by F. G. Smith and others—is dead. During its heyday its radical ideas drove the engine of our movement and gave it the cohesiveness and toughness born out of deeply held convictions. There are some fairly serious matters facing the movement today, but none more serious than the need of a clear articulation of those central views which yet remain as a time-tested part of our heritage.

The goal now was for the seminary faculty members "to come forward with a clear and ringing statement of their present perspective on who we are as a [Church of God] movement, from whence we came, and where we now stand." In the months to follow, this difficult writing task was supervised by Dean Callen, completed successfully, and distributed widely.

President Reardon's instincts about the status of the Church of God movement soon appeared accurate since the years following 1979 saw the seminary's "We Believe" booklet circulate by the tens of thousands of copies and be translated into three languages other than English. In 1978 Reardon had written a brief essay for a popular church heritage book edited by Barry Callen, titling the essay "A Glossary of Church of God Terms." It detailed the meaning of the distinctive and now dated language of what the president judged the dying "reformation theology," a language he knew so well and many younger people in the church did not know at all (*A Time To Remember: Evaluations*, 1978, 24-27). Nonetheless, despite these popular and clarifying publications, campus relations with the Church of God movement went significantly sour in early 1980, keynoted by a deliberately inflammatory mailing sent to President Reardon by Pastor Leroy Oesch of South Carolina, with copies mailed simultaneously to hundreds (thousands?) of church leaders across North America. The mailing obviously had been timed to inflame unrest against Anderson College just prior to the gathering in June, 1980, of the General Assembly.

The Oesch letter was a broadside charging that "liberalism" was running rampant on the Anderson campus. Prime examples given were a sociology course on human sexuality, Bible courses not insisting on biblical "inerrancy," and a general deterioration of holiness standards related to student conduct on campus. Sexually explicit drawings lifted out of context from the sociology textbook were included in the mailing for dramatic effect on readers. As church historian Merle Strege later summarized: "Oesch's letter and its allegations stormed to the front and center of attention. The entire [Church of God] movement seemed up in arms. College supporters rushed to its defense in the name of reason and enlightened toleration. Opponents attacked it for its departure from the truth and descended on Anderson for the annual convention demanding to know what was going on at the college" (*I Saw the Church* 336). The air on the east side of Anderson, Indiana, in June, 1980, was full of ominous electricity. It was at once a scene of the centennial celebration of the church and turmoil strident enough to threaten the ruin of any celebration.

The dispute erupted openly on the floor of the General Assembly, convened that year in the college gymnasium because the centennial celebration of the church had swollen the attendance beyond normal. Numerous international church delegates, many visiting the big Anderson event for the first time, were "treated" to a series of ugly harangues from various floor microphones—some by persons not even belonging in the Assembly but there anyway because of the anticipated conflict and the opportunity to air a personal complaint against the campus, sometimes unrelated to the Oesch letter and many years old. The Assembly's leadership was unable to keep any rational lid on this boiling pot that saw the Anderson campus and at times President Reardon personally being attacked in the harshest of terms. It was not a time when any real explanations or defense could be mounted, so those under attack sat through it as gracefully as possible. The matter finally was resolved—at least gotten off the floor—by the hasty appointment of a committee charged with investigating the whole matter and reporting back to the following year's Assembly.

The 1980-1981 year was certainly uncomfortable for the campus administration. The review committee that had been appointed jointly by the Chairs of the campus Board of Trustees and the General Assembly proceeded to receive numerous and highly opinionated communications from interested parties on all sides of the issues. In the late summer of 1980 the committee met, determined its recommendations, and sent them to the Board of Trustees for consideration in its fall meeting. They included removing the instructor from the sociology class in question and changing the controversial textbook. The Board, knowing its central responsibility in matters involving campus policy and personnel, created its own Trustee Advisory Committee that began meeting monthly to review these recommendations, take whatever actions appeared appropriate, plan for its own communication with the church, and ready a formal report for delivery to the 1981 General Assembly. Members of the Trustee Advisory Committee were Marvin W. Baker, Esther K. Bauer, James W. Bradley, Ronald J. Fowler, William J. Gaither, and Keith Huttenlocker, all people of high church credibility and trusted friends and colleagues of President Reardon.

This Trustee Advisory Committee worked closely with the campus administration and reaffirmed its full confidence in President Robert Reardon and Dean Robert Nicholson. Rev. Ronald Fowler, member of the committee and coming to new leadership as Chair of the Board, reflected later on the selfless way that President Reardon handled himself in the midst of all this. Reardon knew that his own heavy stamp on the eventual report to the Assembly would prejudice it unnecessarily in the eyes of critics. He also trusted the people working on the problem. So he asked for and received a two-month sabbatical, during which he spent personal time doing family heritage travel in Ireland. As Fowler saw it, Reardon "was big enough to do the right thing, backing off and allowing others to lead. His natural instinct was to stay in Anderson, with hands on and actively defending himself and the campus, but the president stepped aside, showing humility and great confidence in the wisdom of his staff." This confidence was well placed.

Dean Robert Nicholson and Doctors Barry Callen and Larry Osnes assumed key roles in working with the Board of Trustees in the preparation of a major written report to be delivered to the 1981 General Assembly. It was a pivotal time in the life of the Anderson campus and certainly a defining one in its church relations. The issues involved the control of the campus and the integrity of the academic enterprise itself. President Reardon knew that the campus was locked in a very serious battle, not unlike the one President Morrison had been forced to wage in the 1930s. Reardon wrote this in his private journal on May 12, 1981: "There are some bitter days upon us just now. There is a resurgence of narrowness buoyed on by the conservative winds blowing in the country. The move is to have all pastors and colleges take the 'inerrancy oath.' What a return to cult-like thinking this might be!"

Anderson School of Theology faculty and staff, 1980. Seated third and fourth from the left are Dean Barry L. Callen and President Robert H. Reardon.

The formal report of the Anderson Board of Trustees, published jointly with the committee appointed by the previous Assembly, was delivered in an electric atmosphere of nervous anticipation. It was forthright and detailed. It sought to make clear that the Board was in charge of campus life, had done its homework on the contested issues, was prepared to yield at some points, and on principle would refuse to yield at others. The professor in question was to remain separated from the controversial sociology class, but the class on human sexuality would continue, as would the textbook that had been attacked. The campus would not espouse any "secular humanism" and would continue to affirm the centrality of the Bible, but without accepting "inerrancy" language as the norm for the church's understanding of biblical authority. No formal doctrinal test would be mandatory for faculty members, although the application for campus employment would be revised to include clearer statements about the institution's mission, church relatedness, and ethical expectations.

With the passing of a year and the substantial work and report of the Board of Trustees, cooler heads now prevailed in the 1981 General Assembly. President Reardon had believed that moderates in the Assembly would come to see reason when the real facts were put forward fairly. He was right. The Assembly overwhelmingly accepted the Board's report and the controversy quickly subsided. Reardon wrote this in his private journal in late June: "It was an historic Assembly decision that rejected fundamentalism. The air is cleared, thank God!" The pain had been great, but finally rationality had prevailed.

A more conciliatory environment returned to national church life, with attitudes exhibited that were more in character with how Reardon had concluded his preface to the 1979 "We Believe" statement of the School of Theology: "It is a labor of love offered to the Church of God as together we seek God's guidance for the future." Reardon cared deeply both about the integrity of the academic processes on campus and the church's future. While he had good listening skills and could give fair consideration to an opposing point of view, his friend Carl Erskine, a fifteen-year veteran of the Anderson College Board of Trustees, says of Reardon: "Nothing would deter him from what he believed to be right. He was not a man led around by popular opinion. He was a solid Christian who stood his ground."

Trustee William "Bill" Gaither recalls having spent twenty-seven days on the campus during 1980-1981 struggling with the church relations challenges and the issues related to them. He had joined his governing colleagues in listening carefully to the criticisms of aspects of campus life. "In all fairness," he later recalled, "there were some things we needed to look at again and we had to come up with some kind of intelligent responses. We said to each other, 'What do we learn from all of this and how shall we live after all of this experience?' I think we came out of this with good wisdom and in a Christian way. I am proud to have served." Gaither believed deeply in the person of Robert Reardon and knew that, despite the pain of it all, spirits were right, commitments were solid, and good things would follow. They would indeed. On May 11, 1982, for instance, Reardon recorded this in his private journal: "Last week I spoke at Gulf Coast Bible College in Texas. I think I built some new bridges, including getting better acquainted with President John Conley" [who had been one of Reardon's opponents in the recent confrontations in the General Assembly]. It was time to move on.

Even with such constructive bridge building, however, for President Reardon the whole "open letter" affair was a low point of Robert Reardon's presidency. Geraldine Reardon reflected later, "It took some of the joy out of the work for Bob." So much was this the case that soon it would be one factor that would lead to his decision to retire early.

Brothers and Sisters Together

Good perspective often is hard to gain. For instance, one might conclude from the campus-church conflicts identified above that Robert Reardon was a combative, even an anti-church personality regularly creating and then living in the midst of church turmoil. Such would be very far from the truth. Given the strong identification of Reardon's name with the Anderson campus, one might conclude that his commitments and concerns were rather exclusively focused on this one institution. Such also would be considerably wide of the fuller truth. Reardon was a true churchman. Often he acted on a campus issue while thinking about the whole church, its heritage, theology, ministerial leaders, and institutions. The Church of God movement was his home. So far as he was concerned, he and the church's membership were brothers and sisters together.

The Anderson campus was not seen by President Reardon as an entity unto itself, but as a key part of the church's larger life. For example, once when the college faculty was discussing reducing or even making optional the traditional Bible requirements for all undergraduate students, Reardon spoke to the faculty unexpectedly and with a stern voice. To him, such a move suggested a diminished relationship of the campus to the church and probably a lessened ability of the campus and its graduates in the future to effectively serve the church. He made it clear to one and all; the faculty is in charge of the curriculum—unless a faculty move such as the one then under consideration deeply violated the very church-related nature of the institution. In such a case, and only as a last resort if absolutely necessary, this president would intervene and be the one to keep things on what he judged the right course. He did just that in this case—and some faculty members did not appreciate his sudden "executive interference" in their domain. To this president, the right course involved thinking of the Anderson campus as intertwined with the larger life of the Church of God movement nationally and internationally. Intervene he would and did.

Back in the 1950s in his previous role as Executive Vice-President just before becoming the president, Robert Reardon had "engineered" the significant work of the President's Study and Planning Commission that had been established by the Board of Trustees in 1955 to assess the issues and plan for the future of the college. He took pride in having made sure that the key Anderson church leaders were deeply involved in the process. They were brothers and sisters together in a common enterprise under God. They had a deep commitment to each other, the College to the Missionary Board, the Gospel Trumpet Company (publications) and the Board of Christian Education to the College, etc. Then, soon after his becoming president in 1958, a major crisis developed in the work of the church nationally that tested this togetherness.

A winter storm in March, 1960, collapsed the roof of the big wooden tabernacle that had housed the large gatherings at Anderson Camp Meeting for forty years. Harold Phillips, then Editor of the church's national publication, wrote a famous editorial that May on "The Death of Brother Tabernacle" (*Gospel Trumpet*, May 1, 1960). What should be done? A debate developed among church leaders about whether to attempt a repair of the old structure or erect a brand new one. Some, like T. Franklin Miller, Steele Smith, and Charles Weber, felt it was time for change and a significant step forward. Others, including Robert Reardon, William E. Reed, and Paul Tanner, resisted the idea that major funding be directed to new construction of a very large building to be used only one week a year and likely to be built at the expense of existing ministries (like Anderson College). Reardon, says Tanner, "was a known tiger when it came to a debate over issues that really mattered to him." So Reardon, Reed, and Tanner refused to sit still. They went to Indianapolis to visit Harold Achor, a close friend of Reardon's and the Chief Justice of the Indiana Supreme Court.

Achor was pleased to help. He arranged for a meeting with the State Building Inspector to discuss his stance on the viability of the tabernacle's repair. It turned out that the Inspector thought repair was a workable plan, the opposite of what those church leaders favoring new construction had implied was his view. The report of this meeting was not appreciated in some quarters back in Anderson. Despite the new information, a magnificent new structure, Warner Auditorium, was built by decision of the General Assembly of the church, as was a process of repairing relationships among opposing leaders. Church executives began a pattern of meeting on a regular basis to share, think beyond the work of individual ministry agencies, and embrace the work of the whole church. These staff luncheons continued for the next forty-five years.

Reardon was on the losing side of this heated issue, but he had a way of winning even in the midst of apparent loss. The new Warner Auditorium for many years has been the proud scene of the commencement ceremonies of Anderson University. Reardon quickly emerged as a natural and highly respected leader in the staff luncheons. With the controversial decision made, the new building erected, and the church crisis past, the Anderson church leaders managed to again become warm brothers and sisters together in God's work. Robert Reardon remained a major player in the midst of things.

President Reardon became the point man on a range of other church issues over the years. Locally, he negotiated with the Gospel Trumpet Company (Warner Press) about various land issues, usually wanting to purchase more church property for the expanding needs of the campus. "Although Steele Smith and T. Franklin Miller were dear men to me," says Reardon, "I fought them for every inch of land." He added with a glint in his eye, "We had a lot of sparks flying sometimes, even though I doubt that God in heaven cared much about the whole thing!"

Succeeding most of the time in managing to buy or secure a longterm lease on desired church land, Reardon nonetheless made sure that new campus buildings were made available for multi-purpose use during the annual Anderson Camp Meeting. The campus and church were to remain helpful partners regardless of who owned which pieces of adjacent property. Nationally, clear examples of his active churchmanship included the "Open Door" racial policy resolution that he personally sponsored in the 1968 General Assembly of the Church of God and his launching and supervision of the development of the "We Believe" booklet of Anderson School of Theology in 1979. These illustrate well his deep caring about the well being and integrity of the whole church and its mission in the world.

On a more personal level, Robert and Geraldine Reardon nurtured long friendships with scores of church leaders. One welcome tool for this hospitality was the construction of Boyes House in 1968. A highlight of each year was when the Reardons opened the doors of this presidential home to members of the Executive Council of the Church of God as it gathered in its annual session. Many of these church leaders from year to year were Anderson College and/or School of Theology graduates. These wonderful occasions featured serious talk, laughter, and a time of singing as Geraldine played the grand piano and then Robert would play his little pump organ, usually to encourage people to sing some of the heritage hymns of the Church of God movement. These times together were a mixture of church celebration and alumni reunions. The Reardons were natural networkers of people. While there always was an element of intentional church relations involved, such hosting was also a sincere way of caring about many very special friends, brothers and sisters together in the work of Jesus Christ.

Beyond relationships with key people, President Reardon was committed to ministerial education. This commitment was rooted in his love for the church and its need for well-informed and mature leaders. He was passionate about such education and, with the writing assistance of Dr. Barry Callen, Dean of the School of Theology in the 1970s and early 1980s, he supervised the development and release of the document "Anderson College: In Partnership with the Church." A key paragraph in it states well Reardon's own thought. Anderson College and School of Theology

> ...values the church relationship in which the thought and practices of the church and the methods and perspectives of the academic disciplines are enabled to probe and inform each other. The College assumes that the theology and life of the whole Christian community, and of the Church of God Reformation Movement in particular, is worthy of orienting and enriching the educational process. It is equally aware of its responsibility to be a source of research, rethinking, and renewal in the church. Formulations of theology are never fixed or finished, and church traditions lose their significance apart from fresh analysis and an understanding of contemporary relevance.

The vision of President Reardon always has been practical in nature and global in scope, never failing to embrace concerns for the well being of the larger church. The beginnings of the campus TRI-S program in the 1960s is a prime example. The president wanted opportunities for students to be able to travel, experience, and serve in relation to the church's larger mission in the world. Maurice Caldwell served three five-year terms on the Anderson College Board of Trustees during the Reardon presidency. In his view, Reardon will be remembered especially for the TRI-S program, just as President John F.

Kennedy is remembered for launching the Peace Corps on a national level.

An element on the agenda of each annual meeting of the campus Board of Trustees was the report of Norman Beard, longtime Director of TRI-S. Caldwell recalls vividly the meeting of the Executive Council of the Church of God when Robert Reardon first shared his dream of a global Anderson College program based on the general strategy and ideal of the Peace Corps, but motivated by Christian faith and implemented in relation to the larger mission work of the Church of God movement. In the years to follow there would be numerous Anderson College students inspired by their TRI-S experiences and then becoming full-time missionaries serving through the Church of God around the world. Reardon took great pleasure in this.

Church leadership was, of course, a particular concern of President Reardon given the minister-educator he always has been. Beginning with his masters thesis at Oberlin Graduate School of Theology in the 1940s, he persistently expressed a deep caring for the heritage and trending of the whole Church of God movement. He became an enthusiastic supporter and early part-time faculty member of the School of Theology that was new on the Anderson campus in 1950. In the late 1960s and early 1970s, when enrollments were down in the seminary and its viability and relevance to the ministry of the church had come into question, he refused to sit quietly on the sidelines. The issues for the campus and church were too crucial.

Being a man of action, a "fixer" by nature, President Reardon set a major study in motion. Largely fueled by his own initiative and imagination, its work eventually led to a greatly revised set of seminary degree structures and the founding of the Center for Pastoral Studies that was designed to reach out in new ways to the real and practical educational needs of pastors, including ones without educational credentials and thus not potential seminary students. He cared greatly about the church's leadership, not just the ministers who could be brought into the standard academic programs of the campus. The curriculum of the seminary had to be relevant to the church or its integrity would be compromised, a significant portion of its purpose aborted, and its financial lifeline cut.

On occasion, President Reardon exercised a prophetic voice to the church at large from his campus base in Anderson. Some years he would choose to deliver himself the major address at the Anderson College and School of Theology commencement ceremonies that were held in front of crowds of thousands as the beginning event of the annual Anderson Camp Meeting of the Church of God (he did this in 1956, 1964, 1967, 1973, 1978, 1980, 1983, and 1992). He took advantage of one such occasion to point out to the crowd his personal pleasure at the group of women in the seminary graduating class. Then he lectured the crowd rather sternly concerning the shame that ought to be felt about the sad fact that the Church of God movement was weakening in its commitment to valuing and placing women in key leadership positions as God chose to call them. To him, controlling the education and placement of church leadership with the subtle use of any racial and gender distinctions among ministers called by God was a blight on the integrity of God's church!

Reardon also served quietly in other ways to minister to the church at large. For example, in 1966 Warner Pacific College, a sister school to Anderson College located in Portland, Oregon, was experiencing great financial difficulty and turned to the national Church of God movement for help. Robert Reardon became Chair of the Emergency Fund Committee established by the General Assembly. He worked actively behind the scenes and soon was able to report considerable improvement in the financial circumstances of that college. Anderson was his home, but in many ways the whole church was his parish. The pain of one was the pain of all. Gifts should never be wasted. When key church leaders retired from national responsibilities and were still able to be productive in Reardon's view, he reached out and gave them new challenges on the campus. Examples of vital post-retirement ministries with Anderson College and School of Theology include Lester Crose (missions in the seminary), T. Franklin Miller (the seminary's Center for Pastoral Studies), Harold Phillips (New Testament in the seminary), with William E. Reed, Hillery Rice, and Ann Smith who gave years of valuable service in campus development and church and alumni relations.

President Reardon also had influence on a personal level not seen in public. In the church agency life of the Church of God at the national level, for instance, Rev. Paul Tanner reports, "I never would have resigned as Director of World Service to become Executive Secretary of the Executive Council of the Church of God without the gentle persuasion of Bob Reardon behind the scenes." At the level of local churches, there are scores of stories like that of Rev. James Cook. In 1971 bad weather stranded Cook in the Indianapolis airport while he was trying to get back to Chicago to finish his last year of seminary. He encountered the arriving Dr. Reardon who offered him a ride to Anderson for the night. On the way, the president asked about Jim's plans for ministry after graduation. There were none; he was still "waiting on the Lord." Reardon gathered more information and said he would try to help. One week later, while at an Anderson College alumni event in Garden Grove, California, representatives of the Corona church asked the visiting president if he knew of coming seminary graduates who could be considered as their future pastor. "Call James Cook," he told them. They did and he pastored in Corona for eight years, later becoming a leading Church of God pastor in Michigan, Ohio, and Indiana, including functioning as a Trustee of the Anderson campus and always a very appreciative friend of Robert Reardon.

The president of Anderson College and School of Theology was always at work on behalf of what he saw as the well being of the church as a whole. He may have been the president of the largest of the institutions of higher education in the church, arguably the most influential of all the church's institutions, but he also thought of himself and the church at large as brothers and sisters together. Teasingly, he sometimes said that the two best times each year in Anderson were when all the "saints" drove into town for the big annual Camp Meeting and then when he saw the waves of them driving away! In his eyes, the growing educational endeavor of the Anderson campus was a genuine ministry (see Appendix G). He truly loved his brothers and sisters in the faith and sought to serve their best interests through the enlightened education of many of their young.

President Reardon often was honored by church and campus,
this recognition presented by Theodore Baker.

President Robert H. Reardon leaves the presidential home, Boyes House,
for retirement and coming years of new ministry beyond the Anderson campus.

CHAPTER *Six*

Moving Out and Moving On

A t the 1978 celebration of his first twenty years as president of Anderson College and School of Theology, Robert Reardon was presented with a personal gift, an original cartoon drawn for him by his artist friend, the famous Charles "Sparky" Schulz. Speaking through the usual Charlie Brown characters, the text reads: "American college presidents usually don't last for twenty years, but old Reardon was too stubborn to know the difference!"

Good-natured kidding aside, transition does come in every life. In Reardon's case, leaving the presidency came

Cartoon created by Charles Schulz in 1978 honoring Robert H. Reardon on the occasion of his twentieth year as President of the Anderson campus.

in 1983 after twenty-five years in office and only because of his personal decision to retire. Things were going well on campus and he surely was welcome to continue, but he judged that, for very personal reasons mostly, it was time to go. Back in 1957-1958, Reardon had witnessed at close hand and benefited personally from a carefully planned and peaceful presidential transition from the leadership of John A. Morrison to himself. He now initiated

183

a similar process in 1982-1983 that would lead from himself to the new presidency of his longtime Dean, Robert A. Nicholson.

Meanwhile, President Reardon chose to speak himself at the June, 1983, commencement ceremony, the last over which he would preside. He began his address to the big crowd with the usual touch of humor, saying: "I would like to thank the special committee that chose the commencement speaker this year. It was composed of my wife, Jerry, my secretary, Virginia, and Shirell Fox. I know they searched far and wide and finally saw the wisdom in selecting me!" Then he posed this question about his own retirement: "How does one know when it is time to quit?" For him, it was really quite simple, he reported. Barrett Bates, the campus basketball coach, had sent his twelve-year-old son Ryan over to the president's home to get something. Once back home, the boy's mother, Roberta Bates, said to him, "Did they ask you in?" "Yes" was his reply. She continued, "What did you see inside the house?" Ryan's response was, "Just a couple of antiques." So Reardon announced to the crowd, "I knew then that it was time to quit!"

Letting Go of the Presidency

Having been elected and ratified to a new five-year term as president in June, 1978, Robert Reardon informed the campus Board of Trustees that October that likely he would not serve beyond the conclusion of this new term. By then (1983) he would have reached the age of sixty-four, including thirty-six years with the campus, twenty-five of those as president. Whenever the time of his choosing would come, he made it clear that he had no intent of encouraging any search process for his successor to begin prematurely, leaving him a lame duck president. "The changing of the guard in the halls of ivy," he said, "is often a painful and debilitating experience for the institution and those most centrally involved. We must not let this be our experience here." He was a strong and respected leader. His wishes in this regard were honored by the Board of Trustees.

Eventually more clarity about exact timing for his retirement began to dawn on Reardon. While in Chicago one day working with a colleague on behalf of the Indiana Association of Church-Related and Independent Colleges, there came frustration and reflection about the future. It was a cold day of waiting much too long to visit a chronic non-giver who should have been contributing to the cause of private higher education in Indiana that clearly was of benefit to his business. In the wasted interim of waiting, the colleague said to Reardon, "Do you remember the 1949 drama *Death of a Salesman?* The main character, Willy Loman, had given all of his life to his company, but now he was nearing a breaking point. He was tired and his dreams had faded. This is where you and I seem to be today, Bob!"

This comment by a frustrated colleague helped Reardon to begin reflecting privately on where he was in his own professional and personal lives. He then was sixty-two years old, in good health, but definitely tired. He

President Robert H. Reardon

said the following to the college chapel audience on February 1, 1979: "At one point I really worried about Anderson College—there were real financial and constituency problems. I had walked from Boyes House past Wilson Library and down College Drive carrying all this on my back." Then the Lord had said to the fretting president: "For your information, Bob, this college belongs to me. If I need any help from you, I'll let you know!" Faith had to be strong; the problems were real and often little understood beyond the president's office. Reardon was still full of sturdy faith, but his energy and drive were not quite what they once were.

In the January to April period of 1980, Reardon did some serious thinking about his personal future, with specific reference to Warner Pacific College in Portland, Oregon. This sister institution of Anderson College was nearly bankrupt and needed visionary leadership to assure survival. Reardon was inclined to become involved directly, admitting to himself that he was "coasting somewhat" at Anderson since he now was surrounded by "strong people carrying the load well." He thought his role on the Anderson campus might be coming to an end. He said "yes" to whatever God wanted (see Appendix G), noting in his private journal (February 17, 1980): "Pulling up the roots of a lifetime would be an emotionally exhausting experience." With the help of Dean Robert Nicholson, a plan was created for managing the future of Warner Pacific College. Trips were made; the plan was adopted; Dr. Milo Chapman emerged as the man to carry it out initially. So by April 4, 1980, Reardon could write in his journal, "The burden had lifted." He would stay at Anderson College, but not for much longer.

President Reardon was sensitive to the passing of a generation. He wrote in his private journal on April 22, 1980, about the retirements that June of six of his Anderson faculty friends and colleagues of many years, including Dr. Val Clear and Dr. Gene Newberry. Then on May 25, 1980, he noted the death of his beloved Sunday school teacher, Dr. David Gaulke. On October 27, 1981, he wrote this private note to himself: "I am really weary of fundraising in the worst possible times in Anderson, Indiana, with its large General Motors layoffs. Since we have several million dollars to raise for the new [Reardon] Auditorium, we have a big mountain to climb and people expect us to perform another financial miracle. I will need all the help from the good Lord that I can get—plus the luck of the Irish!"

The Anderson campus and its president suddenly were struggling through some very deep waters in church relations (the "Open Letter" affair). The June, 1981, meeting of the General Assembly of the Church of God had laid this big and bitter controversy to rest for the most part. Relative quiet had returned in campus-church relations and likely would remain for at least a few years. President Reardon thought to himself, "this would be a good time to call it quits." He and Jerry talked about this on walks together in Maplewood Cemetery just behind the backyard of Boyes House, their presidential home. She says, "he wanted to go when things were going well—and we did have some other things we wanted to do." All six of their immediate family had graduated from the Anderson campus (Robert, Jerry, and their four children). Now appeared to be a good time for Robert Reardon, highly successful and rather tired, to "commence" in a new way.

If a coming retirement were to be announced, what kind of transition would be good for the school? Reardon certainly wanted the campus to stay on its historic mission course and he realized that, beyond himself, his college dean since 1958, Robert Nicholson, was the pervasive influence in the institution and a few years younger than himself. A plan formed in his mind and he decided to act on it. Soon the Board of Trustees was informed that the

Robert H. Reardon breaks ground for Reardon Auditorium, 1982. With him, left to right: Wilbur Hardacre, Keith Huttenlocker, Esther Bauer, Bill Surbaugh, and Helen Shoemaker.

president would retire after the Board had chosen a successor and that person had been able to benefit from a one-year time during which the president-elect could function by Reardon's side to allow an ideal transfer of power. Such an arrangement would enable an unhurried presidential transition, much like the Morrison-to-Reardon experience decades earlier.

Although clear that choosing his successor was the business of the Board of Trustees, not his, Reardon nonetheless went so far as to name Robert Nicholson to the Board as the obvious presidential candidate in his view. In a closed session with the Board, he observed to the members that if anyone else were named, Nicholson would be *de facto* president by common perception—a most awkward circumstance, even though the gracious Nicholson would surely do all possible to minimize such a problem. Nicholson was the most knowledgeable person on campus; people would naturally look to him for wisdom and leadership; and he often had acted presidentially in the past, by Reardon's permission and request. In fact, Nicholson recently had functioned as Acting President when Reardon took a brief sabbatical. Having known Nicholson briefly in that role was surely significant to the Board's perspective on his potential candidacy.

Robert Reardon and the beloved "Nick" had been a special leadership team for twenty-five years and Reardon now saw wisdom in the continuity that would occur if Nicholson were named president. The Board listened carefully, proceeded with its own deliberation on this important matter, and

*President Robert H. Reardon and President-Elect Robert A. Nicholson
at the presidential inauguration of Nicholson, 1983.*

soon agreed with Reardon. Dr. Robert A. Nicholson was elected to be only the third president in the institution's history. Many years later Reardon wrote this about Nicholson's years of service as dean of the College that covered the entire tenure of the Reardon presidency: "For twenty-five years we worked together, supported each other, friends, confidants, and joyous servants in a cause we profoundly believed in. He was a major player in building the faculty, designing a host of educational facilities, presiding at faculty meetings, and adjudicating conflicts with wisdom and grace."

Following the 1982-1983 year of preparation and mentoring for the presidential office, and on the very day that Nicholson officially assumed the office, July 1, 1983, the new president sent his dear friend Robert Reardon a handwritten letter, saying in part:

You have been absolutely great to work for and with. I mean that sincerely and fully. You have dealt creatively with matters of presidential importance, and then you pressed/lured each of us to grow, stretch, and learn as we managed our respective areas. You have been a superb model in this, as in many other things. I haven't completed a full transition yet to the office, even with the year's transition opportunity. But I must—and I shall. There are many other things which could be said, but for today a simple and sincere "Thanks!'"

To the Board of Trustees, Nicholson reported the following: "At the beginning of this period [presidential-elect year], President Reardon and I made a commitment to each other and to the Board that we would do everything in our power to make the transition a constructive one for the College and for each of us. I believe, under God, we both have been able to say, 'we did it and did it well.'" The Board heartily agreed and with deep appreciation voted to grant an honorary Doctor of Laws degree to Robert Reardon at the 1983 commencement ceremony.

A wonderful portrait of President Reardon had been commissioned years earlier and was displayed proudly in Decker Hall, accompanied by a handwritten letter from him now appropriately framed and displayed (see Appendix G). Soon President Nicholson presided over setting the cornerstone of the magnificent new Reardon Auditorium that would house college chapels in the future as well as many conferences and concerts for the campus and community at large—an obvious fulfillment of Reardon's vision of campus and city, faith and learning. At the opening night celebration in the new Auditorium in February, 1984, the great crowd honored Robert Reardon and was entertained by the Anderson Symphony Orchestra and the famous jazz musician Dizzy Gillespie.

While approaching his retirement and managing a thoughtful time of transition to future campus leadership, President Reardon had received many honors and expressions of congratulations and best wishes. Included were the Liberty Bell Award from an association of lawyers, the Toner Award for contributions to international understanding, and the Doctor of Laws degree from Oakland City College where he was the commencement speaker in 1979. In 1982 the Distinguished American Educator Award came to him from the Eisenhower Memorial Scholarship Foundation and in 1983 he received the Distinguished Service/Ministry Award of Anderson School of Theology and the honorary Doctor of Laws degree from the deeply appreciative Anderson campus. Also received from the office of the governor of Indiana was the prestigious Sagamore of the Wabash award. It said of Robert Reardon that he was "distinguished by his humanity in living, his loyalty and friendship, his wisdom and counsel, and inspiration in leadership."

Such qualities had been of benefit to the Anderson campus in the person of Robert Reardon since 1947. Now things would be changing. One day Barry Callen walked with Reardon into his garage in University Village, his Anderson retirement home in 2003. He took me there to view all of these awards displayed on a wall. He looked at them and commented to me: "There's not a single award on that whole wall that will get you into heaven!" The awards that really mattered to him, he insisted, were the campus alumni who occasionally would approach him to report how enjoyable and profitable it had been for them to have attended Anderson College or School of Theology under his presidency. When such graduates reported how anxious they were to see their own children come as students to the Anderson campus, said Reardon, "that is more important to me than any piece of paper or plaque I could be given!"

December, 1982, marked the last presidential Christmas card sent out by the Reardons to the world of faculty, staff, alumni, and friends of Anderson College and School of Theology. It recalled the December, 1974, campus production of Charles Dickens' *Christmas Carol*. Kevin, six-year-old son of Professor Fred Shively and his wife Kay Shively, had played Tiny Tim, the crippled son of Bob Cratchett. All went very well until that time near the end when, with old Scrooge redeemed and a gracious Christmas dinner provided for the Cratchetts, Tiny Tim was to say those familiar words, "God bless us every one!" Instead, out came "Er-ah-well, God bless everybody!" So President Reardon now wrote in the card:

> In a few short months, Jerry and I will conclude thirty-six wonderful years with Anderson College. The understanding, support, and love you have shared with us and our children are gifts we always shall treasure. So, in this our final College Christmas greeting, we send along to you Kevin's version of those familiar lines of Dickens, "Er-ah-well, God bless everybody!"

Letters flooded in at the time of Reardon's retirement events. Both what they said and who they were from spoke loudly about the man and his many accomplishments. Acting President John Hicks of Purdue University said: "When I think of Herman Wells, Fred Hovde, Isaac Beckes, Ted Hesburgh, and you [Robert Reardon], I can only believe that Indiana has produced more outstanding college presidents in the last forty years than any other state." President J. Lawrence Burkholder of Goshen College observed, "There are few

Presidents who leave so many visible and invisible evidences of strong Christian leadership. You have done a magnificent job!" From Rev. William E. Reed, senior executive of the North American work of the Church of God movement, came this: "There has been an affinity of spirits between us, Bob, as we have worked together in national church work. We have taken on some tough assignments together; fortunately, we have survived, and so have some of the causes for which we took a stand." A courtesy letter came from the White House in Washington, D. C., with four paragraphs that began, "Nancy and I [Ronald Reagan] are pleased to offer our heartfelt congratulations on your retirement as President of Anderson College."

A more personalized letter came to Robert Reardon from a close acquaintance, the honorable Richard G. Lugar, United States Senator from Indiana. He wrote: "I know of few other college presidents who are so loved by students, faculty, and alumni. Your friends and family should be very proud of all that you have achieved." Anderson faculty member Dr. Merle Strege, American church historian, observed the following in his letter to the retiring president: "You may have retired from the A. C. presidency; you have not put aside the mantle of authority that dignified that presidency and gave it credibility for over two decades. The qualities that come from within cannot be put off so easily as mere retirement." Thinking historically and knowing that Reardon would agree fully, Strege concluded his "congratulations and sincerest good wishes" with this: "We are like dwarfs sitting on the shoulders of giants; we see more things and things that are further off than they did—not because our sight is better, or because we are taller than they were, but because they raise us up and add to our stature by their gigantic height." Reardon had stood on tall shoulders indeed, including those of his father Eugene and President John Morrison. Now he himself had both benefited from the past and raised the bar even higher for those still to come. The torch was passed peacefully and successfully to Robert A. Nicholson.

Immediately following President Reardon's retirement, a book was published in his honor. Titled *Educating for Service* and released in 1984, its editor, Dr. James Earl Massey, said of Reardon in the preface: "Your life and labors have personified the close ties that exist between life and learning, study and service, wisdom and work, the church and the academy. You belong to the company of the Doctors of the Church" (vii). Reardon's friend and colleague Dr. Gene W. Newberry added this (5):

Left to right: James Earl Massey, Robert H. Reardon, and Robert A. Nicholson, with the book edited by Dr. Massey and published in Reardon's honor.

Bob is a minister-educator with about equal weight on each of the two. If these two are at the bottom corners of the triangle, Christian (husband, parent, friend) is at the top, and integrity forms the gridwork across the center. No one places a finger on Bob as hard worker, creative, gutsy leader, ally in battle, responsible citizen, Christian brother, and gentleman with class.

Early into Reardon's retirement, president-emeritus John Morrison, still living close to the campus, found a way to honor the special man whom he had mentored, who now had succeeded him in the presidential office of Anderson College and School of Theology, and who had served well in that office for a quarter of a century. The major Christian periodical *Christianity Today* ran a "Select Sermon Series" in 1961 to feature Christian messages representative of the best of evangelical preaching in the American churches of the time. Morrison successfully nominated Robert Reardon whose sermon "The Great Question" appeared in the July, 1961, issue. The sermon was printed with Morrison's comments about it. He said he was impressed by the sermon's simplicity, adding: "Great preaching is never pompous. Effective preachers do not itch to parade a vocabulary.... Who wants to carry a dictionary to church to find out what the preacher is saying?... When preaching comes to be academic, it ceases to be preaching. It is lecturing. New Testament preaching was serious business. It was the business of the heart, the soul, the whole life, the total personality of the preacher." This prominent publication, a generous gesture of Morrison, was truly an honor for Reardon and gave him and his obvious preaching gift national exposure in the wider Christian community.

Additional exposure soon came for Reardon in quite another way. The campus's national alumni association commissioned the chair of the Department of Art of Anderson College, famous sculptor Kenneth G. Ryden, to produce a bronze bust of the beloved President-emeritus. It took many months of work and finally was unveiled in September, 1986, and installed in the center of the spacious lobby of Reardon Auditorium on campus. It stands on an elevated pedestal that is positioned so that thousands of college students and community residents will file by it annually to attend scores of events. Graduates Todd and Beth (Hazen) Callen later were married at Park Place Church of God across the street and had their reception in the Reardon Auditorium lobby. They arranged for the Reardon bust to be dressed properly for the

The bronze bust of President Robert Reardon, located in the lobby of Reardon Auditorium.

occasion with a white scarf swirled about the neck and a black top hat placed with a slight angle on the noble head, a fitting tribute to a man of dignity in permanent residence in the midst of celebration.

The heritage of stability remained with Anderson's presidential office. Nicholson proceeded to serve well for the next seven years until his own retirement, with Reardon remaining in the immediate community but choosing to stay off campus in order to allow Nicholson the ability to function without a trace of distraction from him. When Nicholson's time of retirement came in 1990, the choice of his successor would turn out to be another man gladly affirmed by Robert Reardon. James L. Edwards had been a young staff person in Reardon's administration, serving during his seminary years as Director of Recruitment before pastoring in Michigan. He came back to campus in 1972 as Director of Church and Alumni Relations and then in 1975 became an Ohio pastor, earning a doctorate in higher education administration at Ohio State University. Reardon rejoiced when Edwards became president in 1990, thereby reassured that the campus was still going to be kept on a good and steady course, whatever changes were required by new times. As would be expected, Reardon was chosen as the obvious person to offer the inaugural prayer as Dr. Edwards was installed in the presidential office in October, 1990. Reardon's heart and counsel flowed out in these prayerful words to God on behalf of President Edwards:

> We pray for him when he succeeds. Walk beside him to remind him of how many there are whose hands have borne him up. When he fails and the office grows lonely and the way dark, send Thy own strong presence to strengthen and guide him. Save him from the folly of always needing to be right, the need to make everyone happy and to appear in every faculty committee meeting. Remind him of the futility of long, dreary speeches, the temptation to say something profound on every occasion, and to consult the polls before calling the shots. We pray for Thy blessing on him that he may be a good husband and father to his family, a friend and counselor to the students who shall often hear him in this place [Reardon Auditorium], and, O God, in this confused and strife-torn world, grant him the ability and the zeal to fire this community and us all with the vision of faith and learning that are eternally bound together in the service of all mankind.

Such a prayer was filled with echoes of God's faithfulness in Reardon's own past. He was grateful for what had been and for what yet would be.

Reardon soon was affirming in a very public way another development that he saw as crucial for the integrity and future of the campus. The year 1992 was the seventy-fifth for the school and that year there was released a major book, a full history of the Anderson campus. On the cover of the book *Guide of Soul and Mind: The Story of Anderson University* appear these words of Robert Reardon: "There is a sense in which institutions, like persons, have a soul. Soul is a curious, mystical quality that draws together from the past all the various threads of being and weaves them into a tapestry of common experience. In a warm and thoughtful way, Dr. Barry L. Callen, the book's author, leads us on an instructive pilgrimage through the birth, development, and coming of age of Anderson University." The tapestry of memory, vision, people, and common experience in a faith and learning community like the Anderson campus had something of a sacred quality to it for President Reardon.

For the first twenty years of his retirement, Robert Reardon did not become involved directly in campus affairs, even though he and his wife Geraldine lived on Falls Court just opposite one of the men's residence buildings. The Reardons, of course, did stay very active in Park Place Church of God as laypersons and did attend occasional campus events. He was invited to speak to the undergraduate student body in chapel at least once annually— chapel convened in Reardon Auditorium with Robert Reardon's bronze bust standing high on a pedestal to greet all who entered into the spacious lobby area. There were two reasons for his staying completely clear of all campus administrative affairs after retirement. First came his ethics and thus his intention that Robert A. Nicholson and then James L. Edwards be unhindered by him in their own presidential lives. There also was his desire to get on with other things in his own life—such as ministering on an interim basis to a series of hurting churches and relating closely with his wife, children, and grandchildren now scattered across the country. By 2003 there were six grandchildren. Travel and emails were commonplace.

The self-imposed isolation of Robert Reardon from the official life of Anderson University ended in 2003. President James Edwards approached Reardon and requested his assistance in the substantial fundraising necessary to meet a large challenge grant being extended to the campus by Lilly Endowment, Inc. Millions of dollars were involved potentially and Edwards had full confidence that Reardon, now eighty-four years old, still had personal contacts and influence, could therefore be of considerable help, and would proceed to work on special assignments in a manner free from awkwardness for the current campus administration. Reardon was being offered and willingly accepted yet another opportunity to keep the campus on its historic course while also crossing important new frontiers. He had been doing just that for the school since 1947 and still was willing to do so into the twenty-first century.

On the Road Saving Churches

Over the decades, Robert Reardon often had been on the road for Anderson College, with all experiences not pleasant. For instance, he and Gene Newberry traveled around the world together in the 1960s. When they arrived in Singapore from Cambodia, the president's luggage failed to arrive. After multiple days and the filling out of duplicate papers and still no luggage, he insisted rather sternly that something be done. Finally, he announced to airport officials that he was not a well man, his medicine was in the bag, and his country would hold them responsible if something happened to him (in fact, hay fever was his only ailment and the only medicine!). The airport police took him seriously, toured with him to some possible sites in and out of the airport where luggage could have been mislaid, and eventually arrived at a nearby dump. There it was! Reardon's suitcase was sitting quite visibly in the middle of a mountain of refuse! The police waded out and retrieved it for him, speculating that likely it had arrived on a flight without him, sat unclaimed, and was judged by someone to be suspicious—potentially abandoned with a bomb in it. So it had been removed carefully to a place where it could do little harm.

One could wish that problems that sometimes happen during travel would not ever inflict Christian congregations as they move through their own years. Unfortunately, congregations also and too often experience relational explosions that do great harm. People find themselves discarded, some come to feel violated, leadership disappoints trusting people, and fellowship fractures. When it happens, the intervention of a wise man with a warm, patient heart and a wonderfully supportive wife can make a real difference. Later in his life, Robert Reardon clearly was that kind of person with that kind of wife. The result was the evolution of a pattern of calls for assistance, churches in need taking Robert Reardon back into the pastoral setting. As he says, "We went on the road saving troubled churches."

The years in administration on the Anderson campus may have been many and truly significant, to say the least, but after retirement Robert Reardon was blessed to be able to say that a key contribution of his life was still ahead. He was a practical churchman with a rich ministerial heritage from his father and a wife who had been a successful evangelist as a teenager. His own philosophy was that "it's not real if it doesn't work locally." So he found himself returning to local churches, trying to make faith and vision real in circumstances much less than ideal. "I became a parish priest again," he said, "and found it one of the most rewarding things of my whole life."

The new Reardon role would be interim minister, with the occasions several and the settings very wide-ranging (see the table for detail). It was to be something like being a "flying minister" as were the earliest ministers of the Church of God movement. Always by his side would be his wife Geraldine who joined him in finding true happiness in this way and at this time of life. She had retired from public school teaching in Anderson and together the Reardons were back into the local ministry, something they had not known since the 1940s in Pennsylvania—except for brief interim ministries in Whittier, California, in the summer of 1971 and in Kendall, Florida, in the winter of 1980. Together they would go from place to place, usually for months at a time, often having to bridge wide gulfs of relational ruptures by being agents of Christ's reconciliation among good but hurting people.

It began with an Anderson College trustee, Gilbert McBride, who had worked closely with President Reardon and was a member of the congregation in Denver, Colorado, pastored decades before by Rev. E. A. Reardon. Then it was the vision and persistence of Rev. Maurice Berquist that helped put Robert and Geraldine on the road as interim ministers serving congregations of the Church of God in transitions of various kinds. Berquist insisted that the last thing Anderson, Indiana, needed in the 1980s was another retired Church of God minister (including the one who had been a college president). The Reardons listened, prayed, and responded, first to the call to Denver, the scene of Bob's boyhood. While in Denver, they took full advantage of the setting. Some of the people in the church taught Robert how to snow ski. Daughter Connie flew to Denver to visit. She and her dad skied together; she was so impressed by his interest and developing skill.

In Denver and in all the churches to follow, things were challenging but went well and were most rewarding. Usually after a stay of about six months there was stabilization in the church, new congregational leadership on the horizon, and arrival of the time for the Reardons to go home to Anderson, Indiana, for a while and then move on again to more ministry in another place. Geraldine was extraordinarily helpful in these situations. She was winsome and gifted, relating to people so graciously. In the meantime, Robert sometimes had to make some hard decisions, even at the risk of appearing abrasive, finally saying to a church what should have been said much earlier by someone else—

"This has got to stop!" He, half teasingly but quite seriously, observed that there developed in their experiences a simple three-part formula for saving a troubled church—preach many sermons on love and reconciliation, have many casual meals and candid conversations in the private homes of the members where they are relaxed and really feel heard, and rely on Jerry to affirm, charm, and support person after person. She sang in church choirs, played the piano as needed, and was capable of preaching when the opportunities presented themselves.

Through the call of Maruice Berquist, the next stop after Denver, Colorado, was with the congregation in Vernon, British Columbia, then with churches in Olympia and later Seattle, Washington. A large congregation in Dayton, Ohio, had a leadership failure that stunned the national church. As usual, it was time for the Reardons. A scenario of unfortunate turmoil developed later in Grand Cayman in the Caribbean. The call came and the Reardons went. This amazing ministry went on and on from place to place. The range of interim ministries soon came to stretch all the way to East Africa.

Rev. Eugene and Pearl Reardon, Robert's parents, had spent the last year of their lives together in Kenya in the middle 1940s just before Eugene's sudden death. It had been a troubleshooting venture of loving intervention, a model for their son Robert to follow decades later. Since the 1940s, African children had been born and given names honoring the elder and beloved Reardon. African graduates of Anderson College had returned home to assume responsible positions of leadership in the Kenyan government and church. So Robert Reardon had a built-in interest when the Missionary Board of the Church of God, like it had done earlier with his parents, called for his help in Africa. It sought temporary ministry services on behalf of a large congregation in Nairobi that was beginning a significant transition. It was building a large facility and needed help in designing and implementing a much-increased range of programming. They wanted the wisdom of an elder minister who could preach, lead, and help them manage major change. Robert was all of that; even more, he carried the good name of Reardon that was revered in the Kenyan church.

With the support of the Missionary Board in the United States and a gift of $10,000 from Park Place Church of God in Anderson for Reardon to use in supporting the Kenyan ministry as he saw fit, a wonderful six months in Nairobi, Kenya, began for Robert and Geraldine. They enjoyed the active support of missionary leaders Robert and Janet Edwards who were on the scene and lived near the apartment where the Reardons were comfortably housed. Soon the Edwards children were calling Robert "Uncle Bob." The Buru Buru congregation in Nairobi that he now was leading temporarily was fundraising for a major new building. The American interim pastor arranged to have erected in front of the congregation a very large thermometer that dramatically registered the upward progress of necessary giving. With the $10,000 of Anderson's Park Place Church of God that he had with him to use as he saw fit, he challenged the people, promising that he would match dollar-for-dollar everything that came in until they had $20,000 in hand. The red column rose as the money arrived. Excitement and pride grew. Leadership made a difference. Reardon knew how to do such things very well.

Then it happened. It was one of those visual symbols that captures the minds and hearts of a people. As the magnificent new structure rose, there was a large blank wall in the front. A very sizable cross appeared to be needed. Reardon commissioned an African man to make it while others in the church planned and practiced a passion drama for the coming Holy Week. On Easter Sunday morning there were costumes, a great choir, and riveting drama as down the center aisle came the suffering Christ. With realism that was almost frightening, he was pulled upward in front of the big congregation and apparently nailed to the big wooden symbol of terrible torture. Then the soldiers climbed on big extension ladders and lifted the cross into its permanent place high on the front wall. Jesus died, was taken down, and disappeared from view. The choir began singing the "Hallelujah Chorus" and suddenly the African actor playing Jesus appeared from the back of the church in a white gown and with his arms raised in victory! The crowd of African Christians and its interim American pastor shouted in spontaneous and grateful delight at the amazing grace of God. It was a scene that Robert Reardon would never forget, a memorable Easter service in Africa, one skillfully created by Robert Reardon and his African friend Peter Lukoye.

Finally, the African sojourn ended and the Reardons returned to Anderson, Indiana, on Robert's seventieth birthday. Ahead lay other ministries, especially with the congregation in Clearwater, Florida, where they spent six months stabilizing a divided and demoralized congregation. Then, as they wintered in Florida over the coming years, they would maintain a long relationship with this church in Clearwater as supportive laypersons. Rev. Charles Tarr came to pastor there and later Rev. Tom Bates.

The story seemed to be much the same, whatever the location, in these retirement years of continuing ministry. Robert Reardon could build bridges among people, make the hard decisions needed, use humor in a timely way, bring back dignity to a broken situation, spread some love about, relish the presence of his gifted and gracious wife, and get a campus or church back on course. See the table that lists the twelve interim ministries of Robert Reardon stretching from 1985 to 2001.

Interim Pastoral Ministries in the Post-Retirement Years of Rev. Dr. Robert and Geraldine Reardon

Denver, Colorado, 1985

Vernon, British Columbia,1986-1987

Olympia, Washington, 1987

Dayton, Ohio, 1987-1988

Nairobi, Kenya, East Africa, 1988-1989

Lexington, Kentucky, 1989-1990

Anderson, Indiana (North), 1991

Seattle, Washington, 1991-1992

Georgetown, Cayman Islands, 1992

Clearwater, Florida, 1993

Tampa, Florida, 1994

Muncie, Indiana, 2001

Family Transitions

Family always has been a very precious thing to Robert Reardon. He came from a stable and loving home and was privileged to marry a very special Christian woman devoted to home and children. Soon after they had relocated back in Anderson, Indiana, in 1947, Robert and Geraldine (Jerry) Reardon had completed their own immediate family of four children with the birth of Gene. Jerry had been a student for two years at Anderson College many years earlier and then had focused her major attention on being a loving wife and devoted mother. In the 1960s she went back to school, finished her degree at Anderson College, and then earned a masters degree at nearby Ball State University. Soon she developed a strong interest in literacy and became a beloved teacher in the Anderson public school system.

Geraldine Reardon's graduation from Anderson College in 1967 was unusual in that the commencement occasion included her daughter Connie graduating in the same class, while her son Gene was graduating from Anderson High School. The next year, because of a generous gift from Donald Boyes, former general manager of Delco Remy Division in Anderson and vice president of the General Motors Corporation at his retirement, it became possible for the campus to build on the edge of the campus a beautiful new home to be the official residence of the president and family. Mrs. Reardon had the privilege of influencing greatly the design of the interior of the new Boyes House. The Reardons hosted numerous occasions in this home involving thousands of students, faculty and staff, trustees, and campus friends from church, industry, foundations, and the local city.

Over the years, and despite a heavy preoccupation with matters of campus and church, the Reardons were an active family. Robert put real energy into making fun things happen. When the children were still young, he arranged to be the summer preacher for a church in Oceanside, California, meaning that the family got to spend a summer on a lovely West Coast beach. At another time he arranged to deliver a Cadillac convertible to someone in California, meaning that the family had opportunity to ride out with him.

There was much more. Robert bought a ski boat that often was taken to Florida, usually during August and the Christmas holidays. Daughter Kathy fondly recalls the family out on the water daily, "Dad pulling the four children, one at a time, out of the water on skis. I never thought of this as a task for him.

He loved it." During the summer of 1961 the family spent three months in Europe, made possible in part with Robert's careful planning and persuasion of friends at General Motors to donate a car for the family to drive to many very interesting places. Kathy says that her dad was "continually up for fun." He would say things like, "Sure, I'll ride the ferris wheel." "How about a chocolate covered frozen banana for everyone? We'll all head for the ice cream store when the dishes are done." "Let's go to the Good Earth for supper." He would ask, "Anybody want to go for a spin in the new car?"

As a father, Robert Reardon was an active encourager in the lives of his children, even at times when their decisions were questionable in the eyes of loving parents. Son Gene says, "Dad was always ready to help if the request made sense to him. I have always known that, were I in trouble, Dad would not only be there to help me, but he would be able to help me, know just what to do." Daughter Connie shares similar examples from her life. During the 1970s she decided to take a year off from teaching to travel around Mexico and Central America with friends known to her only a few weeks. She had a telephone conversation with her dad during which he told her that he disagreed with her choice, but loved her regardless and would be there for her when she decided to come home. In 1983 she had been living in Europe and decided to come back to the United States. Her dad encouraged her to explore graduate school opportunities at nearby Ball State University, leading to a program in exercise physiology that was key to her future. Later, while living in San Diego, California, and wanting to return to Indiana and be involved in the new Wellness Center on her home campus, Connie's dad helped her focus on the wisdom that can be gained during trying times of necessary waiting. Finally, the waiting ended and her hopes came true.

Encouragement also came to Kathy from her dad. Once she "snagged a Florida boyfriend for a few weeks of fun that Dad never questioned." When he had questions, however, he did not hesitate to ask them. He cared deeply, although he sought to be wise in whether to intervene in any awkward circumstance related to his beloved children. After Kathy later married George Ramsey, Jr., the day came for the birth of their first child, Tito. Her dad got the news on October 4, 1981, and shortly the proud and excited Grandma Geraldine was on a plane to Seattle to bring all the assistance she could. Grandpa Robert was set to reflecting now that he was a grandfather for the first time, writing this in his private journal: "A new person has come into the world, a new pair of hands to do good things, a new pair of eyes to see and ears to hear the sweet-sad music of life. One stands in awe of the great tree of life that reaches back to the beginning of time."

When President Reardon's retirement came in 1983, he and his wife moved to a private residence on Falls Court, only blocks from Boyes House. They took with them a stunning gift that had been given to Jerry by the faculty/staff women's organization of a grateful campus. A year-long project that had been kept totally secret, the gift was a large memory quilt made up of thirty-five squares, each made by a different person and designed to celebrate some significant aspect of the

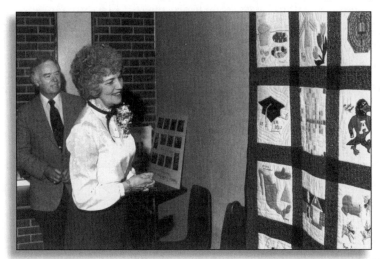

Robert and Geraldine Reardon admire the gift quilt in 1983.

first lady's personal or professional life. Karen Nelson headed the group and reported that Treva May had finally put it all together. There were different fabrics appropriate for the different lands the Reardons had visited and served. One square was a piano reflecting Jerry's love for music, another an ash tree under which Robert had proposed marriage to her, still another a pirate to commemorate the Buccaneers of Southside Middle School in Anderson where Jerry was an English teacher from 1969 to 1976.

After living a few years on Falls Court in Anderson, during which they often were gone for extended periods of time doing interim ministries across the United States and around the world, the Reardons moved again, this time to University Village located only blocks from the main campus. The Village is a development project of the campus, a beautiful setting of retirement condos. Residents buy property and gift it back to the school upon their deaths. Such a move was one more way Robert Reardon could make a substantial gift to the campus and, in the process, be sure that Jerry would have a secure, convenient, and lovely home should anything happen to him. They also were now wintering in Florida and traveling, especially keeping in touch with children and grandchildren. Kathy, now living with her family in the Northwest, recalls lovingly that her mom and dad have "hung out with us, taking more photographs and movies than anyone could view in a lifetime!"

Late in her life the campus invited Geraldine Reardon to speak in college chapel. She had been a gifted and well-known preacher in her teenage years and still could deliver well the Word of God! Then Anderson University celebrated her life and service by granting her an honorary doctoral degree. In September, 2001, her death came suddenly and quite unexpectedly. While with her loving husband Robert and close friends Paul and Jean Tanner, Maurice and Dondeena Caldwell, and others having dinner at the Anderson Country Club and reminiscing about children and the many years of friendship, Geraldine collapsed and died soon after. It was a great shock and loss for Robert. He adored her and had leaned on her in many ways. Life now would be lonely, but he was a survivor and would go on. At age eighty-two at the time of Geraldine's death, Robert still had his health and many reasons to continue an active life. He declared a year of mourning. There would be no sudden changes, no abrupt decisions. The magnitude of this loss would take time to absorb.

How pleased Reardon naturally was in 2002 when his daughter Connie, so like her mother in many ways, returned with her husband Barry Hippensteel from years in San Diego, California, to assume the directorship of programming for the magnificent new Kardatzke Wellness Center just built on the Anderson University campus. Connie was again close to her widowed father who now used the new Center and her services regularly. She has found this period of her life "especially sweet with my dad." She and her husband Barry have enjoyed their many times together with Robert. After having dinner, for instance, Connie reports that "we play piano duets, play games, talk about world events, or walk around the lake at University Village where he lives. He loves to read us Irish stories and we love to be read to."

Connie, a physical fitness professional, has been impressed at how her father has handled his time after her mom's death. He rises early to walk and spend time with God. He has focused "not on what he has lost, but on what he has left." Knowing her dad in his retirement years has been a blessing indeed. When roller blading first became popular, Connie and her husband Barry bought blades and skated around a lake near their San Diego, California, home. When her dad came out to visit in 1997, he wanted to try these new skates. Connie was afraid for him, but he insisted, saying that he had grown up on ice skates in Denver. So, at age seventy-eight, he skated around the lake with Connie and Barry—no problem. His daughter was impressed and relieved.

At the time of the writing of this biography, the Reardon children had long since settled into their adult lives and careers. Except for daughter Connie who had recently returned to Anderson, Indiana, to work on the campus as director of programming at the new Wellness Center, the others were scattered around the continent. Becky was living in New Mexico, unmarried and still pursuing her entertainment career while maintaining a "day job" in the health care field. Daughter Kathy and her family were living in the Northwest. She was an educator with three children, the pride and joy of Grandpa Reardon. One was in high school, two were college students, one carrying the name Robert in honor of his grandfather, and another the name Lydia after Robert Reardon's grandmother. Son Gene was living in the Cleveland, Ohio, area and functioning as a clinical psychologist based in a hospital associated with the famous Cleveland Clinic. He also had three children, for a total of six grandchildren for Robert Reardon. See Appendix H for a brief family tree.

Memories That Never Die

During his retirement years, Robert Reardon looked for ways to bring honor to people he considered unusually worthy. Included was Charles Naylor, church songwriter to whom Reardon owed a personal debt from his own early life. In June, 2003, largely through Reardon's personal efforts, a beautiful new gravestone was erected and celebrated by a large crowd of people who stood in the Maplewood Cemetery adjacent to the Anderson University campus and sang some of the Naylor songs in his honor. Included also in Reardon's parade of honorees was Dondeena Fleenor Caldwell. A longtime friend of Reardon's, he wrote a well-crafted foreword for her 2003 book *Amazon Adventures*. When Joseph Anderson, husband of Cleda Anderson who served so well in the Reardon administration, died in September, 2003, Robert Reardon, dear friend of this family also, was asked to deliver the memorial meditation in Park Place Church of God. In it he recalled that fifty-five years earlier he had played the pipe organ in the old Park Place Church of God during the wedding of Joe and Cleda.

President Robert Reardon initiated the honoring of his deceased friend, Charles Naylor, in June, 2003, with the erection of a new monument for his grave in Anderson, Indiana.

There was so much to recall and celebrate, so many friends to honor, too many funerals at which Reardon was asked to share personal reflections. The retired President Reardon looked for ways to help the next generation remember and truly appreciate the treasures that, in his judgment, were needing passed on to the future. Barry Callen also judges it important to preserve in book form the lives and wisdom of thirty-two of the outstanding leaders of the Church of God tradition (*The Wisdom of the Saints*, 2003). Included in this book of biographies and teachings is, of course, a featured chapter on Robert H. Reardon.

Dr. T. Franklin Miller has been a close friend of Robert Reardon's since those times in the early 1930s when Miller had led the church youth group in Anderson that young Bob was in. They once were longtime neighbors on Seventh Street in Anderson. On several critical occasions over the many years of their acquaintance and friendship, Reardon had turned to Miller for advice. In 2003, when both men were long retired and Miller was being interviewed for this present book, he said he had some summary comments about Reardon that he had never shared with him, but should. They were:

> Bob, I'm impressed with your irrepressible sense of humor. You
> have gone through so much and have managed to see something

funny in each situation. I'm impressed with your innovative and imaginative abilities. You can dream about a better future and be faithful and disciplined on the way toward achieving it. I'm impressed with your deep insights into human nature and the spiritual and professional potentials in people.

Miller spoke with great appreciation. Over the years from the 1930s well into the twenty-first century, thousands of people had experienced and benefited directly from Reardon's insight, vision, leadership, and humor.

A life as full as that of Robert Reardon becomes laden with memories of all kinds. In Reardon's case, a few of his memories are as precious as they are enduring. Their nature says much about the man doing the remembering. Following are eight examples of moving memories that for Reardon would never die. They are snapshots of deep reality that are also windows into the man who continues to be moved by them.

1. Saintly Parents. There was that moment in his youth when Bob Reardon walked into the dining room of his Walnut Street home in Anderson, Indiana, and saw his father, the beloved local pastor, sitting by the window in his favorite chair. Eugene was in prayerful meditation, with an open Bible in his hands. The early morning sun was shining through the window and dancing on the humble man. Bob could almost see a halo glowing on his head. Here was a man of God, a model of the right way to go in life.

There was another moment in his youth when Bob got home from church first and looked back up Walnut Street toward Eighth. His father, Pastor Eugene Reardon, had just preached at Park Place Church of God in his usual Prince Albert coat, a picture of dignity. Now the pastor was seen coming home, sitting in a wagon being pulled by several local children—his coattails flapping behind him. The children loved him and he loved them!

Robert Reardon also carries a beautiful memory of his mother. As he reported it to the Anderson College chapel audience on November 22, 1977: "I remember lying in bed as a child and hearing my mother playing the piano downstairs and singing her favorite song." The first verse says: "Tis so sweet to trust in Jesus, Just to take Him as His word, Just to rest upon His promise, Just to know, 'Thus saith the Lord.'" He would fall asleep with these thoughts filling his mind.

2.   Roots, Books, and Hope. In 1978 Robert Reardon was guest preacher one Sunday on the Christian Brotherhood Hour, the national radio broadcast of the Church of God movement. He spoke of being accepted by God as loved children through amazing grace. Then he turned to something very personal, saying to the radio listeners:

> A few months ago in the town of Limerick, Ireland, I found the record of my grandmother's baptism in the great cathedral there. It was a moving experience to turn those pages back through time to February 11, 1857, and see before me the record of someone I never knew, yet to whom I owed my life. When I walked out of the cathedral that day with a copy of that record in my hand, there came flooding over me the words of a familiar song: "My name is in the Book of Life, O bless the name of Jesus; I rise above all doubt and strife and read my title clear." I affirmed again my own sonship as a child of the Heavenly King, a restored, forgiven son.

What a moving memory this is!

3.   A Tree of Peace. Fixed always in Robert Reardon's memory was the planting of the Ginkgo tree of peace in the central ravine of the Anderson campus after President Richard Nixon had ordered the bombing of Cambodia. In the midst of the horrors of war, there suddenly had appeared on the campus a living symbol of the ancient tree of life. What Reardon would never forget were "the faces of those wonderful kids, shining with idealism, distressed by the course events had taken, but determined somehow to relate their young lives to the pain and agony of the world." Reardon loved young, idealistic people, especially when their spiritual lives and social consciences were active and about God's business in this world. He recalled this event for the Anderson College campus and alumni world in his 1973 presidential Christmas card, writing:

> Tonight the first snowfall of the year began to lay its white blanket over the campus as I walked home past the little Ginkgo tree. It is alive and well, its roots reaching down into the soil and its branches up to the sky. I stopped for a moment to salute this tree of peace and to recall for a moment the students now gone from the campus who faithfully are carrying out the promises made to their Lord on that memorable day. Praise God!

4.   Respect, Skill, and Class. In the early 1980s President Reardon traveled for two weeks with the Male Chorus of Anderson College as they sought to share their faith with the Finnish people. The thirty-three singers were hosted by the Free Church of Finland and assisted greatly by one of their members, Jarmo Kormu, an Anderson College student from Finland who functioned as interpreter and guide. Reardon had the joyful task of introducing the impressive Chorus to crowds in city halls around Finland from night to night. He was a musician himself and appreciated greatly the outstanding performances of these special men and their skilled director, Dr. M. Eugene Miller.

One day something happened that would never be erased from the president's memory. The Chorus gathered at the monument of a national hero of Finland, a world-class musical composer. The Anderson College men got off the bus dressed smartly in their matching blazers, gathered reverently in careful formation at the monument, and sang the national anthem of Finland in the Finnish language. There were numerous local citizens standing about this shrine to their national soul. They froze in amazement that an American group of young men would show such respect, do it with such skill and class, and know how to do it in the local language. Reardon stood close by, watching, listening, and being very proud. He loved good ceremony, good music, and gifted young men who know how to show proper respect.

5.   A National Prayer Breakfast. Not long before the wonderful Finland trip, the Male Chorus of Anderson College was privileged to stand immediately in front of President and Mrs. Ronald Reagan and hundreds of the top officials of the government of the United States to sing at the National Prayer Breakfast in Washington, D. C. President Robert Reardon sat close by and beamed with understandable pride. The young men moved this prominent crowd with an inspired rendition of the song "Precious Lord, Take My Hand!" that featured the gifted black soloist Milton Hines. These were memorable moments indeed. The young men, cream of that generation's crop, were a class act, witnessing to Jesus Christ in front of the people who were wielding great power in this world.

6.   Resurrection Indeed! There is that enduring memory of the Easter drama in Nairobi, Kenya, in 1989. Robert Reardon had engineered this amazing event. The large new wooden cross was raised dramatically in the proud facility of the Buru Buru Church. The crucified Jesus had disappeared from sight and suddenly reappeared in the back of the crowded sanctuary. The African actor playing Jesus had first inspired crying by the congregation as he died and now shouts of resurrection joy as he lived again! The scene became a mental picture Reardon would always remember. The actor wore a white gown that stood out against his dark skin. Down the aisle he came with arms raised in the air, a huge smile on his brightened face, saying, "Hallelujah, hallelujah! Jesus lives!"

7. A Vision of Tolerant Love. One undying memory of Robert Reardon is intensely personal. On his 80th birthday in April, 1999, he wrote to his beloved daughter Becky to tell her of a "vision" he had experienced in relation to her personal identity as a lesbian. His campus friend Dr. Val Clear had helped him to alter his attitude about the morality of one's basic sexual identity, coming to think of it as a given for some people as much or more than as a learned behavior. He wrote the following with a heart of fatherly compassion:

Hello, Sweet Rebecca.

This morning your mother and I were at the breakfast table with waffles and maple syrup. I fell into a kind of trance in the quiet time that followed. It was nothing spooky. I saw myself in Park Place Church of God in Anderson. I had taken you by the hand and led you up the stairs to the chancel. We were not on Rev. David Coolidge's order of worship. It got very quiet as we stood there for a moment, looking into the faces of those assembled who were waiting with some unease to learn what this unstructured event was all about. Then I heard myself saying:

This is our daughter Becky whom many of you know. She grew up in this great church and was nurtured by this great community of faith. She is gay. She has come home to be with us for the summer and her father and mother have two questions to ask. Can you receive and accept her for who and what she is, a fully human being? Can you make this place a sanctuary of understanding and love? If you can, stand up!

210

It was quiet for a moment, and then one by one they all stood up and the whole place was filled with light!

Love, Your Dad

8. The Lights Are Still On! Robert Reardon would never forget the throes of the Great Depression of the 1930s and the near financial demise of the Anderson campus. What he especially recalled was that conversation between President John Morrison and his father, Rev. Eugene Reardon, that culminated in the pastor saying: "See those campus lights, J. A.? We'll never let them go out!" President Reardon wrote this in his 1969 presidential Christmas card:

I write these lines thirty-six years later on a December evening as another quiet snow is beginning to fall and the street is filled with passing students. As I look out my window, the lights are blazing out of Wilson Library, Olt Student Center, and Morrison Hall, and I think of that special band of men and women in whom the heavenly light shone, whose lives unlocked for us the unspeakable treasures of Christmas. When I hear our students singing carols, these songs of praise, joy, and hope, I think I hear Dr. John, Dean Olt, Dr. Martin, and all the others join in the heavenly music, and suddenly it sweeps over me how grateful we should be for their gift. Although Old Main and its flood of memories is gone, new lights are coming on which will light our way in the future and bear witness to the One in whom there is no darkness at all.

These eight moving memories have never weakened for Robert Reardon. Sometimes he used them as his story approach to a range of audiences. He was exceptional at conveying treasured traditions and values through well-told stories. For instance, alumni by the thousands recall vividly his "Uncle Barney" Christmas story told annually at the campus Christmas chapel (see the full text in Appendix A).

In 1983, President-Emeritus Reardon retired, moved out, and moved on to new dimensions of life and ministry. He took his memories and stories with him and made good use of them in many settings. They are rich in meaning and have kept sustaining him and inspiring others.

President Robert H. Reardon addressing a homecoming football crowd at Macholz Stadium on the Anderson campus. During his presidential years and for more than two decades since his retirement in 1983, his has been a respected voice of authority and wisdom.

CHAPTER Seven

Direction and Destiny

··

"Staying on course," the phrase that serves as this biography's title, implies awareness of diversions from the right track and deliberate effort to avoid any veering from the proper path. There are ever-present alternatives that have a way of forcing themselves forward. Effort to avoid the diversions is an exercise in wisdom and balance that sometimes requires considerable skill and courage. Robert Reardon has been masterful as a sailor on the sometimes rough seas of personal, church, and academic life.

Here is how Dr. James Earl Massey put it in his dedicatory letter to Reardon that appears in the front of the 1984 book *Educating for Service* (vii) edited by Massey and published in Reardon's honor: "Your high scholarship combined with a devout faith and an unfailing commitment to service have long since marked you as an exemplary figure among us." In this tribute lie the basic elements of a right direction and worthy destiny as Robert Reardon has understood them. They require a careful balancing of serious scholarship, devout Christian faith, and disciplined leadership.

Reardon once said of himself that a key contribution of his to the Anderson campus was "my ability to see strength in people and bring them into the right place." He recalled and strongly affirmed some administrative advice he had heard from Ralph Noyer back in the 1950s: "Bob, if you hire weak people, one day you will wake up knee-deep in midgets. So, bring people smarter than yourself, free them to function, and they will keep you out of trouble." President Reardon practiced this wisdom, championed strong people, usually managed to position them wisely, and sought to keep their eyes fixed on key issues and the larger picture. The best way to stay on course, he sometimes said, is to keep the destination in view and keep pointing it out to others.

When Reardon invited Dr. Barry Callen to assume executive leadership of Anderson School of Theology in 1973, he gave the much younger man some advice. It came in two parts. First, the president gestured out his office window in Decker Hall to the distant Maplewood Cemetery and asked, "Barry, who over there is not dead?" Callen did not know how to respond and then heard the answer: "Those who wrote!" Reardon saw writing potential in Callen and challenged him not to get so lost in the details of administration that he neglected to think and communicate for the wider church world. Callen heard him well and did as instructed for decades to come.

The second piece of advice had to do with how to keep one's composure in the conflicts of administrative life. He observed that Callen would be in regular trouble now that he was a graduate school dean. Some people

President Robert H. Reardon

would be unhappy at decisions made, whatever they were. The advice? Locate your own star in the sky, that which is the right one for your own calling under God. Keep your eyes on that star, follow it through your days, and act accordingly. Doing this will not eliminate the critics, but it will choose them and thus allow good sleep at night! It comes down to one's own God-intended destiny and the steady maintenance of movement in that direction, regardless of circumstances and critics.

For President Reardon, giving definitive direction to the educational enterprise, his obligation as the executive leader as he understood it, may have kept the Anderson campus on its historic course, but it also was viewed by some as occasionally a little heavy handed. In response to such periodic criticism, Reardon insisted that his campus administration over the decades was definitely not "dictatorial." All issues of substance were discussed openly by the whole executive staff and few if any major decisions lacked general staff awareness and support. The group of strong executive leaders at Anderson

College and School of Theology believed in their president and knew where he was coming from in terms of basic values and commitments. He functioned with a clear philosophy that he once put very simply: "I learned early on that the responsibility of leadership is to lead." Worthy leadership is deliberate and directionally focused. The Reardon campus years (1947-1983) surely reflected such focus. He did not hesitate to accept the responsibility of leadership. Being a committed churchman, his leadership often extended beyond the campus to the Church of God movement at large.

Ruts in the Road of Reform

What is the central view of institutional destination that should keep the life of the Anderson campus on course? Robert Reardon once stated his preoccupation with the "inner life" of Anderson College. To him it was a "great myth" that it is ever adequate for the campus to claim success because it has a great physical plant, plenty of dollars, and a large collection of faculty members with earned doctorates. What gives life is the Spirit of God. In short, "an institution is not an end to be served, and it is only as we are able to become a servant educational community that our corporate life will be found" (*Anderson College News*, December 1965).

The meaningfulness of the church relatedness of the campus was foundational, not optional in his view. Reardon was driven by a vision. He told the Board of Trustees in April, 1983, that it was a vision that allowed him to see "a resurgence of deeply rooted Christian faith to give the dimension of depth to learning, to nourish its value system, and to graduate students ready to use their education in lives of service." His church-related educational vision was rooted particularly in the heritage of the Church of God movement which he once described as "a great outburst of idealism. . .a call to return to the 'early morning time,' to a church 'without spot or wrinkle,' to a life of perfection and holiness, to a union of the saved and sanctified, drawn out of sin and the confusion of sectism" (*This Is the Way It Was* 16).

So far as the Anderson College (University) campus is concerned, after his retirement Robert Reardon looked back with pride and gratitude on his decades of leadership. He wrote these unpublished lines in 1988: "I am proud that with God's help I left at the end of my tenure a strong, vital college and seminary, poised for the future years, leadership in place, with a continuing strong bond with its sponsoring church and other vital constituencies." His concern was always with more than the academic institution. He was a Christian minister, God's humble servant, a gifted preacher. So he also wrote: "I would like to be remembered as a preacher who gave his best to youth conventions, camp meetings, ministers' meetings, in college chapel across the years, with some finding salvation, others making decisions for the ministry or teaching, and just encouraging others." He assumed a Christian theological stance that could be described as "orthodox" and that he judged critical to the Anderson campus and to his own life's ministry. Finally, he concluded, "It is Christ and His Kingdom which draw us on, and it is His loving, guiding, chastening, encouraging, empowering presence which enables us, even in our sometimes stumbling ways, to fulfill our mission. I should like to be remembered as one who tried to keep the dream alive" (*Some Anderson College Reflections*, 1983).

Robert Reardon has always tended to be forthright in his judgments, including about the Church of God movement of which he has been a part all his life. On the positive side, he characterizes his pilgrimage with this particular people of God as a journey that has left him with "a heart of great love and appreciation." Many of the prominent leaders of this reform movement over the decades "have been like an extended family that has shaped my life and everything good that has happened to me" (*The Early Morning Light* 11). On the more negative side, he believed in the admirable holiness-unity vision of the movement's pioneers and also spoke openly of their clay feet in ways not intended to lessen appreciation for them, only to enhance adequate understanding and current relevance.

The Rev. Paul A. Tanner has been a special friend and ministerial colleague of Robert Reardon since the 1950s. He judges with admiration that "Bob gave his primary attention to things that mattered. He never got bogged down in petty issues or minor disputes. He always managed to see the large picture." Tanner adds: "When Bob spoke, people listened. In small groups he usually influenced the course of conversation. If no agenda existed, he was sure to have one up his sleeve." One agenda he had consistently at hand was the current health of the Church of God movement. It appeared to him that, like all vigorous reform bodies, the Church of God movement at times has gotten a little off the track. When it did, he or his father before him was right there, dared to grasp the wheel and seek to steer things in a better direction.

Reardon was a pilot by instinct and was committed to maintaining a good course for campus and church. He said in his 1943 Oberlin thesis that church movements are like living organisms and never remain static. For the approximate period 1920-1943, he identified some significant trending in the reform movement in which he was reared and which he loved (see Appendix E). Generally affirming of this trending personally, much later Reardon reflected on common pitfalls that have troubled the journey of the Church of God movement.

Four ruts in the road, four dangerous obstacles on the path of reform, are identified and elaborated. They are enlightening as one seeks to understand about both the Church of God movement and Robert Reardon. The following summarizations are drawn from Reardon's book *The Early Morning Light* (1979) and from a later private interview with him on the subject.

Rut #1.   Extremism.   Robert Reardon once wrote: "The most dangerous people in any reform movement may be the extremists who advocate it. This extremism is generally characterized by pushing a valid thing to its outward boundaries where it becomes distorted and untenable" (*The Early Morning Light* 82). Reardon saw this unfortunate tendency characteristic especially of the earliest decades of the Church of God movement.

Extremism is said to have impacted the life of the Anderson campus heavily in the early 1930s when President Morrison's presidency was challenged, again in the 1940s when the "watchmen on the wall" challenged the whole network of Anderson-based church agencies, and certainly in 1979-1980 as Reardon's own presidency and the very integrity of the academic programs of Anderson College were confronted vigorously by the "open letter." It was in these times of great stress that Reardon tended to see the Church of God movement at its worst. Good people and honest rhetoric were perverted by their extremism. One can tell a vicious lie by focusing exclusively on only half of the truth, so much that true perspective disappears.

Rut #2.   Narcissism.   In ancient Greek mythology, Narcissus fell in love with his own reflection in a pool of water. Preoccupation with self can be a fatal flaw. Observes Reardon: "As time passed, much writing [in the Church of God movement] began to focus on who we are. This preoccupation often led us away from the Christ whose message of redemption we were called to deliver" (*The Early Morning Light* 85). Reardon lived through decades of this

217

preoccupation with "we" and came to resist it in significant ways from the presidential office of Anderson College and School of Theology. He witnessed at close range this struggle, with himself and his father before him sometimes in the middle of the fray. Reardon's mentor, John Morrison, was a stalwart in the struggle, with the great 1934 confrontation over his ratification for another term as president of Anderson College being a major chapter in the story. Reardon evaluates that confrontation this way in his *The Early Morning Light* (73-74):

> At stake was how the church was to address itself in the future—
> as a cult, calcified, turned in, windows closed; or as a people twice
> liberated from the rule of new and sterile creeds. I believe that no
> other single action by the [General] Assembly has had more effect
> on the future of the Church of God movement. And we can be
> grateful for the men and women whose vision of the church was
> so true that they suffered, fought, and persevered for the
> principles that we enjoy today.

One core principle affirmed by Reardon was that the focus of the church must be on Jesus Christ and his mission in the world, not on any particular grouping of his disciples being of paramount concern.

Completing the picture of the 1934 struggle, giving room for the grace of God working over time, and recalling that John Morrison and F. G. Smith represented opposite sides of the struggle during the 1920s and 1930s, this also should be noted from the writings of Robert Reardon (*The Early Morning Light* 75):

> In their mature years, F. G. Smith and J. A. Morrison met, broke
> bread together, and came to a blending of spirits drawn from the
> deepest wells of human existence—a common Lord, a common
> faith, and a profound love and commitment for the church.
> Together they found validating evidence of the centrality of that
> unity of the spirit which transcends the doctrinal impulse to seek
> unity in creed and ritual. F. G. and J. A. have now entered into
> that celestial city where our human frailties and the struggle to
> comprehend the Truth are only shadows of yesterday. There the
> lamp of Truth shines forth in its majestic brightness and eternal
> flame.

Narcissism is always a potential rut in the road of reform. Also a persistent potential is the grace of growing wisdom and reconciliation.

Rut #3. Dogmatism. It is the case, Robert Reardon has observed, that keeping a community of believers doctrinally sound has often been in tension with making room in that community for individuals who dare to think their own thoughts before the Lord. He warns, "the search for truth, the practice of it, and the testing of it provide a continuing challenge to the church. It is there. But our perception of it is never so complete that we can claim an exclusive franchise to it" (*The Early Morning Light* 85-86). Reardon was influenced by the fact that, even in the early years when the curriculum was limited and the sponsoring church was quite provincial, the Anderson campus was not sheltered from a range of stimulating ideas. President John Morrison and Dean Russell Olt were committed to academic freedom to a degree that spared students and faculty members from "the narrow, fundamentalist, dogmatic approach to learning" (*The Way It Was* 90). There were outstanding faculty members who exemplified this open tradition and directly impacted Robert Reardon for the good.

For example, at Russell Byrum's death at age ninety-one in 1980, Reardon spoke as the president of Anderson College and School of Theology, the school for which Byrum had taught decades before. He lauded Byrum's contributions to the campus and church, saying: "It was Russell Byrum who threw open the windows and doors of learning…. It was largely through the breadth and vision of this man that we were saved as a movement from theological rigidity and the same kind of closed-mindedness our movement had come into being to oppose" (*Vital Christianity*, May 4, 1980, 5). Byrum was pictured as having taken "his scholarly key and demanded entrance into our doctrinal museum to raise questions about some of the exhibits there" (*The Early Morning Light* 81). Comments Reardon in his private journal (February 20, 1980), "After Byrum, it was OK to think!" The "heresy trial" of Byrum in 1929 and the subsequent resignation from his teaching post at Anderson College elicited impassioned judgments from Reardon. It was, he said, "one of the worst, most useless, painful—and shameful—episodes in our history" (*The Early Morning Light* 53). Reardon, of course, would be quick to say with pride that much of what was good in Russell Byrum also characterized his own father, Rev. E. A. Reardon, who was an irenic pastor with both conviction and compassion, a respect for heritage and an openness to honest exploration on the part of others. Robert Reardon certainly aspired to such a stance himself.

Rut #4. Exclusivism. Too often in its first fifty years, the Church of God movement interpreted "Be ye not unequally yoked together with unbelievers" to include those in sin and "Babylon" or sectarian confusion. Concluded Reardon: "That left precious few besides ourselves. This exclusiveness manifested itself in complete separation from other religious groups.... The view that God had abandoned the denominations and was no longer at work in them left us with a very difficult position to defend, namely, that God was restricting his activity to our reformation movement. Fortunately, this impossible assumption did not prevail" (*The Early Morning Light* 86). But such a view was defended vigorously by many leaders through the years of Robert Reardon's young adulthood. It often was argued that the great church reformation that God had set in motion about 1880, the time of Daniel Warner's emerging ministry, had at its center and most prominent and faithful voice the reforming people who became known as the Church of God movement (Anderson).

A central support for the argument of exclusivism was a prophetic calculation that many movement leaders found in the Bible, especially in the biblical books of Daniel and Revelation. There was seen a divine timeline featuring the year 1880, thus highlighting the Church of God movement as a chosen herald of God's great work of gathering all true believers into a Spirit-enabled unity before the end of the age. Such a biblical reading came from Daniel Warner himself in his final years (d. 1895) and was furthered significantly by F. G. Smith (d. 1947) in the first decades of the twentieth century. Although in later decades there would be numerous voices in the movement differing from the Warner-Smith perspective, Reardon's included, the narrower view placed a deep stamp especially on the early history of the Church of God movement.

Robert Reardon judged that such a reading of Scripture's prophetic writings "unleashed a powerful driving force" for all those who "saw the light." But by Reardon's seminary days at Oberlin in the 1940s, his own father and some younger leaders like Otto Linn were raising serious questions and cautions. In fact, Linn and soon Boyce Blackwelder, Adam Miller, Fred Shoot, Marie Strong, and others on the Anderson College and School of Theology campus openly contradicted the earlier approach to reading the Book of

Revelation and offered an informed and thoughtful alternative. Reardon documented with appreciation in his 1943 Oberlin thesis this alternative way of reading Scripture (already prominent in the 1940s) and understanding the nature and role of the Church of God movement (see Appendix E). Exclusivism as a viable stance was slipping away, introducing an identity crisis for the movement, one that has persisted to the present time. The widespread collapse of "last reformationism" opened a theological vacuum with traumatic effect on the movement. Reardon concludes that the movement was left without distinctives and comrades in arms since it had trashed and alienated the whole landscape of traditional (denominational) Christianity and nurtured few friendships outside its own immediate circles.

Ever since the 1930s and 1940s, various leaders have been attempting to rebuild on firmer ground the Church of God movement's biblical reading and theological foundations. The result in Reardon's eyes is this (*The Early Morning Light* 88):

> No one yet has been able to come up with a substitute which places the [Church of God] movement in a place of such exclusiveness and uniqueness that it elevates us above and beyond all other beliefs. It is doubtful that any one will.... Our mission is hardly to come forward with an irrefutable argument that, of all believers, we enjoy a special status with the Almighty. Rather, we must accept the pain and embarrassment of our frustration with humility before the Lord and lay again those great, supporting, biblical timbers that will support the true Temple of God.

What are these biblical timbers? Reardon went on to identify several, especially the foundational position of Jesus Christ, the central place of the revealed Word of God, an authentic vision of the church, a hunger for the presence and power of the Spirit of God, freedom from sectarian bondage, and a global vision of the church's mission. He calls these the "marks of greatness" (*The Early Morning Light* 88ff). Here is Reardon's summary statement made in 1978 in Barry Callen's book *A Time To Remember: Projections* (19):

> It is the conviction of this writer [Reardon] that we should not be overly concerned about our future as a movement. If we will take our heritage humbly and honestly, continuing to examine it in the

light of God's Word, daring to live out that heritage in our individual lives and in our mission as a people, keeping our hearts open to what the Holy Spirit is saying to us about our mission of redemption and reconciliation in today's world, then in obedience and servanthood we will find our place and God will be able to carry forward his work through our lives. Today I find the Reformation Movement open and seeking, casting free from some of the outworn baggage of the past, and earnestly seeking to respond to the ancient call of our Lord, "Come, follow me."

Reardon delivered a presidential directive to Dean Barry Callen and the School of Theology faculty in 1979 on the eve of the centennial celebration of the Church of God movement. They were to write together a statement of such timbers as one way to fill the aching void for the movement. The result was the *WE BELIEVE* booklet, something widely circulated for many years. Reardon believed strongly that the Anderson campus should take the lead in thought formation in the church, something it often had done on many fronts since early in the twentieth century. As president, he intended to be a man of action on a front as important as this. His vision was clear, his roots deep, and his strong commitments unshaken. Reardon wrote this (*The Early Morning Light* 96):

> It is time to ring again this great reformation bell. The centennial [1980] is no time to cast a quick, curious eye on the past or to study our history as a movement from a detached cultural perspective. It is time to look long and hard at those great pillars of fire in our night which lit the way for our fathers. It is time to discard the old wineskins that can never take the sweet new wine of truth. It is time to break free from every trap set for us by the enemy and to climb out of every pit into which we have fallen.

God is still carrying on a redemptive mission in the world and Robert Reardon has wanted passionately for the Church of God movement to be a significant part of it. In the late 1970s and early 1980s there had been a strong move by the most conservative leaders in the movement to restrict the life of the Anderson campus by legislating some tight fundamentalist guidelines. As president, he stood firm, determined to keep the campus on its historic course, successfully resisting "those who would drive us down a cultish road."

Marks of Enduring Greatness

In 1976, at the heighth of Robert Reardon's presidential tenure and accomplishments, he told the Board of Trustees of Anderson College and School of Theology about various ways that he and his administration were being innovative and even risk taking in finding the best ways for the fulfillment of institutional mission in changing times. He admitted, "there is some pain in this.... We are making some mistakes, but dead and unresponsive we are not. This is no 'steady state' for us. It is a time of high adventure." The president was a progressive conservative who both engaged in high and innovative adventure and "held the line" where campus mission and church-relatedness required.

It had been helpful for Reardon to have known personally Anderson College in its infant days of struggle. Especially during his student years in high school and college, he had caught the dream of the school's purpose and future as originally held by President Morrison and Dean Olt. So, for Reardon, adventuring was always to be done in careful continuity with the school's rich heritage, very much including its church heritage. He identified for the Board of Trustees in 1977 some core characteristics of the church community that first came to Anderson, Indiana, at the beginning of the twentieth century, the faith community from which the campus had emerged in 1917. These characteristics, he suggested, have enduring meaning and the potential "to create a thriving and innovative educational community unique in the annals of higher education in America." If properly engineered, he concluded, "we may be on the threshold of the most exciting development in our sixty-year history."

What were these pivotal characteristics of community vitality and potential? Among those visionary pioneers who established the Church of God movement in Anderson, the womb from which the Anderson campus was given birth, there was "a centrality of faith and purpose. . .which gave meaning to their lives and to those who came to join the community." There was, explains Reardon, "a deep sense of destiny" accompanied by a strong sense of stewardship of life in response to God's love. There was "a fundamental feeling about the dignity of labor." All members worked for the good of the whole community. The apprentice method was common for the learning of necessary skills. Life was hardly mundane and colorless. The arts flourished. There were active poets and painters and an outpouring of new musical literature. It was a cohesive and creative community of faith and learning. Thus, the president concluded: "It just may be that God is at this time calling us out of the educational lockstep to a higher level of activity more compatible with the Christian faith and with the aspirations of the church which brought us into being."

In no technical sense has Robert Reardon ever considered himself an accomplished philosopher or theologian despite his ordination to Christian ministry and his excellent theological education. Nonetheless, he always has been a serious churchman, a thoughtful educator, and an unusually committed disciple of Jesus Christ.

Robert H. Reardon

When he and his wife arrived back in Anderson, Indiana, in 1947 for him to first assume teaching and administrative duties, they came with some core convictions which Robert reaffirmed at his inauguration as president in 1958 and in light of which he has lived and served ever since. As published in the *Alumni News* (November 1958), these convictions were:

> We believed that the youth of the church and the nation are our greatest wealth, deserving our best since what happens to them will happen to the future; that the heart of a Christian liberal arts college is a qualified and inspired faculty; that there is an essential unity in the truth and no honest Christian student need repudiate his or her faith to maintain integrity; that without the claims and insights of religion, education loses its way and may easily turn into a sort of Frankenstein monster. . .; that learning is neither for wealth nor prestige, but for responsible Christian citizenship; that a church that will take a college and seminary to heart. . .will reap rewards in enrichment of its own life....

In 1979, on the eve of the Church of God movement's centennial celebration, President Reardon published his personal reflections on this particular people of God who were beloved in his eyes. He saw enduring genius in central features of the thought of this reform movement and gladly set them forth as his own. His reflections, as in his book *The Early Morning Light*, follow here in brief.

1. **The Centrality of Christ.** Jesus Christ is the core of Christian faith; the hunger after Christ-likeness is what Church of God people have meant by "holiness." Reardon: "Our forefathers had a deep, relentless, searching hunger after Christ and a profound commitment to be like him in spirit and conduct" (88).

2. **People of the Covenant.** The Church of God movement has deep roots in the long history of God's working to form a people loyal to the divine plan of redemption. Reardon: "God has acted in history to bring into being a people, called by his name, through whom he was going to attempt in a special way to do his redemptive work. This ancient article of faith, born in the time of Abraham and fulfilled in the commissioning of the early church, is as valid today as it has ever been. It is this ancient root system that anchors our [Church of God] movement into the vast, universal, catholic church" (89).

3. **Freedom from Sectarian Bondage.** All of God's people are to be united with each other because of their common relatedness to Jesus Christ. Reardon: "There was the strong ring of truth in our early preaching that called for the redeemed to renounce every vestige of sectishness and step out into a life of freedom to join heart and hand with every child of God on the face of the earth.... This membership in the great family of God through the new birth, standing in Christ alone, reaching hands in fellowship to every blood-washed one, is still a powerful, scriptural, and compelling idea" (90-91).

4. **Where the Action Is.** God's united people are to be vibrant with the amazing life of God in their midst. Reardon: "There was a refreshing spontaneity and excitement [in the early Church of God movement]. Church was where the action was: testimonies to salvation, witnesses

to miraculous healing, ringing songs of victory, powerful and stirring preaching, lives being saved and transformed" (91).

5. **Central Place of the Word.** The call of the Church of God movement always is to come "back to the blessed old Bible" as foundational for church life. Reardon: "The pioneers were first, last, and always students of the Bible. It was the written Word that gave authority; the Word that was the vehicle of the light; the Word that spoke to the kind of lives we were to lead; the Word which provided guidance, direction, and food for the soul" (91).

6. **Hunger for the Holy Spirit.** "Sanctification" is a crucial doctrine of the church. Humans long for the purifying gift of "holiness." Reardon: "The biblical doctrine of sanctification is a beautiful gift to believers that sets their lives apart for the Lord, strengthens and empowers them for service, assures them of the undergirding presence of the Holy Spirit, and purifies their inner being. It is one of the great treasures of the Church of Jesus Christ. Rightly and sanely understood, it bears witness to one of the timeless hungers of humanity—the yearning after holiness" (91-92).

7. **Inspired Hymns and Spiritual Songs.** Unified and holy people of God burst out in joyous song that is attractive to the world. Reardon: "One of the great legacies of our [Church of God] movement is our treasury of song.... One of the most attractive features of our early work was the singing.... It was ringing, boisterous music, and it attracted and inspired people everywhere" (93).

8. **A Vision of the Church.** Jesus Christ is Lord of the church. Only in him can true Christian unity be found or effective mission be accomplished. Reardon: "This vision of the people of God. . .called for a 'called out' community of the firstborn, the entire congregation of the redeemed, with Christ as the head, the door, the energizer, the organizer, the Lord who sets the members in the body, distributing gifts and callings through his wisdom.... This vision is the only basis upon which true unity between Christians can come" (94).

9. **A Global View.** The Church of God movement is to be driven by God's gracious mission to the whole world. A great God sends his people on great adventures! Reardon: "From the earliest days our leaders saw theirs as a global mission.... Something dynamic and exciting had broken into their time, and their vision was to get the message out to the whole world.... This vision of great adventures and victories for God challenged the pioneers to new and creative methods of evangelism and outreach" (94).

In the view of Robert Reardon, these nine features of enduring Christian greatness have always held obvious significance for the mission of the church's Anderson campus. For instance, at his retirement in 1983 Reardon told the church why, in his view, there had been so much campus growth during his twenty-five presidential years. He observed: "Young Christians and their parents want a school that has standards of behavior, that has a framework of faith, a religious root system, but where there is a strong academic program, a strong sense of freedom to think, to explore within a sense of community where people come to know one another and participate in one another's lives" (in *Vital Christianity*, September 11, 1983, 11). The Anderson campus had been founded by a special people of God and always had been guided by a special mission under God. For decades, Reardon had determined to keep this specialness on its appointed course. The right path must have both deep religious roots and serious academic pursuits.

President Reardon much appreciated the observation that Dr. Gilbert W. Stafford offered in a personal letter to him on October 17, 1977: "I am grateful that you have not allowed Anderson College to drift into being either a merely vertical nor a merely horizontal institution. I like the horizontal dimension that is characterized by TRI-S and I like the vertical dimension that is symbolized by the chapel steeple. Furthermore, I am glad that the two dimensions are not compartmentalized." This was the reflection of a grateful faculty member on a true leader who had a strong sense of what was right and the discipline to see that things stayed on the right general course.

Rev. Marvin W. Baker was a campus trustee from 1958 to 1988, the full tenure of Robert Reardon's presidency and beyond. Baker marveled at President Reardon's gifts of faith and leadership. They were contagious, helping the Board of Trustees to believe that things were possible even when the challenges sometimes appeared overwhelming. From a church perspective, says Baker, "Bob always understood who we were and worked hard to lead the school and church in that direction."

The Polar Star of My Life

On May 1, 1952, Robert H. Reardon addressed about five hundred Church of God high school juniors and seniors who were visiting the Anderson College campus in an attempt to determine their futures. In a time of rampant materialism and despair when, as Reardon explained, "the draft threatens, the international scene is incendiary, and life is cluttered with a thousand uncertainties," there nonetheless had never been a better time for productive Christian service. God does call and provide. Grateful obedience, he explained to the young people, "sanctifies labor and brings inner joy and satisfaction" (in the *Gospel Trumpet*, June 21, 1952, 3-4). The Apostle Paul had recalled the numerous trials of his own troubled ministry and finally confessed that he did not count his life of any value in itself; he only wished to finish the course of Christian ministry that is called to testify with joy to the good news of God's grace (Acts 20:24).

Reardon was persuasive on that 1952 occasion as the strength of his conviction spread across the youthful crowd. Such strength of personality and conviction, by the grace of God, poured forth from Reardon and spread across numerous crowds for over fifty years. So has Reardon's subtle humor, earthy practicality, and disciplined leadership. For instance, he said the following to the crowd in October, 1958, as he spoke at his own inauguration as the second president of Anderson College:

All week, especially today, I have had the same uncomfortable feeling that came to me as a boy in the grades out in Denver, Colorado. The teacher held up a paper that had particularly pleased her and, looking in my general direction, began to extol its merits—good penmanship, spelling flawless, grammar sound, punctuation accurate. I was carried away. She was talking about me! I smiled and nodded to my classmates. Then she mentioned the name on the paper and the boy behind me stood up. All week [as so many wonderful things have been said about the new

Anderson College president] I have been waiting for the boy behind me to stand up. Perhaps he will yet!

No other boy ever did stand. This time it really was Robert Reardon that they all were talking about! The decades to come would prove that all of the good things being said about him were richly deserved.

President Robert H. Reardon held generations together with his memories and vision, tied a campus to a city with his networking ability, and was a progressive and a conservative at the same time, enabling quality education and viable church relations. He vigorously advocated the ideal relationship between religion and education, as President John Morrison and Dean Russell Olt had done before him. He fought the good fight, testified persuasively to the good news of God's grace, and always stayed the course of personal faith and campus mission.

Bill Gaither once observed: "A key quality the Anderson campus has had is a wonderful balance between a solid theological base and a creative flexibility that encourages innovation. There is a spirit of openness that remains tied to something basic and sound. The resulting tension is an ongoing struggle, of course, but one well worthwhile." Robert Reardon has been a masterful pilot in this regard, handling the inevitable tension and keeping the campus on course.

Piloting through social turmoil, economic crises, and the political minefields sometimes appearing in campus-church relations has not been personally comfortable for the man who usually appeared so under control and even regal in his presidential style. Robert Reardon's personal faith and practical humanity helped make the difference for him when times were hard. In 1973, for example, he wrote this in his private journal:

The things that give me the greatest satisfaction and support are:

—A quiet benediction by the Park Place Church choir on Sunday;
—A good meal in the family dining room with old friends;
—Feeling that students love and respect me;
—Creating and preaching an exciting sermon;
—A long, tight hug from my kids;
—A quiet walk through the cemetery in October with Jerry;

—Jerry's closeness at night;
—Seeing Anderson College realize its dreams;
—Watching college kids mature;
—Playing the piano and pumping the old organ;
—Seeing signs of faith coming on strong in my children.

*Left to right: Robert Nicholson, Robert Reardon (himself
a skilled organist), and Willard Reardon, the President's brother.*

It is Robert Reardon's personal testimony that "all of my life I have lived
with an awareness of the Eternal.... This awareness of the Spirit has been the
polar star of my life, supported by the Word and illumined in the face of Jesus
Christ." He has believed deeply that this "inner light" is the "great human
treasure, transcending all reality, giving fulfillment to personality in this life and
beyond" (in *Vital Christianity*, November 9, 1980). Whatever else he has been,
Reardon always has been a Christian disciple and minister. Being a man of
considerable energy, high vision, and personal drive, his own spiritual journey
has been central to his life—and not always the most comfortable.

In February, 1956, Reardon, then a busy young executive and professor
on the Anderson campus, recorded some candid reflections in his private

journal. He had just served as a pall bearer at the funeral of Lucena Byrum, causing him to write: "Such an event brings life back into focus and speaks of the shortness of time and the necessity to work while it is yet day." Soon he would be president of the campus and was widely perceived as gifted and ambitious, competent and self-assured. Nonetheless, he added this candid self-insight: "I am not satisfied with myself. I find it hard to live with my limitations and faults. And yet my weak confidence rests in the grace of God which I increasingly fail to understand but which I accept with humility and gratitude." His acceptance never wavered in the decades to follow.

Over the many years of his campus leadership, Reardon had the primary and persistent intention of making Jesus Christ central. He put this in the form of a story as he addressed the Anderson College chapel on September 4, 1975. A male student inherited a playboy roommate who put degrading pictures on the walls of their room. What should be done? Rather than scold the roommate directly or just take the pictures down when the playboy was out, he chose to say nothing, but placed on his desk a framed picture of Jesus. Two weeks later he came into the room one day and the Jesus picture was the only one left! The story's intended message for the student body? "There is something about making Christ central in this community and in our lives," announced President Reardon, "that sets a tone and shapes the whole value system of the institution—and that's what we are after around here."

In July, 2002, then eighty-three years old and widowed, Reardon recognized that he was beyond his life expectancy and admitted that his thoughts sometimes turned to the subject of heaven. His testimony was shared as follows in Barry Callen's book *The Wisdom of the Saints* (229): "The Master assures me that there is nothing to fear, that heaven will be home, with plenty of room that reflects the love, light, joy, and unimagined possibilities of the character of the God revealed through our Lord Jesus Christ." He added with appropriate caution: "We must not stray far from what our Lord said about the future, and he said very little." How, then, should one live out the fleeting days of this present life? Reardon's answer was the one that Jesus himself once gave in replying to a question from one of his first disciples: "Don't be afraid. Trust me. There will be a place for you in the Father's house where there are many rooms, and I will be there to welcome you" (John 14:2-3).

Bill Gaither produced a "Homecoming" video in 2003 featuring Christian views and music about heaven. He asked prominent and wise Christian leaders like Billy Graham and a range of gospel music greats to provide sung and spoken testimonies on the subject of the Christian's ultimate hope. Robert Reardon was a natural for Bill to ask since he had been the president during the college days of both Bill and Gloria (Sickal) Gaither on the Anderson College campus. They also had been longtime friends of Reardon and benefactors of the College, with Gloria teaching occasionally and Bill serving for many years on the campus Board of Trustees. On the video, Reardon spoke briefly and very much to the point. He shared what he understands to be most important about the heaven theme, simply quoting again the words of Jesus: "Don't be afraid. Trust me. There will be a place for you in the Father's house, where there are many rooms, and I will be there to welcome you" (John 14:2-3). This is exactly what Robert Reardon deeply believed and was anxious to share.

When asked for the purpose of this biography what he would want written on his tombstone some day, Robert Reardon's reply was quick and straightforward: "Trust the Lord!" This, he said, is what he had tried to do over the years and also what he had tried to get students to do. This attitude makes the obvious even more plain. Reardon is a man of considerable complexity and great accomplishment; he also is a man of deep Christian faith that is well focused on what is finally most basic—trust and witness. The whole earth is the Lord's and there is good news to be shared. Reardon did all he could to enable future generations of the church's youth to deepen in faith and widen in witness.

Reardon accepted as enduring the wisdom of his beloved mentor, John A. Morrison, that life should be spent for something greater than itself, something that will outlast it. Carl Erskine observes that his dear friend Robert Reardon "should be remembered for one main thing, that he has been a minister of the Christian gospel, something you don't usually expect from a college president. One of his marvelous skills has been preaching, using simple illustrations in graphic ways." The illustrations often pointed listeners toward a vision greater than themselves and encouraged them to give themselves away in its service.

It also was in 2003 that Robert Reardon was asked to share on the subject of Christian hope before the large crowd gathered at the 117th North American Convention of the Church of God convened as usual in Anderson, Indiana. He recalled movingly that sixty-three years earlier on those same grounds he had successfully proposed marriage to the beautiful Geraldine

Hurst. Having now lost her in death in 2001, he admitted that he longed to see her again and had been forced to realize that it would not be in this world. Then he posed this question for the large crowd: "Had Jesus ever lost hope?"

The answer to this question given by the wise and now elderly Robert Reardon radiated faith and reassurance across the massive Warner Auditorium. Jesus was rejected in Nazareth, disappointed by the very disciples who were with him for three years, wept over a faithless Jerusalem, and faced on the cross what seemed a glaring fact, that everything possible had gone wrong. Did he give up hope? No! Three days later the stone was rolled away and God took the worst that humans can do and turned it into the best thing that has ever happened on this planet! What, then, is the source of our hope? Concluded Reardon with evident emotion: "It is the promise of the presence of our Lord Jesus Christ. That is our great prize! Hallelujah!!"

At Christmas each year President Reardon hosted students
with organ music and the telling of the "Uncle Barney" story.

The "Uncle Barney" Story

A Christmas story told annually for many years in the
Anderson College Christmas Chapel by President Robert H. Reardon.
It originally was written by Leah Neustadt and published in
Guideposts magazine with the title "Let's Go Neighboring."
Copyright 1954. Used here by permission.

This is a country story about a Christmas away back in 1876. Uncle Barney was a just and kind man in his ideas of right and wrong. His nearest neighbor was Ed Newton, a good farmer who had a severe struggle to get along.

Ed Newton watered his milk and was caught at it. You would have to be country bred to know the enormity of the offense. It was on a par with horse stealing, and men have been hanged for that. But we are not all built with stiff backs and incorruptible morals. Ed Newton fell, and was detected. It required money and influence and the tears of a distracted wife to keep him out of jail. After that he was kept in fierce isolation by his neighbors.

There is no more cruel sentence than to be ignored. When Ed and his family were left alone, Newton became a silent, aged, downcast man. It nearly killed Mary, Ed's wife. She was never again seen at church or at any meetings. You never saw lights in the Newton house at night, and Mrs. Newton nursed one of her girls back from the portals of death without even calling the doctor.

The Christmas season of 1876 was a stem-winder, with the wind blowing great guns, and the snow drifting until the fences were lost and the roads were almost obliterated. It was bitter cold and the children were sent home from the little red schoolhouse. But on Christmas morning the sun shone, and God Almighty showed what a wonderful picture He could make when He set His mind to it.

Simple gifts had been hung in front of the fireplace and there were raisin clusters, stick candy, peanuts, and a great deal of the greatest gift of all, human love in a happy home. The chores had been done, and Uncle Barney sat by the fire roasting his shins and thinking.

"Miriam," he said in his rich voice, "you and me and all the children are going visiting. Ed Newton has lived in hell long enough. Even God Almighty don't aim to condemn a man for one slip. Get the dinner fixings together for we are going to eat our Christmas dinner where we ain't invited."

He chuckled and then said, "Maybe I don't look much like a good Samaritan, but I'm going over to try to move a load off a man's heart." The children helped to hitch the horse to the big bobsled with straw in the box and blankets and robes. And the turkey and mince pies were loaded in the clothes basket. Away they all went, down the road, snow flying, crisp air making their cheeks tingle, bells making music, and they swung in the Newton driveway and through a great drift and were at the side door.

The two women cried out, "Miriam!" and "Mary!" and threw their arms about each other, crying.

Then Uncle Barney said, "We've come neighboring, Ed, just as we used to do, and we want this to be a Merry Christmas for all of us who need each other.

Ed Newton went over to the settee and held his head in his hands, then he got up and kissed his wife and Aunt Miriam and all the girls. And the children got together and played and showed each other's gifts. All the strangeness disappeared.

The women folks then went into the kitchen and started on dinner, while the men folks went out to the barn to look at the stock. The children played in the snow and had a bully time. At last, Mrs. Newton rang the big farm bell on the kitchen roof and they all gathered for Christmas dinner.

Ed Newton said the blessing and choked up so badly that he could hardly get through with it, and his wife laid her worn hand on his while he was praying. Yes, siree, that was some dinner, with two helpings of everything and cider and apples, and nuts in the parlor afterwards.

Well, the best of things come to an end. Uncle Barney and his family had to go home for their chores. But visits were promised and all the old troubles were buried deep under the snow and out of sight. There was more kissing and, as Uncle Barney turned back for another handshake, he said, "May God bless this house and all who are in it."

Back in his home, Uncle Barney started for bed when Aunt Miriam said, "Barney, you are a good man, a blessed good man. God cannot forget what you have done this day."

**Text of the 1968 Presidential Christmas Card sent to
the faculty, staff, alumni, and friends of
Anderson College and School of Theology
by Robert and Geraldine Reardon**

A few days ago a speeding car careened out of the night and ended the life of a beautiful and radiant girl, sophomore Wanda Blocher. There were the wailing sirens, the telephone conversations with her parents, the lights burning late in the hospital intensive care ward, the gathering of concerned students in quiet circles of prayer, and the anxious ride on a chilling fall night by a mother and dad in the desperate hope that the slender thread of life might yet hold.

Now the memorial services are over. The long lines of friends, the endless procession of faces lined with grief have all passed away and the snow lies deep upon this fresh grave, with the trees standing like giant sentinels keeping their mournful watch in the silence of the night.

I write this at Thanksgiving, with only a few days left before Christmas. Today a letter came from Wanda's parents: "God has been so good to us! This has been a difficult time, but the deep loss we feel is offset by the joy of knowing we are in God's will. So life goes on. Our prayer will always be one of thanksgiving for the rich fellowship we have felt through the greatness of God's love."

The snow is falling softly outside. A few leaves from the giant oaks stir in the winter's dusk. Wanda is gone. But the stars are out tonight and I know there will be carols and candles of faith and hope at Christmastide in the Blocher home this year.

Note: These sensitive comments, written by President Robert H. Reardon, show clearly the pastoral style of his presidency. Note elsewhere in this biography how the Reardons later ministered in a special way to two later students, Wanda Blocher's sister, Greta, and her soon-to-be husband, David Reames.

Robert H. Reardon (left) and Bob Holstein.

Bob Holstein Mimics Robert H. Reardon

Dr. Robert Holstein recounts in 2003 for this biography
two dramatic incidents between himself and President Reardon
that occurred on the Anderson campus in the early 1970s.

From the moment that I heard him speak at my first chapel service as
an Anderson College freshman, I was endeared to the man. His humor,
unique mannerisms, and gift of storytelling all captured my heart and
my fullest attention. He was Mark Twain himself, and until that moment, no
one in my lifetime had so personified the wit and wisdom of that great
American humorist. Reardon and Twain became the objects of my affection
and my primary course of study. And study them I did.

Mark Twain, Batman, and Robin

I don't recall the very first time that I imitated Dr. Reardon in the public
arena, but my experiences through the drama department at Anderson College
afforded me many opportunities to do so. It was an emulation born out of a
deep love, admiration, and respect. It created a bond between two people that
could never be broken.

Initially, the imitation of Dr. Reardon occurred solo. However, I soon
wanted his participation. While he was a very well liked and respected
president, he was considered by some of us to be too "presidential," too formal
and untouchable. I had an idea that would change that image forever, but
would he possibly consider such a challenge?

I had been asked to serve as Master of Ceremonies of the upcoming
Vocation Days Variety Show in the spring of 1972. I would come on stage as
President Robert H. Reardon imitating Batman. Then, he would appear
imitating his sidekick Robin. I knew in my entertainer's heart of hearts that it

would be an unforgettable moment that would bring down the house. . .an Anderson College first.

To get him to do this would be no small endeavor. I'll never forget how intimidated I felt to schedule an appointment with him one afternoon to discuss the idea. I sat in his massive office with a lump in my throat and shared with him the most ridiculous proposition that he had heard all year (save any from one of the previous General Assembly meetings of the Church of God!).

While his reaction at first was a little stunned and required input from an equally skeptical Dean Robert Nicholson, who I am certain thought that this whole thing was a little out in left field, the president turned to me and said, "Do you think it will be funny?" When I replied, "Yes, I do. I know it will be funny," he said, "Then I will do it. Just tell me what you want me to do."

The impossible had been accomplished. I left that office a man. I was relieved and proud. The man that I most admired, that I had imitated out of love, believed in me, had confidence in me, and placed his reputation in my hands. He had a way of doing that with students. He believed in them and was willing to be vulnerable for them because he loved them. Yes, he loved the institution greatly, but he loved the students intimately.

But love alone would not get us through that night, for love is rarely funny. To save us both, it was imperative that we be funny, VERY funny. I sent him his script through his secretary, Virginia. She wasn't sure she could trust me since I once telephoned her, imitating Dr. Reardon and instructing her to write a check for $500.00 and place it in Bob Holstein's college account!

On the night of the Vocation Days Variety Show, Dr. Reardon was to meet me in the men's locker room at a specified time in order to change into the Batman and Robin costumes. Timing was essential. This needed to occur between acts that were concurrently taking place onstage. We needed to appear on cue, so we had only a few minutes to prepare.

Dr. Reardon was promptly in place backstage. With some hesitancy, he put on the Robin costume, repeating often, "Robert, this is not going to be funny!" I constantly reassured him that it was going to be great, but desperately needed someone to quietly reassure me of the same. It was a memorable moment walking down the dark corridor to the stage with our capes gently flowing in the breeze, Batman and Robin, the dynamic duo, lowly student and esteemed president. He continued to mutter, "Robert, this is not going to be funny!"

The moment on stage was unforgettable. I imitated Dr. Reardon as Batman to a receptive audience as he remained backstage in the dark. But it was the president's entrance as Robin that was the highlight of the evening. He delivered his lines as rapidly as possible to an overwhelmed audience. "Golly, gee, Batman. We better get in the Bat Mobile and apprehend the Penguin before he robs the Gotham City Bank!"

Reardon did it!! The challenge had been met. His presidency would never be the same. And it was good. And he rested, greatly relieved.

This event was, to me, the highlight and most memorable of my experiences imitating Dr. Reardon; but he enjoys bringing up another event. He relishes telling of the time that I "streaked" in chapel while imitating him. He did not, however, seem to relish the incident at the time that it occurred (to put it mildly!).

The Infamous "Streaking" Incident

It was my senior year and the streaking craze was sweeping across America. People were running naked in public. The city of Anderson had experienced such behavior in various restaurants and business establishments. There were murmurings that it was inevitable that the AC campus would have a streaking incident at anytime. Students and faculty were often commenting that someone would probably streak in chapel where everyone was gathered in one place. Dr. Reardon even had several streaking jokes up his sleeve.

So, what would be more appropriate than for the tension to be relieved and the anticipation to be satisfied by a streaking parody involving President Reardon and his secretary, Virginia Johnson Reardon (she married Robert's brother Williard). It sounded funny to me. When I shared the idea with Roger Shoot, Director of Student Activities, he thought it would be hilarious and told me what he knew about the format of the planning for this particular chapel session. This was all the encouragement I needed.

I knew the president's routine at the chapel service immediately preceding Easter break. It was always the same every year. He would tell a few jokes, deliver his Easter message, and end with a reminder for the students to travel safely to their homes and communities. So, as I hid backstage wearing his well recognized half-moon glasses, shirtless and in flesh colored leotards with a fig leaf appropriately placed, I listened for just the right time to appear.

The Anderson College choir had just finished a very moving song, followed by a brief applause. Dr. Reardon began speaking. His voice, though faint, could be heard by me, but just barely. "What was he saying," I wondered. "Is this the time?" It was now or never. It should have been never!

A bewildered and shocked president watched as I streaked right in front of him across the front of Park Place Church of God, saying in his familiar baritone drawl, "Keep running, Virginia, and don't look back or they will catch you for sure!" I disappeared into the wings to a standing student ovation. The president recovered, as expected, with humor and his battery of streaking comebacks, one of which was, "The Bible speaks of streaking. 'Repent and be baptized. . .for the end is in sight'." What I had not realized was that just prior to my grand entrance and ridiculous run, he had just reprimanded the student body for applauding after the choir had presented such a beautiful and spiritual rendition. Now he was not in the best of humor. And I was in deep trouble.

I received word within hours to report to Dean Cleda Anderson's office. She shared with me that Dr. Reardon was quite angry about my debacle and wanted to know the names of those involved with this outrageous spectacle. He was convinced that it was a conspiracy among the students, an attempt to publicly humiliate him, and that the applause following the choir was a planned cue for me to appear. I could not possibly tell them that the only ones who had foreknowledge of this event were myself and the Director of Student Activities. I knew that if I shared this information, there would be much more fallout from my poor judgment. I could only reassure Dean Anderson that it was, indeed, not a conspiracy, nor an attempt to embarrass the president. It was my idea alone and I was fully responsible.

I was immediately placed on probation and informed that I would be expelled from Anderson College if there were any further infractions during the remainder of my senior year. I had offended the man whom I most admired. I accepted my well deserved punishment and wondered if he and I would ever be friends again.

It wasn't long, however, before the president was smiling again. He would just look at me and shake his head. When opportunities arose for him to introduce me at subsequent public speaking events, his favorite memory to share about our relationship was the streaking incident. He sent me a card the year prior to my attending medical school and wrote, "All is forgiven." I knew he meant it. We have laughed together many times since.

I will always love, admire, and respect this man who touched the lives of so many. He touched my life with his humor, his regency, his love for God and man. He was a minister, a sage, the man that I always wanted to be. And for a brief span in my life, I *was him*. And it was good.

The Booster Song

∙∙∙

Arranged by Charles Stanley, Booster graduate, 1953,
with lyrics by the Booster Club that was founded in 1936 by
David Houghton, Robert Reardon, and Mitt Williams,
with Robert H. Reardon named the club's president for 1938.

If you're looking for a friend on whom you always can depend,

Just look for Boosters, those humble Boosters.

They can give a joke, a laugh, a slap on the back, and then, my friend,

You'll know tomorrow, you'll have no sorrow!

You'll find there's consolation when you haven't got a dime;

Just ask your Booster buddy for a carefree time.

We're all pals together, comrades, birds of a feather,

Hootin' pals, rootin' pals, shootin' pals, tootin' pals,

In rain or sunshine,

Pals say they're brothers, pull for each other.

If you row your own, you're not alone, for now you belong

To the A. C. Boosters, man to man!

Excerpts of the thesis by Robert H. Reardon, titled "The Doctrine of the Church and the Christian Life in the Church of God Reformation Movement," submitted to the faculty of the Oberlin Graduate School of Theology in partial fulfillment of the requirements for the degree Master of Sacred Theology, 1943.

Note: Robert Reardon dedicated this thesis to his wife Geraldine, "whose encouragement and understanding have been a constant source of strength," and to his parents "who for more than forty years have given their finest efforts to the church of God." He says, "it is customary in this Movement to spell the word 'church' with a small 'c.'" He follows this custom by referring to the Movement as the "church of God Movement." The trends in the Movement documented in this thesis in the early 1940s were soon used by Rev. Earl Slacum and others in the Movement to justify strong criticism of the Movement's changing reality. Reardon was comfortable with the general trending and became a leader of it in the decades to follow. The following are from pages ii-iii, 90, 105-106, 110, and 118 of the thesis.

Sixty years have elapsed since D. S. Warner and his handful of followers severed their ties with "man-made" organizations and took their stand for the "Truth." The story of this Movement during the ensuing years—its titanic struggle with truth and error, its grappling with the perplexing problem of Christian unity, its frontal attack on the organized church—is a fascinating story indeed.

I have attempted the study of this group as one who has been born and reared *within* the group, but who has studied *without*. It is not my purpose to maneuver the church of God movement into the limelight of respectability so that it might be held in proper esteem by the larger denominations. God forbid! Rather, it has been my purpose to set forth, in an objective manner, the real picture of the church—both historically and doctrinally....

My reasons for writing this thesis have been several: to enlighten and inform those sincere souls who seek to know the church of God better; to correct misunderstandings which have sprung from a confusion of the church of God Movement with the myriad other groups calling themselves by like or similar names; to expose the distorted caricature of the church of God drawn by Elmer T. Clark in his book *Small Sects in America*; to make those within the church aware of the subtle changes which are imminent, and to speak a word to encourage a spirit of honest brotherliness as these changes are met; most important of all, to set before the present generation of the church a clear understanding of its past, that it might build upon that past toward a more glorious future....

Movements, like living organisms, never remain static. Either they continue to grow and develop, or they cease to grow and die. As the word "movement" implies, the church of God Movement has been "moving." In the sixty years of its history, it has grown from a small, well-knit fellowship of a few hundred people, to a recognized church group of some 132,000 adherents. It growth has been marked by much joy and much pain. Many things, which seemed quite certain to Warner and his associates, seem not quite so certain today. Many things that were learned have had to be unlearned. At times, these growing pains have hurt; but "whom the Lord loveth He also chasteneth"....

In the last decade, there have come revolutionary developments within the church of God Movement. Many of the orthodox beliefs on the doctrine of the church have undergone radical change. Voices from many quarters are crying "Restatement!" Some of these upstarts have succeeded in scaling the high walls of orthodoxy and have seen "glimpses of new truth" which they have called back to their brethren below. To a marked degree, the period from 1920 to 1943 has been a period of critical questioning of existing beliefs, and out of this period has come this demand for restatement.

We may summarize the trends in the doctrine of the Christian life as follows: greater emphasis is being given to the sins of attitude, sins of omission, social and economic sins. The methods of evangelism have changed from the exclusive use of the revival to include other significant methods. There is great emphasis on the doctrine of the new birth which includes more than forgiveness. Evidence points to the conclusion that this first work is becoming so inclusive that it has meant the purifying of the moral nature. There is less emphasis given to the second definite work of grace....

There is a definite trend in the church away from a particular interpretation of prophecy as a rationale for the church's existence. The church is no longer trying to justify its name and mission by an interpretation of the book of Revelation. There are two aspects of the New Testament church as taught by Warner which have undergone considerable revision—the exclusive nature of the church and the unity of the church. [A growing majority group within the Movement] claims no magical formula for suddenly transforming a divided Christendom into a united church. This group regards unity as the goal of a slow process of evolutionary growth. It has joined in spirit with men of all denominations who are traveling the thrilling but dangerous road of ecumenicity.

The following are samples of comments of appreciation by Anderson College faculty and staff members. They were written on April 20, 1978, to honor President Robert H. Reardon and his wife Geraldine on the occasion of the twentieth anniversary of his presidency. Over 400 letters were collected (including from many students) and bound into an impressive book of memory.

1. **Dean Cleda Anderson:**
   "President, It is difficult to find a way to convey my gratitude and joy in serving on your 'team' here at A. C. [Dean of Students]. I love you and respect you and so value your leadership as our beloved President. Not only is Anderson College blessed, but so are those of us who participate with you in living out your 'dream' for her."

2. **Mr. Barrett Bates:**
   "Dr. Robert Reardon, Thanks for a job well done. I was a student in your first year as president and I appreciate you more now than I did then. I appreciate your complete dedication to Anderson College."

3. **Dr. Milton Buettner:**
   "Dear Bob, I know of no college president who has equaled you in balancing physical plant growth with spiritual growth on a campus. The 'new broom' we welcomed twenty years ago is still sweeping clean. How often can that be said?"

4. **Rev. Donald Collins:**
   "Dear President, It is an incomparable experience to have my position [Campus Pastor] on a campus whose executive leader, through his idealism and personal example, creates an atmosphere of faith, hope, and love. Thank you for who you are and the priceless gift you give to us all."

5. **Mr. Shirell Fox:**
   "President Reardon, I've worked on many chapels, but this one surely is 'the one that was.' The excitement, sincerity, and spontaneity of response by students and faculty-staff alike reminded me once again,

and so forcefully, of just how much a real part of our own personal lives you and Jerry have been for such a long time."

6. **Mr. Edward Oldham:**
   "President Reardon, Congratulations! Perhaps the most important part of your administration to me has been your determination to uphold on campus the traditions and standards of the Church of God Reformation Movement. I know the pressures to conform to the trends of the times have made things not always easy. Please be assured that God will be with you when right is at stake."

7. **Dr. Frederick Shoot:**
   "Dear Bob, It is with a deep sense of appreciation that I express to you my gratitude for the superb leadership you have given us during these twenty years. Some thought the institution would not survive with you at the helm, but there were the others of us who felt that it would not have survived without you."

8. **Professor Robert Smith:**
   "Dear President, It is difficult to find words to express how much I've appreciated being a part of this campus—and a great part of it is because you have been the president of the college. I can't honestly say I've always agreed with you at all times, and I'm sure you've not always agreed with me. However, I greatly appreciate your support in my endeavors."

9. **Professor Marie Strong:**
   "Dear Bob, Thanks for a beautiful twenty years. Much of what we now enjoy of unusual facilities, large student body, and freedom of expression has been due to the dynamic furnished by you and Dean Nicholson. This is a warm and beautiful place. It has a heart and when the going gets tough for students or faculty, we/they know someone cares in very realistic ways."

Some thoughts to myself – and other college servants.

Find something you believe deeply in and give yourself to it. Be a part of its life. If need be, suffer with it, prosper with it, plan for its fulfilment within the context of the Great Commission. Worry not about salary or titles. Worry about matching your gifts with the institution's needs. Stay until you can honestly say that God has released you for another assignment in His Kingdom. Love, support, and encourage your colleagues. Rejoice when God uses them to do successful things. Keep your own house in order. Put your ideas forward modestly and contend strongly for them. If they be received be grateful. If not, retreat with grace and good spirit. Remember that leadership rests on trust, a commodity to be desired above great riches, or a large throne. It is helpful to remember that it is God who is the author of our gifts and that there are few greater joys than the certitude that He is using us. Anderson College is part of an ancient tree whose roots go back to Jerusalem and Athens. This great tree if cultivated will bear fruit in God's great plan for mankind with coming generations enjoying its rich bounty no matter what sweeping changes may come and go on the passing scene. Rejoice to be a part of it.

R. Reardon

A handwritten letter of Robert H. Reardon on servant leadership.
See Appendix G for a printing of its text.

This letter from President Robert H. Reardon is handwritten and addressed to the whole Anderson College and School of Theology community. It says much about his personal values, commitments, and style of leadership. The original now is framed, hangs alongside a large portrait of Reardon displayed prominently on the second floor of Decker Hall, and is reproduced on page 250.

October 3, 1975

Some thoughts to myself and other college and seminary servants:

Find something you believe in deeply and give yourself to it. Be a part of its life. If need be, suffer with it, prosper with it, plan for its fulfillment within the context of the Great Commission of Jesus. Worry not about salary or titles, but worry about matching your gifts with the institution's needs. Stay until you can honestly say that God has released you for another assignment in His Kingdom.

Love, support, and encourage your colleagues. Rejoice when God uses them to do successful things. Keep your own house in order. Put your ideas forward modestly and contend strongly for them. If they are received, be grateful. If not, retreat with grace and good spirit. Remember that leadership rests on trust, a commodity to be desired above great riches or a large office. It is helpful to remember that it is God who is the author of our gifts and that there are few greater joys than the certitude that God is using us.

Anderson College and School of Theology is part of an ancient tree whose roots go back to Jerusalem and Athens. This great tree, if cultivated, will bear fruit in God's great plan for mankind, with coming generations enjoying its rich bounty no matter what sweeping changes may come and go on the passing scene. Rejoice to be a part of it.

President Robert H. Reardon

Family Tree of Robert H. Reardon

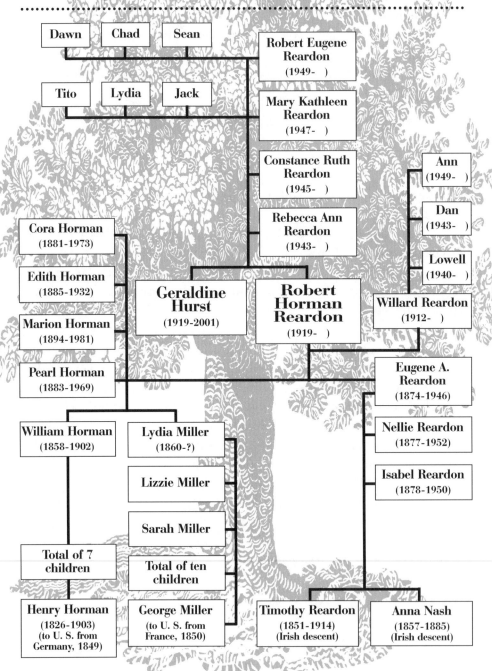

Dawn

Chad

Sean

Robert Eugene Reardon (1949-)

Tito

Lydia

Jack

Mary Kathleen Reardon (1947-)

Constance Ruth Reardon (1945-)

Ann (1949-)

Rebecca Ann Reardon (1943-)

Dan (1943-)

Cora Horman (1881-1973)

Lowell (1940-)

Edith Horman (1885-1932)

Geraldine Hurst (1919-2001)

Robert Horman Reardon (1919-)

Willard Reardon (1912-)

Marion Horman (1894-1981)

Pearl Horman (1883-1969)

Eugene A. Reardon (1874-1946)

William Horman (1858-1902)

Lydia Miller (1860-?)

Nellie Reardon (1877-1952)

Lizzie Miller

Isabel Reardon (1878-1950)

Sarah Miller

Total of 7 children

Total of ten children

Henry Horman (1826-1903) (to U. S. from Germany, 1849)

George Miller (to U. S. from France, 1850)

Timothy Reardon (1851-1914) (Irish descent)

Anna Nash (1857-1885) (Irish descent)

Index of Persons

Phillips, Harold L., 46, 60, 93-94, 176, 180
Pinyoun, Harvey, 56, 64
Pistole, Hollis, 72

-Q-

-R-

Ramsey, George, Jr., 202
Ramsey, Jack, 252
Ransey, Lydia, 205, 252
Ramsey, Mary Kathleen (see Reardon)
Ramsey, Tito, 202, 252
Rankin, Alan, 146
Ratzlaff, Leslie, 62
Rauschenbusch, Walter, 77
Reagan, Nancy, 191, 209
Reagan, Ronald W., 191, 209
Reames, David, 116-117, 237
Reames, Greta (Blocher), 116-117, 237
Reardon, Anna (Nash), 14-16
Reardon, Chad, 252
Reardon, Constance Ruth (Hippensteel), 83, 90-91, 95, 197, 201-202, 204-205, 252
Reardon, Dan (b. 1863), 14
Reardon, Dan (b. 1943), 109, 252
Reardon, Dawn, 252
Reardon, Eugene A., 8, 12-37, 41-46, 49-52, 56, 69-70, 74-75, 83-89, 107, 149, 155, 162-163, 168, 191, 197-198, 207, 211, 219
Reardon, Geraldine (Hurst), 12, 38, 41, 43, 59, 63, 65-67, 74-75, 78-84, 87, 89-91, 93, 95, 97, 103, 105, 114, 116-119, 121-122, 175, 177, 184, 186, 190, 195-197, 201-204, 229-230, 232-233, 237, 245, 252
Reardon, Isabel, 14, 16, 252
Reardon, Mary Kathleen (Ramsey), 40, 83, 91, 95, 201-202, 204-205, 252

Reardon, Mary, 14
Reardon, Nellie, 14, 16, 252
Reardon, Owen, 14
Reardon, Pearl (Horman), 24-27, 34, 36-38, 41-42, 44, 52, 67, 85-86, 198, 207, 252
Reardon, Rebecca Ann, 81, 83, 91, 95, 121, 205, 210, 252
Reardon, Robert Eugene, 40, 83, 90-91, 95, 127, 150, 201-202, 205, 252
Reardon, Robert H.
(numerous references throughout the book)
Reardon, Sean, 252
Reardon, Timothy, 14-16, 252
Reardon, Virginia (Johnson), 104-105, 123, 184, 240-242
Reardon, Willard, 25-27, 36, 44-47, 49, 51, 59, 86, 88, 104-105, 123, 230, 252
Reed, William E., 145, 176, 180, 191
Renner, Glen, 62
Rice, Hillery, 166, 180
Riggle, H. M., 20
Roark, Warren, 76
Robin (see Batman and Robin)
Rock, Robert, 145
Rollings, Mary, 24
Roosevelt, Eleanor, 147
Rowe, A. T., 51
Ryden, Kenneth G., 193

-S-

Sago, Paul, 123
Samuel (biblical prophet), 8
Santa Claus, 119
Sayre, John, 62
Schield, Wilbur, 96, 138
Schminke, Fred, 62
Schulz, Charles M. "Sparky," 10, 117-118, 183